SILVER BURDETT
SCIENCE

Centennial Edition

GEORGE G. MALLINSON
Distinguished Professor
of Science Education
Western Michigan University

JACQUELINE B. MALLINSON
Associate Professor of Science
Western Michigan University

WILLIAM L. SMALLWOOD
Head, Science Department
The Community School
Sun Valley, Idaho

CATHERINE VALENTINO
Former Director of Instruction
North Kingstown School Department
North Kingstown, Rhode Island

SILVER BURDETT COMPANY
MORRISTOWN, NJ
Atlanta, GA • Cincinnati, OH • Dallas, TX • Northfield, IL •
San Carlos, CA • Agincourt, Ontario

SILVER BURDETT
SCIENCE

Centennial Edition

GEORGE G. MALLINSON

JACQUELINE B. MALLINSON

WILLIAM L. SMALLWOOD

CATHERINE VALENTINO

THE SILVER BURDETT ELEMENTARY SCIENCE PROGRAM
1-6 PUPILS' BOOKS
AND
TEACHERS' EDITIONS LEVELS K-6

ISBN   0-382-13108-8

CONTENTS

UNIT ONE

Investigating Our Living World

There is a world of living things around you. Living things can be found on the land and in the air. Living things are also found in lakes, rivers, and oceans. Some living things can even be found in the soil.

In what ways are all living things alike? Why do different kinds of living things live in different places? Why do certain plants grow in meadows but not in deserts? What kinds of animals live in forests? Can the color of an animal help it to survive? In this unit you will find answers to questions such as these.

Chapter 1

Living Things

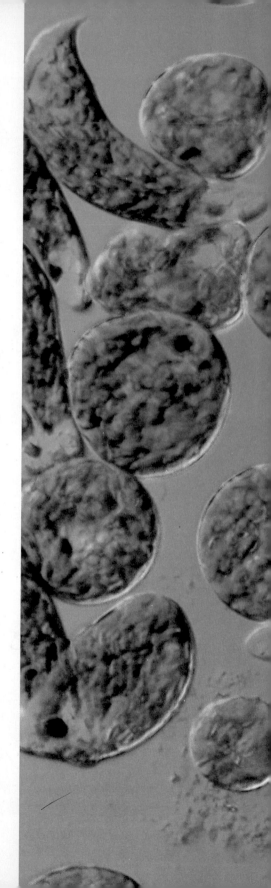

You probably know which things around you are living and which are nonliving. You would call some living things animals and others you would call plants. You might be surprised to learn that there is at least one other group of living things. These living things are so small they can only be seen with a microscope. Such living things are shown in the picture.

There are many different kinds of living things. But all are alike in some ways. In this chapter you will find out how living things are alike. You will also find out how living things differ from non-living things.

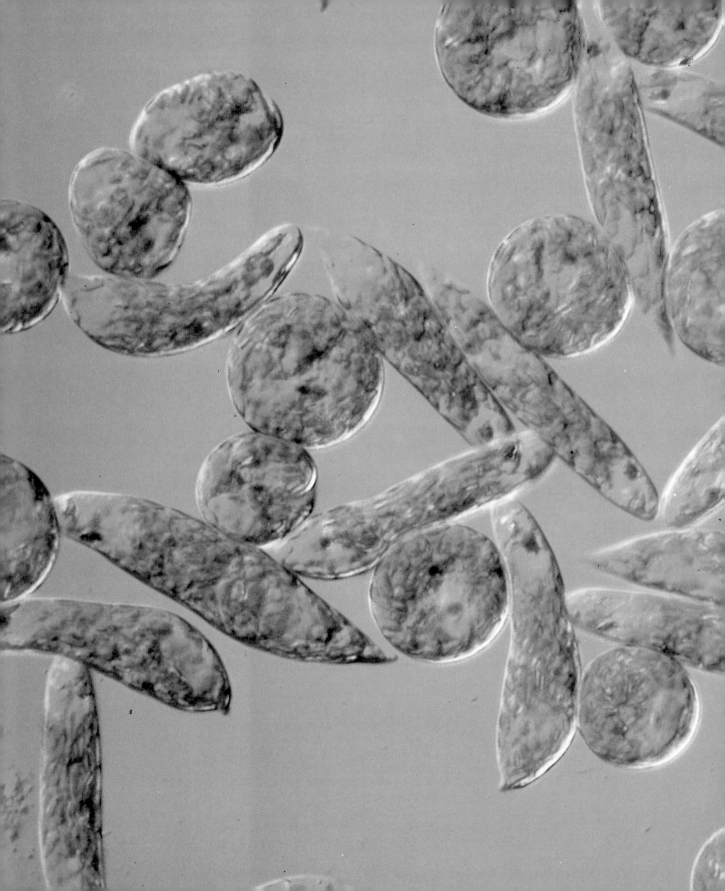

—— LIVING AND NONLIVING ——
How do living things differ from nonliving things?

Triggerfish

Ant

Living and nonliving things are shown in these pictures. What living things do you see? How can you tell whether something is living or nonliving? All living things carry out certain activities called life processes. These life processes distinguish living things from nonliving things.

What are these life processes? First, living things grow. In the spring, plants grow from the soil. New leaves grow on trees, and trees also grow in size. If you have ever had a puppy or a kitten, you have seen your pet grow in size. How much have you grown since last year? Nonliving things, like rocks and stones, do not grow the way living things grow.

Herring gull

Second, living things can respond to the world around them. For example, plants may respond to the sunlight by turning toward it. Flowers may open in the morning and close at night. A frog will jump if you try to catch it. You will move out of the way of a bike coming toward you. Nonliving things do not respond in such ways.

Canada geese

Whitetail jack rabbit

Third, living things can produce more living things like themselves. This process is called reproduction. Different living things may reproduce in different ways. Plants produce seeds that can grow into new plants. Bears have cubs, wolves have pups, and deer have fawns. Chickens lay eggs from which baby chicks hatch. Young lizards, such as the one shown in the picture, also hatch from eggs. Nonliving things cannot produce more of themselves.

Horned lizard

Finally, living things need energy. Living things need energy to grow, to respond to the world, and to reproduce. Where do you get the energy to work and play? Your energy comes from food. All living things need food to get energy to carry out their life processes.

Scientists have a special name for living things. A living thing is called an **organism** (ôr′gə niz-əm). Birds and trees are organisms. But feathers and bark are not. These structures are only parts of organisms. Feathers and bark cannot live alone.

Peacock and feathers

All organisms are alike in that they perform the life processes we have talked about. All organisms are alike in another way. They are all made of cells. A **cell** is the smallest living part of an organism. Many organisms, such as the plants and animals that you know, are made up of millions of cells. The cells of plants and animals are alike in some ways. However, there are some differences between animal cells and plant cells.

ANIMAL CELLS

What are the parts of an animal cell?

Almost all animal cells are alike in certain ways. Most animal cells have a nucleus (nü'klē əs). The **nucleus** is a round body inside the cell. Its job is to control the cell's activities. Find the nucleus in the picture of the cheek cell.

As you can see in the drawing below, the nucleus is surrounded by a membrane called the nuclear membrane (nü'klē ər mem'brān). The nucleus contains threadlike structures called **chromosomes** (krō'mə sōmz). How many chromosomes does the nucleus shown below contain? The chromosomes usually cannot be seen. On the chromosomes are the cell's genes. The **genes** are the units that control most of the cell's activities. It is because of the genes that the nucleus is often said to control the activities of the cell.

Photograph by Carolina Biological Supply Company

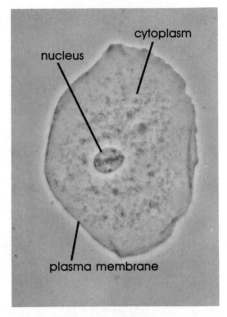

Cheek cell from a human

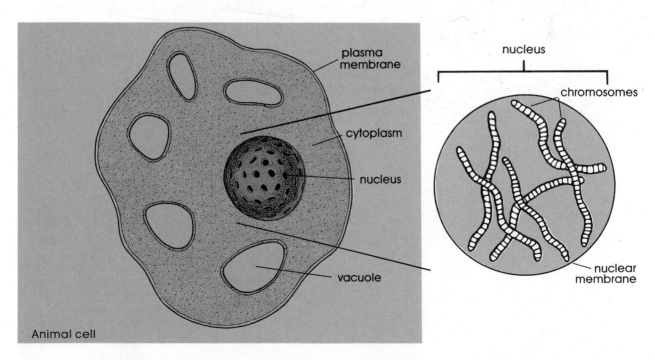

Animal cell

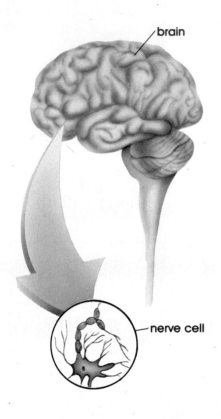

CELLS FROM THE BODY

brain

nerve cell

All animal cells have a jellylike material outside the nucleus. This material is called the **cytoplasm** (sī′tə plaz əm). The cytoplasm has many small structures in it. These structures carry out many of the activities, such as breaking down food, that keep the cell alive.

Sometimes small clear areas can be seen in the cytoplasm. Such areas are actually structures called **vacuoles** (vak′yu̇ ōlz). The clear fluid inside the vacuoles contains stored food for the cell.

All animal cells are surrounded by a **plasma** (plaz′mə) **membrane.** The plasma membrane helps to control the movement of materials into and out of the cell. The plasma membrane is somewhat like a fence around a house. Nothing can enter or leave the cell without going through the plasma membrane. Just as some things cannot get past a fence, some materials are too large to pass through the plasma membrane. Find the cytoplasm, vacuoles, and plasma membrane in the drawing of the cell on page 7.

There are many kinds of animal cells. Different kinds of cells may have different shapes. Some different kinds of cells found in the body are shown here. Compare these cells. How are all of these cells alike? How are they different?

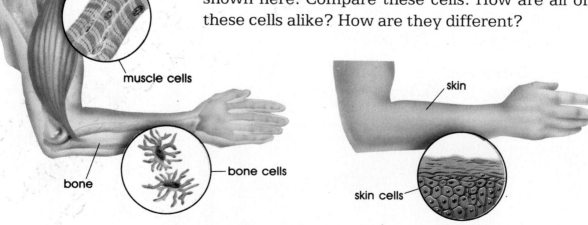

muscle

muscle cells

bone cells

bone

skin

skin cells

What do cells from your body look like?

Materials   microscope / microscope slide / coverslip / medicine dropper / flat toothpick / iodine solution

Procedure
A. The cells on the inside of your cheek are easy to obtain. Use a medicine dropper to put a drop of water on a microscope slide. Using the large end of a toothpick, <u>gently</u> rub the inside of your cheek.

B. Roll the large end of the toothpick in the drop of water. Add a drop of iodine solution to the water. Place a coverslip over the water. Gently tap the coverslip to get rid of the air bubbles.

   1. Why did you add the drop of iodine to the slide?

C. Observe the cheek cells under the low power of the microscope. The cells are irregular in shape.

   2. Draw a few of the cells.

D. Observe the cheek cells under high power.

   3. Draw one of the cells. Label the nucleus and cytoplasm. Also indicate the plasma membrane in your drawing.

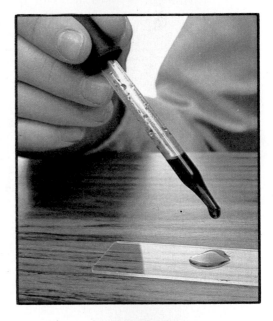

Conclusion
1. Describe what a cheek cell looks like.
2. What differences did you see when observing the cells under low and high power?

Using science ideas
Observe other materials, such as tissue paper and salt grains, under the microscope. How do those materials compare in appearance with cells?

PLANT CELLS
How do plant cells differ from animal cells?

Plant cells, like animal cells, have a nucleus, cytoplasm, and a plasma membrane. However, plant cells differ from animal cells in an important way. Plant cells have a thick wall outside the plasma membrane called the **cell wall.** Find the cell wall in the drawing of the plant cell.

The cell wall and the plasma membrane are different. The plasma membrane is very thin and is a living part of the cell. The cell wall is thick and is a nonliving part of the cell. The cell wall gives shape and strength to the plant cell. Why do plants need cells with strong walls?

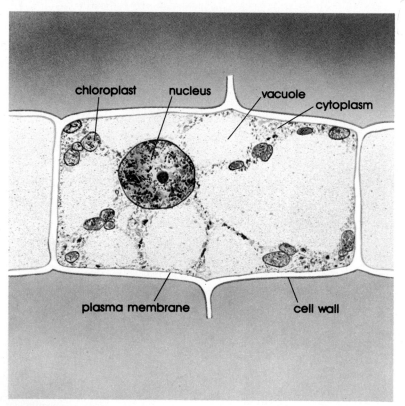

Plant cell

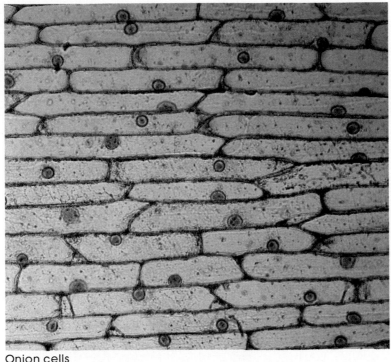

Onion cells

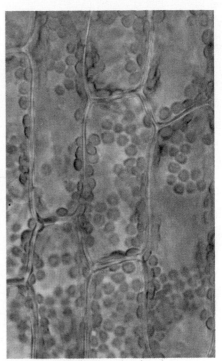

Cells from a water plant

Some plant cells have another structure that is not found in animal cells. This structure is called the **chloroplast** (klôr'ə plast). Plant cells make their own food in the chloroplasts. Chloroplasts contain a green chemical called **chlorophyll** (klôr'ə fil). Those plant parts that contain cells with chloroplasts appear green. Leaves, for example, contain chloroplasts. The chlorophyll traps energy from sunlight. This energy is used to make food. A plant cell may contain many chloroplasts. Chloroplasts can be seen in the picture showing cells from a water plant.

Plant cells also contain vacuoles. However, the vacuoles in plant cells are often larger than those in animal cells. In fact, a single vacuole may take up most of the space in a plant cell, pushing the nucleus to one side.

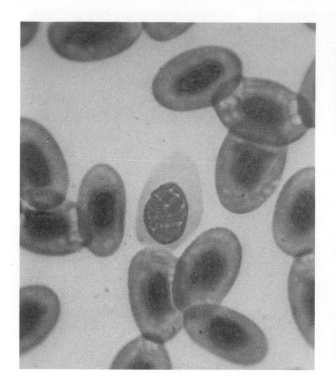
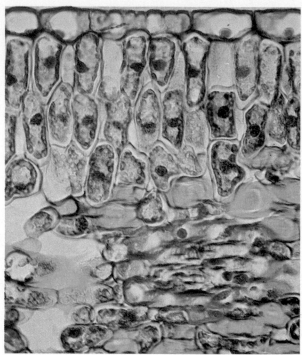

Now that you have learned about animal cells and plant cells, how are they alike? How are they different? Plant cells and animal cells have a plasma membrane, nucleus, and cytoplasm. Plant cells have a cell wall. Animal cells do not. Some plant cells contain chloroplasts. Which of the pictures above shows plant cells? Which structures listed in the table can you identify in the cells in the pictures?

Cell part	Found in animal cells	Found in plant cells
Nucleus	Yes	Yes
Cytoplasm	Yes	Yes
Plasma membrane	Yes	Yes
Cell wall	No	Yes
Chloroplasts	No	In some

What do onion cells look like?

Materials   microscope / microscope slide / coverslip / medicine dropper / tweezers / iodine solution / onion

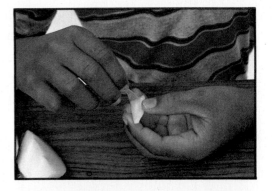

Procedure

A. Put a drop of water in the center of a slide.

B. Obtain a piece of onion. Bend the piece back so that it breaks in two. Slowly pull the two halves apart. A thin layer of onion tissue will peel off. With tweezers or your fingers, remove a piece of this thin tissue.

   1. Why is a thin layer of tissue used?

C. Float the onion tissue in the drop of water. Try to make the tissue flat. Add a drop of iodine to the water. Caution: Iodine stains and is harmful if swallowed. Place a coverslip over the tissue.

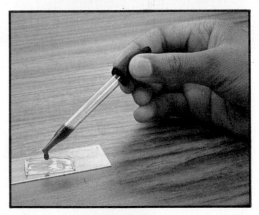

D. Look at the onion cell under low power and high power of your microscope.

   2. Describe the shape of the onion cells.
   3. Draw several of the cells under low power and under high power.
   4. Label the nucleus, the cytoplasm, the cell wall, and any vacuoles that you see.

Conclusion

1. Describe what an onion cell looks like.
2. List all the parts you observed, and describe what they do.

Using science ideas

Observe cells from lettuce leaf, tomato skin, and other plant parts. Compare these observations with those for onion cells.

— HOW CELLS REPRODUCE —
How does a cell divide to form two cells?

Most plants and animals are made up of many cells. You are also made up of many cells. But cells can become damaged or worn out. For example, thousands of skin cells are rubbed off each day as you wash. How does your body replace the cells that it loses?

New cells are made by cell division. During cell division one cell divides into two new cells. This process is called **mitosis** (mī tō′sis). The drawings and pictures show how a cell divides into two cells during mitosis. Check these as you read about each of the steps in mitosis.

1. As mitosis begins, the nuclear membrane starts to break apart. The cell's chromosomes get

Photographs by Carolina Biological Supply Company

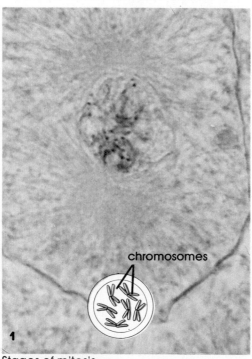

chromosomes

1

Stages of mitosis

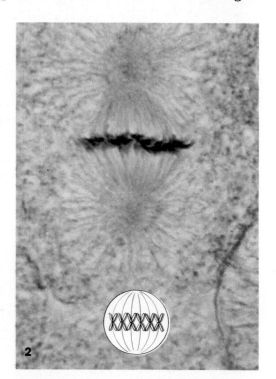

2

thicker at this time, and they become visible. It can be seen that each chromosome has made a copy of itself. So each chromosome is actually two identical chromosomes that are attached.

2. The chromosomes line up in the center of the cell. A web, or network, of fibers appears to be connected to the chromosomes.

3. The pairs of identical chromosomes separate. One member of each pair moves to one end of the cell. The other member moves to the opposite end of the cell. There are then two groups of identical chromosomes at opposite ends of the cell.

4. A nuclear membrane forms around each group of chromosomes. A cell membrane develops down the middle of the cell. As mitosis is completed, two new identical cells are formed.

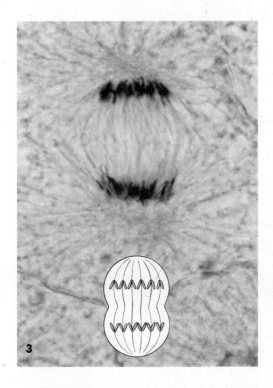

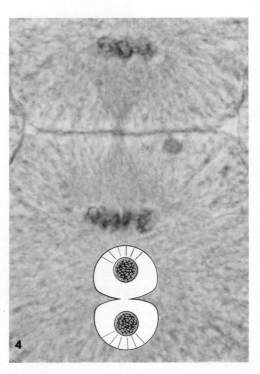

Perhaps you are wondering why the chromosomes made copies of themselves. Remember that the chromosomes contain the cell's genes. The genes control the cell's activities. During mitosis each cell gets a complete set of chromosomes. So each cell gets a complete set of genes. If the chromosomes didn't make copies of themselves, each cell would be missing some genes. The cells probably would not be able to function properly.

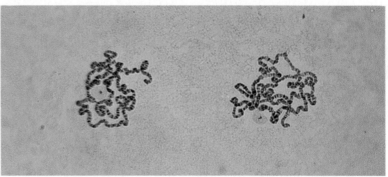

Fruit fly chromosomes

Finding out

Can you make a model of mitosis? Using yarn of two different colors, scissors, index cards, a pencil, and some glue, you can make a model of mitosis. In your model, the cell will contain two chromosomes. Cut eight 1-cm lengths of yarn in each color. The pieces of yarn will represent the chromosomes. Using the drawings on pages 14 and 15 to guide you, make a model of each stage of mitosis by gluing yarn to the index cards. The outlines of the cell and nucleus can be drawn in. Remember that as mitosis begins, each chromosome is double. Therefore, you will have to glue two pieces of yarn together to make doubled chromosomes when these are needed. Glue the index cards in correct order to a piece of cardboard.

SINGLE CELLS

What kinds of organisms exist as single cells?

Some organisms are made up of just a single cell. A single-celled organism is called a **protist** (prō′tist). A microscope is usually needed to see protists. Most protists live in water or in moist places. The protists can be separated into three groups—the animallike protists, the plantlike protists, and the bacteria (bak tir′ē ə).

The animallike protists are called **protozoans** (prō tə zō′ənz). Protozoans do not have chloroplasts, so they cannot make their own food. Protozoans are usually classified by the way they move around in search of food.

Some protozoans, like the amoebas (ə mē′bəz) shown here, move by having their cytoplasm push against the cell membrane at a certain place. The cytoplasm pushes out the cell membrane, as shown in the drawings. These protozoans flow along in the direction of the push, much like flowing syrup. They eat other protists

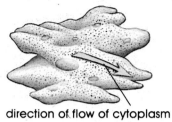

direction of flow of cytoplasm

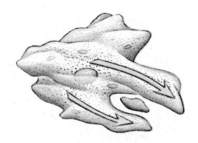

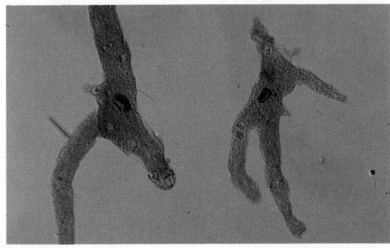

Amoebas

by flowing around and over them. Once one of these other protists is surrounded, it is taken into the cell.

Some protozoans have tiny hairlike structures covering the cell. A paramecium (par ə mē'-shē əm), like those shown below, is an example of a protist with such hairs. The hairs move back and forth and help to move this protist through the water. This is how a paramecium moves around in search of food.

Some protozoans have a taillike structure near one end of the cell. These protozoans move through the water by whipping this taillike structure in a circular motion. A euglena (yü glē'nə) is an example of a protozoan that moves in this way. Euglenas are unusual in that they take in food and also have chloroplasts to make their own food.

A second group of protists are the plantlike protists. The plantlike protists have cell walls and chloroplasts. These protists make their own food.

Photographs by Carolina Biological Supply Company

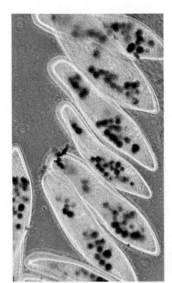
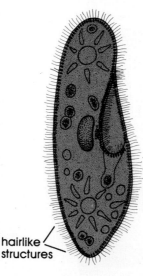
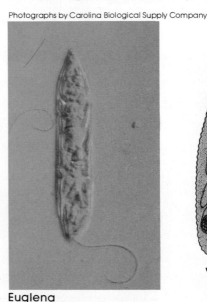
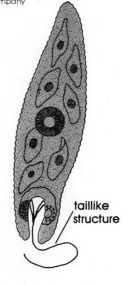

hairlike structures

taillike structure

Paramecia

Euglena

Diatoms

Most plantlike protists, such as diatoms (dī'ə-tomz), float in the oceans. These protists are food for many other living things in the oceans. Organisms that eat the plantlike protists may in turn be food for other organisms. So all organisms in the oceans depend directly or indirectly on the plant-like protists for food.

The simplest protists are the **bacteria.** Bacteria differ in some ways from the plantlike protists and the protozoans. A bacterial cell is surrounded by a cell wall. But there is no nucleus inside the cell. Most bacteria do not contain chlorophyll. So they cannot make their own food. Most bacteria are smaller than the protozoans and the plantlike protists. In fact, several hundred bacteria could fit inside one large protozoan.

Scientists classify bacteria by shapes. As you can see in the drawing, some bacteria are round, others are rod-shaped, and some are spiral-shaped.

Bacteria are found almost everywhere. They live in water, in soil, and in the air. Some types of

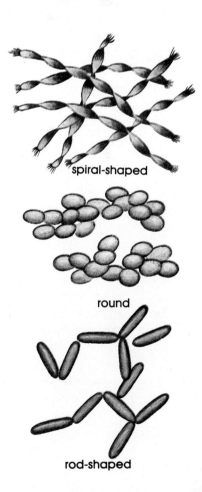

spiral-shaped

round

rod-shaped

bacteria, together with certain other organisms, cause substances to decay. For example, when plants and animals die, bacteria break down the bodies into simpler materials. These materials enrich the soil, making it suitable for new growth. Other kinds of bacteria live inside your body. Many are harmless, and some may be helpful. For instance, certain bacteria form vitamin K in your intestines. However, bacteria sometimes enter your body and cause disease. For example, certain kinds of food poisoning are caused by bacteria.

Do you know?

Have you ever been sick and been told that you had a virus? Well, what is a virus? A virus is not a cell. But a virus does some things that living things do. A virus can reproduce. And a virus uses energy. However, a virus cannot do these things on its own. A virus must be inside a living cell to reproduce. A virus uses the cell's energy to reproduce. Hundreds of viruses may be produced inside a cell. In fact, the viruses finally cause the cell to explode. This is how the viruses spread to other cells.

Since a virus is not a cell, it does not have any cytoplasm. It does not have a plasma membrane. A virus seems to be on the borderline between the living and nonliving worlds.

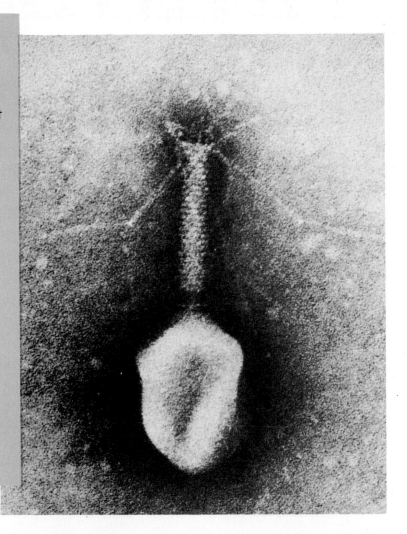

-TISSUES, ORGANS, AND SYSTEMS-

How are cells organized in many-celled organisms?

Plants and animals are made up of many cells. In most plants and animals, different cells do different jobs. Cells that do the same job are like a team. A team of cells in a plant or animal that does a special job is called a **tissue** (tish'ü). The cells in each tissue work together to do a job that helps to keep the organism alive.

The cells lining the inside of your mouth form a tissue. The job of this tissue is to cover and protect the inside of your mouth.

The tissue that covers the outside of a leaf does the same job as the tissue covering the inside of your mouth. The flat cells in that tissue protect the leaf. The cells also keep the leaf from losing water. This helps to keep the leaf moist.

Your body has many kinds of tissue. One kind of tissue is made up of cells that can get longer and shorter. This tissue is muscle tissue. Muscle tissue that is attached to your bones helps you to move. Muscle tissue in your stomach squeezes food and moves it into your intestine.

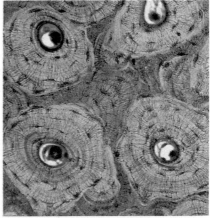
Bone tissue

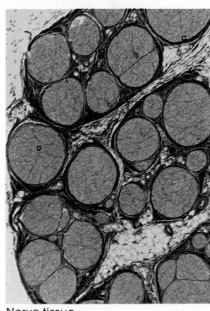
Nerve tissue

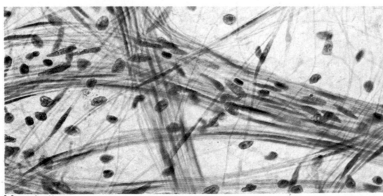
Muscle tissue

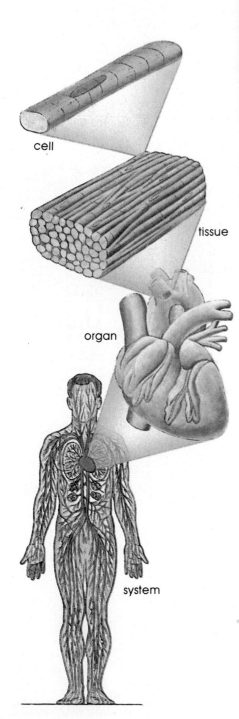

cell

tissue

organ

system

Another kind of tissue is nervous tissue. Nervous tissue is made up of cells that carry messages between the brain and other parts of the body. Nervous tissue is found in the brain, the spinal cord, and the nerves.

Different kinds of tissue usually work together to carry out an important activity. A group of tissues working together to carry out a body activity is called an **organ** (ôr′gən). Your stomach is an example of an organ.

Look at the basketball players in the picture. Could one player do all the work for a team? No. The players work together to score points.

In the same way, one organ alone cannot usually do a major job within an organism. For example, the stomach cannot digest food all by itself. Other organs are also needed to do this major job. In many plants and animals, organs work together to do the major jobs that keep an organism alive. The organs are like the players on a team. Such a group of organs is called a **system.**

Your mouth, teeth, tongue, stomach, small intestine, and large intestine all work together. All of those organs, and others, work together to digest your food. Together they make up the digestive (də jes'tiv) system.

There are other systems in your body that do major jobs to keep you alive. The circulatory (sėr'kyə lə tôr ē) system carries food and oxygen to all parts of your body. The nervous system carries messages to all parts of your body. The respiratory (res'pər ə tôr ē) system takes in oxygen from the air and gives off waste gases. The muscular and skeletal systems support your body and help you to move. What systems are working to help the people in the picture as they exercise?

IDEAS TO REMEMBER

▶ All organisms need energy to grow and to respond to the world around them.

▶ All organisms are made up of one or more cells.

▶ Most cells have a nucleus, cytoplasm, and a plasma membrane. Plant cells also have a cell wall and may contain chloroplasts.

▶ Single-celled organisms are called protists.

▶ A team of cells that does a special job is called a tissue.

▶ A group of tissues working together to carry out an important body activity is called an organ.

▶ Organs working together to carry out a major job in an organism make up a system.

Reviewing the Chapter

SCIENCE WORDS

A. Use all the terms below to fill in the blanks.

mitosis   organism   chlorophyll   bacteria
chromosome   tissue   protist   protozoans

A living thing is called a/an __**1**__. A one-celled living thing is called a/an __**2**__. Two kinds of these one-celled living things are __**3**__ and __**4**__. All living things are made of cells. Cells that work together in a living thing form a/an __**5**__. Plant cells that make food contain the chemical __**6**__. Cells reproduce by a process called __**7**__. In this process, each __**8**__ makes a copy of itself.

B. Write the letter of the term that best matches the definition. Not all the terms will be used.

1. Cell part that contains the chromosomes
2. A group of tissues working together to carry out a body activity
3. Cell part that controls movement of materials into and out of the cell
4. Structures, found on chromosomes, that control a cell's activities
5. Cell part that gives strength and shape to a plant cell

     a. genes
     b. cell wall
     c. system
     d. cytoplasm
     e. nucleus
     f. cell
     g. vacuole
     h. plasma membrane
     i. organ

UNDERSTANDING IDEAS

A. Write the correct term for each number in the diagram: nucleus, plasma membrane, cytoplasm, cell wall, vacuole.

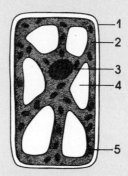

B. Write the names below in two groups: organisms that can make their food; organisms that cannot make their food.

diatoms   trees   grasshoppers   sunflowers
whales   amoebas   grass   zebras

C. The pictures show the stages of mitosis. Write the numbers of the pictures to show the correct order. Describe what is happening in each step.

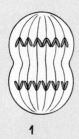

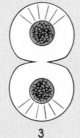

1   2   3   4

USING IDEAS

1. Your body contains many systems. Read about one of these systems. What important jobs does this system do for you? What organs make up the system?

2. Certain human organs, such as kidneys and hearts, can be transplanted. But sometimes the new organ is rejected by the body. Why does this happen?

Chapter 2

Plant Growth and Responses

Imagine that there is a certain tree in your schoolyard. On the tree is a limb that you can just touch by jumping up. Suppose this tree grows 16 cm within the next year. Suppose you grow only 4 cm in that time. Will you be able to touch that limb next year? The answer is Yes. It will also be easier to do because you will be 4 cm closer to the limb.

You may have thought that the growth of the tree would change the location of the limb. But that does not happen. To understand why, you must learn how trees and most other plants grow. In this chapter you will study how plants grow. You will also study how plants respond to the world around them.

HOW PLANTS GROW

How do plants grow in size?

Growth takes place only in certain areas within a plant. These areas are called **growth regions**. There are growth regions at the tips of stems, branches, and roots. Two growth regions are shown in the drawing.

In growth regions there is a special kind of tissue called growth tissue. Many of the cells in this tissue are dividing by mitosis. What steps of mitosis can you find in the picture below? After a cell divides, the two new cells grow larger. They finally become as large as the cell from which they formed. There are many cells dividing and increasing in size in a growth region.

The increase in the size and number of cells causes the tips of stems, branches, and roots to

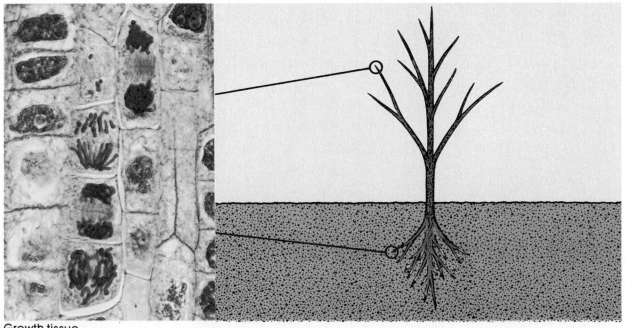

Growth tissue

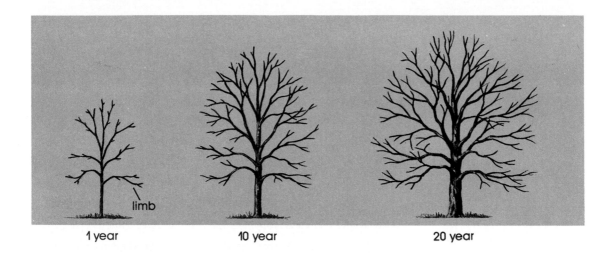

limb

1 year   10 year   20 year

grow longer. That is how the trunk, or stem, of a plant, such as the sequoia tree, grows taller. That is how the branches of a plant grow longer. And that is how the roots of a plant grow longer.

Compare the tree in each drawing above. There are growth regions at the top of a tree trunk and at the end of a limb. A limb can grow longer at the tip. A tree can grow taller at the top. As you can see, the location of a limb on the tree shown above does not change.

Plants have a ring of growth tissue near the outside of stems, branches, and roots. Find the ring of growth tissue in the drawing of the stem. This growth region causes stems, branches, and roots to get bigger around, or increase in circumference.

Look at the drawings of the tree again. What will this second type of growth do to the limb on this tree? In a few years, the limb will be bigger around. If you tie a rope around the limb, it will start to grow over the rope. After many years, the rope will probably be buried in the limb.

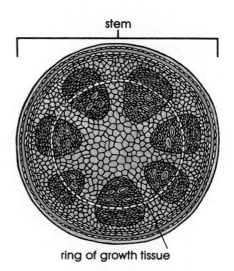

stem

ring of growth tissue

In some areas there is a seasonal change in plant growth. Some kinds of plants grow from seeds in the spring and then die in the fall. Before they die, the plants produce seeds that will sprout when spring returns.

Many kinds of plants live for several years. Some trees may live for hundreds of years. The growth tissue of plants that survive year after year becomes inactive in the fall. Therefore, such plants do not grow during the winter. Although the plants are alive, they are dormant (dôr'mənt), or inactive.

As spring returns, the growth tissue of these plants becomes active. Cells begin to divide again.

Spring

Summer

Fall

Winter

In plants that lost their leaves, new leaves develop. The food-making process begins again, and energy is available for further growth. The plants continue to grow through the summer. As fall returns, growth stops. Then the cycle repeats itself.

This seasonal pattern of growth can be observed in the stems of trees. Notice the rings in the tree stem in the picture. Each ring represents a year's growth. For this reason the rings are called **annual rings.** Each year, the ring of growth tissue in the stem produces a ring of wood. How can you find out how old a tree was from its stem? About how old was the tree in the picture when it was cut?

Do you know?

Tree rings can help scientists learn about the climate in the past. During years when rainfall is abundant, trees produce thick annual rings. During periods of drought, growth is slow, so annual rings are thin. By examining the patterns in annual rings, scientists can determine when droughts occurred in certain places and when years of rainy weather occurred. Tree rings may help show whether conditions of drought and rainy weather occur in cycles.

—— GROWTH AND SURVIVAL ——

How can the way a plant grows help it to survive?

All organisms live where conditions allow them to survive. The conditions that are found where an organism lives are part of its environment (en-vī′rən mənt). The **environment** includes all the living and nonliving things in an area. A plant's environment must have conditions suitable for growth. These conditions include sufficient light and water and a proper temperature range.

If a plant cannot grow in a certain environment, it will die. Often, however, conditions are not perfect, yet plants survive. The plants react to the environment in ways that help them survive. Some of the things that plants may react to are light, gravity, and water. The trees along the cliff live in a rugged environment. But they are reacting to the available light and water and are growing.

The reaction of an organism to something in its environment is called a **response** (ri spons′).

Something in the environment that can cause a response is called a **stimulus** (stim′yə ləs). Pulling your hand away from a hot stove is a response. The stimulus is heat.

Plant responses to a stimulus often involve growth. Look at the picture of the plant that is leaning to one side. What caused the plant to grow in this way? Perhaps you already know that plants grow toward light. On which side of this plant was the light probably the strongest?

Light was the stimulus for the plant in the picture. The growth of the plant toward the light was a response. Plant responses that involve growth are called **tropisms** (trō′piz əmz). The response of a plant to light is called **phototropism** (fō tō trō′piz əm).

How can growing toward light help a plant survive? Many plants grow from seeds that are scattered in the environment. Suppose a seed lands under a bush where there is little light. Does this mean the young plant will die? Not necessarily. As the stem of the plant grows, it may bend toward the light. The stem may bend enough so that the leaves get enough light for the plant to live. When many seeds sprout closely together, as shown, the young plants must compete for light. Those that grow fastest toward the light will survive.

What causes plants to bend toward light? There is a chemical in plants that speeds up cell growth. The chemical moves to the side of a plant stem that is away from the light. This causes the cells on the shaded side to grow faster and larger. The larger cells on the shaded side cause the stem to bend toward the light.

Phototropism

Sprouting seed

33

How can a plant's response to light help it to survive?

Materials 2 paper cups / potting soil / 6 bean seeds / cardboard box / scissors

Procedure

A. Add loose potting soil to two paper cups, leaving a 1-cm space at the top. Use a pencil to poke three holes, each 2 cm deep, in each cup.

B. Put a bean seed in each hole. Cover the seeds with the same amount of loose soil. Add the same small amount of water to each cup.

C. Cut a hole about 6 cm square near one corner of a cardboard box. Put the box upside down in a place where light can enter the hole.

D. Put one of the cups under the box. The cup should be at the end of the box opposite the hole. The other cup should be placed where the developing plants will get normal light. Give all the plants the same amount of water every few days. Do not move the cups when watering them.

    1. Why should you not move the cups?

E. Allow the plants to grow for 10 to 12 days. Then observe the plants for differences in growth.

    2. Describe any differences you observed.

Conclusion

1. In a good experiment, there is one setup that is kept under normal conditions. This setup is called the *control.* All but one of the conditions in the other setups are the same as those in the control. This one condition is called the *variable.* What is the control in this experiment? What is the variable?

2. How did the growth response of the plants under the box help them to survive?

The plant in the tipped-over pot is getting light from all directions. Yet it has started to grow upward. What is this plant responding to?

Plants respond to the earth's gravity. Plant stems grow in the opposite direction to the pull of gravity. So the plant stem in the picture has started to grow upward.

Plant roots, however, respond to gravity in a different way. The roots grow in the direction of the pull of gravity, or downward. How does this kind of response help a plant to survive?

In addition to growth responses, a plant may have special structures that help it to survive. For example, the tough bark of a tree may prevent insects from eating into the tree and killing it. Any structure or response that helps an organism to survive is called an **adaptation** (ad-ap tā'shən).

Finding out

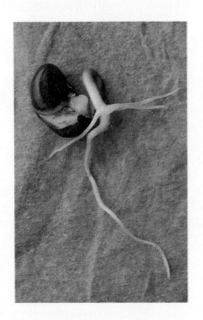

Can you design an experiment to prove that a root grows in the direction of the pull of gravity? You have learned that roots grow in the direction of the pull of gravity. But can you design an experiment to prove this? First you should state a purpose for your experiment. Then make a list of the materials you will use. Next write a step-by-step plan for carrying out the experiment. Remember, every good experiment includes a control and a variable. Be sure that your experiment has each of these things.

After planning your experiment, try it out. Make observations and record data during the experiment. When you have finished, make a conclusion based on your data.

-OTHER ADAPTATIONS OF PLANTS-

How are plants adapted to their environments?

If a seed lands on the soil near its parent plant, it has little chance to survive. As it grows it must compete with the parent plant for water and light. So most seeds have adaptations that allow the seeds to be spread around.

Milkweed seeds are very light and can be carried by the wind. Maple seeds are "winged." The wings help carry the seeds in the wind. Many seeds, such as apple seeds, are hidden in fruits. Animals eat the fruits and seeds, but the seeds are not digested. They pass out of the animals and into the soil. Some seeds, such as those of cocklebur, have stickers that cling to animal fur.

Milkweed seeds

Maple seeds

Cocklebur

The seeds are carried on the animal for a time and then fall off.

Why don't seeds germinate during the winter? Seeds do not germinate if the temperature is too low. During winter, the soil temperature is low. As spring approaches, the soil becomes warmer. So seeds in the soil begin to germinate. What would happen to seeds that germinated during the winter?

Pines, firs, and other evergreen trees have needles instead of broad leaves. The needles are very compact and have a small surface area. The trees lose very little water through their needles. Evergreen trees are abundant in places where rainfall is not great. The needlelike leaves are an adaptation for conserving water.

Evergreen needles

How does temperature affect the germination of seeds?

Materials 50 bean seeds / paper toweling / 2 plastic containers (or other type of container) / tweezers

Procedure

A. Obtain two pieces of paper toweling, each about 30 cm long. Fold each piece of toweling in half lengthwise twice.

B. Soak both pieces of toweling with water. Place the pieces of toweling in separate containers.

C. Place 25 seeds between the first and second layers of the toweling in one container. Place this container in a refrigerator at about 5°C.

D. Place 25 seeds between the first and second layers of the toweling in the second container. Store this container at room temperature (20°–25°C). Place the container in a dark area. Keep the paper toweling moist in both containers.

E. Check the containers each day for 7 days for seed germination.
   1. In a table like the one shown, record the total number of seeds that have germinated in each container each day.
   2. At which temperature did the greater number of seeds germinate?

Conclusion

1. Make a bar graph showing the total number of seeds that germinated in each container every day over the 7-day period.

2. How did temperature affect the germination of seeds in this experiment?

| Day | NUMBER OF SEEDS GERMINATED | |
	At room temp.	At refrig. temp.
1		
2		

Some plants have adaptations that help them live in cold places. Others have adaptations that help them live in hot, dry places. Desert plants, such as cactuses, have thick stems in which water is stored for use during long dry periods.

Cactus

Cactus stem

Many desert plants have long roots that are close to the surface. Such shallow roots are an adaptation for absorbing as much water as possible. Rainwater in the desert does not penetrate very far below the surface.

The seeds of many desert plants have chemicals in the seed coat. These chemicals keep the seeds from germinating until conditions are favorable. But the chemicals can be dissolved with water. A little rain will not dissolve all the chemicals. So the seeds will not germinate. If they did germinate, they would probably die from lack of water. However, a lot of rain will dissolve the chemicals. The seeds will then germinate. There will probably be enough water in the soil for the plants to grow and reproduce.

As the picture shows, a forest fire is a destructive event. However, the seeds of certain plants are adapted to forest fires. The seeds of some kinds of pine trees are held in the cones by a sticky material. Heat from a forest fire is needed to melt the sticky material. The seeds will then be released. When the fire is over, the seeds will germinate.

The seeds of some kinds of shrubs are also adapted to forest fires. The seeds have such a hard coating that water cannot get in. Heat from a forest fire splits the hard coating. When conditions are good, the seeds will absorb water and germinate.

BIOLOGICAL CLOCKS

How is the timing of blooming controlled in plants?

Look at the picture of the crocus in the snow. Crocuses bloom in the early spring. Other kinds of flowers, such as day lilies, bloom during the summer. Some flowers, such as mums, don't bloom until the fall. But nearly all the flowers of any one kind of plant bloom at the same time. As a result, pollen can be transferred among the flowers. Many seeds will then be produced.

Some kinds of flowers, such as morning glories, open in the morning. Other kinds, such as four o'clocks, open in the late afternoon. Still others, such as the moonvine, open just as it is getting dark. But nearly all the flowers of any one kind of

Crocus

Day lily

Morning glories

plant are open at the same time. This allows pollen to be transferred and seeds to be produced.

What causes all the flowers of one kind to bloom at the same time of year? What causes the flowers to open at certain times of the day? These questions puzzled scientists for many years. The answers still are not completely known. Scientists do know that something causes plants to do certain things at certain times. This "something" is called a **biological clock.** A biological clock is not a specific part of a plant. It is a kind of "chemical clock" inside the organism. This biological clock causes certain activities to take place at certain times.

Moonvine

Mums

A plant's biological clock causes the plant to respond to changes in the environment. For example, a plant may respond to changes in the length of day and night. A good example of this can be seen above. In nature, mums usually produce flowers only in the fall. The short daylight period in the fall is a signal to the plants to bloom.

Flower growers have learned how to fool the mum's biological clock. Flower growers grow mums in artificial light. The length of time that the mums receive light each day is the same as the daylight period in the fall. Therefore, the plants can produce flowers all year.

A plant's biological clock may keep the plant from growing in certain places. Ragweed plants produce flowers when the daylight period is just about 14½ hours long. But in northern Maine, the daylight period is longer than this for most of the summer. When daylight shortens to about 14½ hours there, it is nearly fall. The weather has turned cool. The ragweed plants would die before they had time to produce seeds. So ragweed will not grow in northern Maine.

Ragweed

IDEAS TO REMEMBER

▶ In plants, growth regions located at the tips of stems, branches, and roots cause these structures to grow longer.

▶ Rings of growth tissue near the outside of stems, branches, and roots cause these structures to increase in circumference.

▶ Plants respond to the environment in ways that increase their chances of survival.

▶ An adaptation is a structure or response that helps an organism to survive in its environment.

▶ Different plants have different adaptations. A plant's adaptations help it to survive.

▶ The biological clocks of plants control the timing of certain important activities.

Reviewing the Chapter

SCIENCE WORDS

A. Use the terms below to fill in the blanks.

annual rings   phototropism   environment   stimulus
adaptations   growth regions   tropism   gravity

    In plants, growth takes place only in certain areas called __1__. Growth can be observed in many ways. For example, the seasonal growth pattern of trees can be observed in the __2__ produced in the stem. Like all living things, plants respond to conditions in the __3__. Something that can cause a plant to respond is called a/an __4__. Any plant response that involves growth is called a/an __5__. The growth response of a plant toward light is called __6__. Both stems and roots respond to __7__ but in opposite directions. Since these responses help a plant to survive, they are called __8__.

UNDERSTANDING IDEAS

A. State whether each sentence is true or false. Rewrite false statements to make them true.
1. Cells on the lighted side of a stem grow faster than those on the shaded side.
2. Plant stems grow in the direction of the pull of gravity.
3. Growth regions are located at the tips of stems, branches, and roots.
4. The seeds of many kinds of desert plants will germinate only after a heavy rain.
5. A plant's biological clock is an organ in the stem.

B. Study picture **A.** It shows a tree in early spring. Then study pictures **B, C,** and **D.**

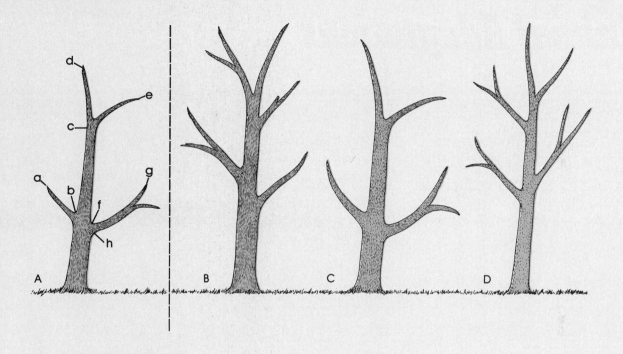

1. Which picture (**B, C,** or **D**) best shows how the tree in picture **A** might look the following spring?
2. Certain areas of the tree in picture **A** are labeled. Identify the areas where increase in length would take place in the tree.

USING IDEAS

1. Set up and perform an experiment to find out if bean stems will grow downward if the only light source comes from below.
2. The seeds of some plants, including many evergreens, must be frozen and then warmed before they will germinate. Use the library to find out how this adaptation helps the plants to survive.

Chapter 3

Animal Adaptations

The bird in the picture is a snowy owl. The snowy owl lives in the northern United States and Canada. The ground there is covered with snow much of the year. The owl's white feathers blend in with the snow. Other birds, and small animals such as mice, have difficulty spotting the owl. These animals happen to be the owl's food. The white color is an adaptation that helps make the owl a successful hunter. Such an adaptation involves the owl's body. In this chapter you will learn about adaptations that involve an animal's body. You will also learn about adaptations that involve the way an animal behaves.

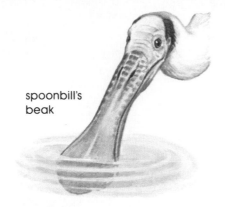

spoonbill's beak

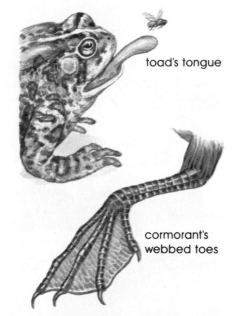

toad's tongue

cormorant's webbed toes

— STRUCTURAL ADAPTATIONS —

How can the structure of an animal's body help it to survive?

An adaptation can be something an organism does that helps it to survive. An adaptation can also be a certain part of an organism. The white feathers help the snowy owl to blend in with the snow. An adaptation that involves some part of an organism's body is called a **structural adaptation.**

Different animals have different kinds of structural adaptations. Some adaptations help animals to feed. Other adaptations help animals to move. Such adaptations can help animals to catch food and escape from enemies. Adaptations may also protect animals from other animals or from a harsh environment. Such adaptations often involve the body covering. Some adaptations are shown here. How might each adaptation help the animal to survive?

The first type of structural adaptation you will study is related to feeding. Different animals may have different kinds of teeth for chewing and eat-

rhino's horn

seal's flipper

turtle's shell

ing different kinds of foods. Birds lack teeth, but they have bills that are adapted for feeding. Birds' bills may be adapted for eating seeds, fruits, or animals. Some insects have specialized mouth parts for feeding on plants. Other insects have mouth parts for feeding on blood.

What is the woodpecker's structural adaptation for feeding? The woodpecker has a sharp beak. The sharp beak is an adaptation that helps the woodpecker drill holes in trees. The woodpecker feeds on insects that live within the wood. The woodpecker may also use the hole for a nest.

Have you ever noticed a butterfly moving from flower to flower? The butterfly has a long tube-like mouth that it can coil and uncoil. This adaptation helps the butterfly to get the sweet juices that are deep inside the flowers.

Woodpecker

mouth tube

Pale clouded yellow butterfly

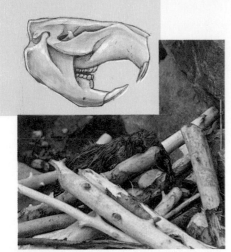

Beaver

The beaver has sharp teeth that help it chew wood and gnaw through trees. As the beaver gnaws wood, it wears its teeth down. But the teeth keep growing. So the beaver can continue to feed. Both the sharpness of the teeth and their ability to keep growing are adaptations.

Grazing animals, such as cows, have large flat teeth along the sides of the mouth. These teeth are called **molars** (mō′lərz). Grazing animals use their molars to crush and grind tough plant materials. This makes the food easier to digest.

Meat-eating animals, such as wolves, have sharp pointed teeth near the front of the mouth. These teeth are called **canines** (kā′nīnz). The teeth are useful in killing prey. The meat-eating animals use their sharp front teeth, called **incisors** (in sī′zərz), to tear off chunks of flesh, which they then swallow with little chewing. Since meat is easier to digest than plant material, the molars of meat-eaters are small. Compare the animals shown on the top of page 53. Which one of these animals eats meat? Which animal grazes?

Cows grazing

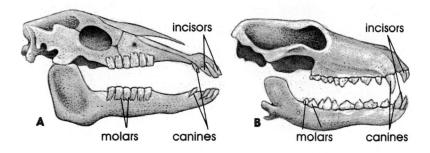

incisors

molars   canines   molars   canines

incisors

A   B

A second type of structural adaptation of animals is related to movement. Such adaptations may involve the ability to run, climb, jump, swim, or fly. Differences in body structure among animals are often related to different adaptations for movement.

Kangaroos are plant eaters that hop about on powerful hind legs. If attacked, a kangaroo will bound away in great leaps. Powerful leg muscles enable a large kangaroo to take leaps of 10 m or more. Such jumps can help the kangaroo escape wild dogs and other enemies.

Kangaroo

Gibbon

Gibbons are small apes that live in the forests of Asia. These animals spend most of their time in trees. Notice how long the arms of a gibbon are. Gibbons use their long, powerful arms to swing among the branches in search of the fruits they eat. Though clumsy on the ground, gibbons swing through the forest with amazing skill. They are the acrobats of the animal world.

The cheetah is a meat-eating animal that lives in Africa. It catches its prey, such as antelope, by running it down with a quick burst of speed. The cheetah's light build and long legs help it to build up speed quickly. In addition, the cheetah has a flexible backbone. As the cheetah runs, its backbone stretches and shortens like a spring. This action gives the cheetah a very long stride, which adds to its speed. Over a short distance the cheetah can run about 100 km/h.

Cheetah

Vultures are birds that feed on the remains of dead animals. Since vultures do not have to catch their food, they are not adapted for speed. Instead, the long, broad wings of vultures are adapted for soaring. Vultures glide slowly in circles while watching the ground. When a vulture spots a dead or dying animal, it will land nearby. When it is safe to do so, it will begin to feed.

Another type of structural adaptation involves the body covering of animals. Some kinds of animals, including worms and amphibians, breathe through their skins. Adaptations such as feathers and hair help animals to conserve body heat. Special adaptations on the skin, such as spines, may protect an animal from enemies.

Salamanders have smooth, moist skin. The moist skin allows oxygen to pass into the salamander's blood. Carbon dioxide can pass out through the moist skin. In fact, some salamanders, like the dusky salamander, do not have lungs. Such salamanders can only breathe through their skin.

Turkey vulture

Spotted dusky salamander

55

Short-horned lizard

Instead of smooth, moist skin, reptiles have a covering of scales. Oxygen cannot pass through the scales. So reptiles cannot breathe through their skin. However, the scales keep the reptiles from losing water. So reptiles are better adapted than salamanders to life on land. Reptiles can even survive in the desert. Salamanders would lose moisture and die quickly in such a dry environment.

As you probably know, animals with hair are called mammals. Hair is an adaptation that helps mammals keep warm. Musk oxen and other

Musk oxen

mammals that live in cold regions have thick coats of hair. The long, thick hair of the musk ox protects the animal from cold temperatures and arctic winds.

Mammals may shed hair as summer approaches and grow thicker coats of hair in the fall. The whitetail deer of the United States and Canada has a light coat of reddish-brown hair in the summer. In winter this deer has a thick coat of grayish hair.

Sometimes an animal's body covering is an adaptation that protects it against enemies. The porcupine is a slow-moving animal that feeds on plants. Its body is covered with long, sharp quills. When threatened, the porcupine rolls into a ball. Its attacker may end up with a mouthful of quills rather than a meal.

The armadillo (är mə dil'ō), which is found in the southern United States and Mexico, is covered with armor plates. The hard plates help protect the armadillo from its enemies, such as the fox.

Porcupine

Armadillo

Finding out

What structural adaptations can help an imaginary animal to survive in this desert? Think of an imaginary animal that lives in this desert. The animal feeds on insects in the early evening and morning. During the day it burrows into the ground to avoid the heat. It is food for a large ground-dwelling bird. List three or four structural adaptations that will help this animal.

How does hair help to keep an animal warm?

Materials 2 tin cans (equal size) / 2 Celsius thermometers / glue / cotton / hot water / clock or watch

Procedure

A. Remove the labels from two tin cans. Coat the outside of one can with glue.

B. Put a layer of cotton over the glued surface. Wait a few minutes for the glue to dry. Fluff the cotton outward.

C. Fill both cans with hot water from the same container. Make sure both have the same amount of water.

   1. What do you think will happen to the temperature of the water in each can?

D. Measure and record the temperature of the water in each can every 5 minutes for the next half hour.

   2. Make a graph of the temperature over the 30 minutes to show your results.

   3. Which can lost heat more quickly?

Conclusion

Using the results of this experiment, explain how hair helps to keep an animal warm.

Using science ideas

Many sea mammals, such as whales, have little hair. How do such animals keep warm in cold water?

LOOKS THAT PROTECT

How can an animal's appearance help it to survive?

There are several kinds of structural adaptations that involve appearance, or how an animal looks. Such adaptations may help the animal to look like something else or to hide in its environment.

One structural adaptation involving appearance is **protective coloration** (prə tek′tiv   kul ə-rā′shən). An animal with protective coloration has a color similar to the color of its environment. As a result, the animal is hard to see. This may give the animal some protection from its enemies. Or it may help make the animal a successful hunter. The white color of the snowy owl on page 49 is an example of protective coloration.

The chameleon (kə mē′lē ən) is a tree-dwelling lizard found in Asia and Africa. Chameleons can change color to match the color of their surroundings. For example, a chameleon will turn green

Chameleons

Snowshoe hare in summer

Snowshoe hare in winter

when it is among green leaves. But when on a brown branch, it will turn brown. The ability to change color allows the chameleon to remain hidden as it hunts the insects that it feeds on.

Some animals change color with the seasons. An example is the snowshoe hare. As you can see in the first picture, the hare is dark colored in the summer. Then the hare blends in with the bushes that it hides in. The hare's fur is white in the winter, as you can see in the second picture. This makes the animal hard to see in the snow. Throughout the year the hare's enemies, such as the bobcat, have difficulty seeing it.

Can you see the insect on the branch in the picture below? It is called a walking stick. The walking stick has a color similar to the branches it lives on. It is also shaped like a small branch. These adaptations make it hard for lizards and birds that eat the walking stick to see it. An adaptation in which an animal looks similar to something in its environment is called **protective resemblance** (ri zem′bləns).

Walking stick

Monarch butterfly

Viceroy butterfly

Certain harmless animals benefit by looking like poisonous or dangerous animals. Look at the pictures of the monarch butterfly and the viceroy butterfly. The body of the monarch contains a poison harmful to other animals. A bird that eats a monarch will become sick. Thereafter it will not eat a monarch. The bird will also avoid viceroy butterflies. The viceroy benefits by looking like the poisonous monarch. Would you be able to tell the two apart if both were on a flower? An adaptation in which an animal looks like a dangerous or poisonous animal is called **mimicry** (mim′ik rē).

— BEHAVIOR AND INSTINCT —
How can instincts help animals to survive?

An adaptation can be something that an animal does that helps it to survive. The activities and actions of an animal are called **behavior.** Behavior includes any activity that helps an animal to survive. Animal behavior includes activities such as the barking of a dog and the singing of a bird.

Some kinds of behavior are learned. For example, a wolf pup learns to hunt by imitating adult wolves. But animals are also born with certain patterns of behavior. Any behavior pattern that an animal is born with is called unlearned behavior, or **instinct** (in'stingkt). The behavior patterns involved in nest building and the raising of young are examples of instinct. Animals usually don't have to learn how to build nests or how to raise their young.

Crocodile on nest

Birds are well-known for their nest-building ability. Different birds build different kinds of nests. Look at the blue jay feeding its young in the picture on page 63. The blue jay builds its nest with small sticks. Then it lines the nest with roots. The nest may be built from 2 m to 15 m above the ground. The blue jay usually builds its nest close to the trunk of a tree. From three to six eggs are laid in the nest. The young birds hatch in 15 to 17 days.

Blue jay feeding its young

The chimney swift often builds its nest on the inside wall of a chimney. The nest is made of sticks. The chimney swift glues the nest to the wall with its own saliva. The saliva hardens and holds the nest in place.

As you can see, different birds build different kinds of nests. Different materials may be used. But in all cases the nest increases the chance that the young birds will survive.

Nest building is a complex behavior. Some kinds of instinct, however, are simple. For example, a young fawn may remain still if something approaches in the forest. Since the fawn blends in with the forest, it may not be seen. The simple act of keeping still is an instinct that may save the fawn's life. Can you think of other examples of simple instincts in animals?

Chimney swift

ANIMAL MIGRATION

Why do animals migrate?

One interesting kind of behavior in animals is migration (mī grā'shən). **Migration** is the movement of an animal or a group of animals over a long distance.

A group of animals usually migrates from one region to another. The animals later return to the original region. The timing of migration is often related to a change in the seasons. Migration is sometimes simply a journey to better feeding grounds. However, many animals migrate to certain regions to reproduce and to raise their young. These regions are called **breeding grounds.**

Many kinds of birds are well-known for their migratory behavior. In the Northern Hemisphere, many birds migrate southward in the fall. This is because winter in the north is harsh and food is scarce. These birds then migrate northward in the spring, when the weather is milder and food is more abundant. Most migratory birds reproduce and raise their young during spring and summer, when conditions are good.

The arctic tern makes the longest journey of any bird. During summer in the Northern Hemisphere, this bird is found throughout the arctic region. It breeds in Alaska, Canada, Greenland, and northern Europe and Asia. In fall the birds leave the arctic. Flying over ocean waters, they travel all the way to the antarctic region. They arrive in time for the antarctic summer. The arctic terns fly north again as the antarctic fall begins and spring returns to the arctic.

Snow geese migrating

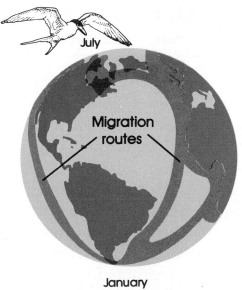

July

Migration routes

January

Arctic tern

Birds are not the only animals that migrate. The picture shows some migrating wildebeests (wil'də-bēsts). Wildebeests are grazing animals that live part of the year on the plains of East Africa. As the dry season begins in June, the wildebeests move west looking for water. A journey of more than 300 km takes them to a region where water can be found. In December the rainy season begins in East Africa. The wildebeests return to the plains, where water is again available.

Wildebeests migrating

HIBERNATION
Why do certain animals hibernate over the winter?

Many animals do not migrate in the winter. They have other ways to survive the cold and the scarcity of food. One adaptation for survival is the deep sleep called **hibernation** (hī bər nā′shən).

During hibernation, an animal's body temperature drops to about the temperature of the environment. However, it does not drop much lower than the freezing point of water. Body activities, such as breathing and heartbeat, become very slow in a hibernating animal.

Many of the animals that hibernate are cold-blooded. A **cold-blooded animal** is an animal whose body temperature changes as the temperature of the environment changes. A cold-blooded animal's body temperature is often close to the temperature of the environment. Snails, amphibians, and reptiles are examples of cold-blooded animals.

Bull frog in pond in fall

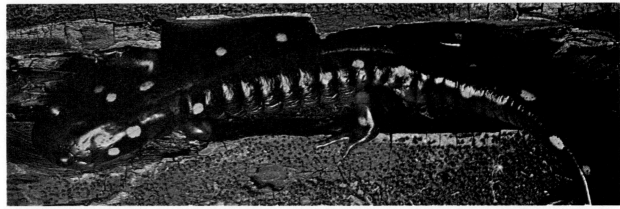
Spotted salamander

Many kinds of animals that live in lakes and ponds hibernate in the mud. Turtles and frogs are among these animals. In the fall they bury themselves in the mud at the bottom of the lake or pond. They survive through the winter even though the lake or pond may freeze over. As spring returns, the frogs and turtles leave the mud and enter the water again.

Some amphibians and reptiles hibernate in the ground. Look at the picture of the spotted salamander. It has crawled into a space in a piece of wood well below the surface. Salamanders hibernate in places like this through the winter. When the weather warms in the spring, salamanders become active again.

Many kinds of snakes hibernate in dens. The den may be a hole in the ground under a large rock. Or it might be a small cave. Different kinds of snakes, such as copperheads and rattlesnakes, may hibernate together. In spring the snakes often leave the den together.

Some warm-blooded animals hibernate also. A **warm-blooded animal** is an animal that has a

Copperheads

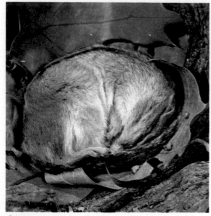
Chipmunk in den

fairly constant body temperature. Birds and mammals are examples of warm-blooded animals.

Some kinds of rodents, such as the woodchuck and chipmunk, hibernate. The woodchuck gets fat during the summer and fall and lives on its fat while it sleeps. Look at this chipmunk curled up in its den. The chipmunk stores food in its den during the summer and fall. It wakes up about once a week during the winter to eat.

Bears, raccoons, and skunks also go into a winter sleep. However, there is some question as to whether or not these animals are really hibernating. For example, the body temperature of a black bear remains near normal during its winter sleep. The heart rate slows but is also near normal. Some black bears even leave their dens and wander around for a time. They then return to their dens.

How is hibernation an adaptation? For some animals, hibernation is a way of surviving the extreme cold of winter. For other animals, hibernation may be a way of surviving during a season when food is scarce.

Grizzly bear in fall

How are body temperature and heart rate related to hiberation?

Procedure

The graph below shows the changes in body temperature and heart rate in the arctic ground squirrel during the year. Use the graph to answer the questions.

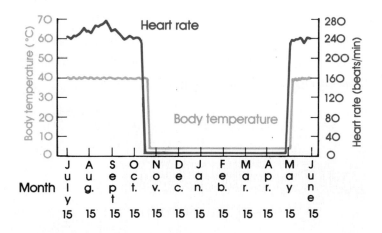

1. During what month does the arctic ground squirrel go into hibernation?
2. During what month does the arctic ground squirrel awake from hibernation?
3. What is the arctic ground squirrel's body temperature when the animal is active?
4. What is the arctic ground squirrel's body temperature when the animal is hibernating?
5. What is the approximate heart rate of an active arctic ground squirrel?
6. What is the heart rate of a hibernating arctic ground squirrel?

Conclusion

In a ground squirrel, what is the relationship of body temperature and heart rate to periods of activity and hibernation?

LEARNED BEHAVIOR

How does the ability to learn help an animal to survive?

Learning is a process that results in a change in behavior because of experience. For example, suppose your dog comes to eat when you shake the food sack each day. Now suppose you stop shaking the food sack at feeding time. Instead, you rattle a can of marbles each day just before you feed the dog. Will your dog learn to come and eat when it hears the marbles rattling? If it does, the dog's behavior will have changed because of a new experience. That is learning.

Raccoon searching for food

Since the environment is always changing, animals must be able to learn. For example, suppose a family of raccoons begins feeding on garbage in cans in a park. For many months the raccoons feed only from the cans. They tip over the garbage cans and make a mess every night as they eat. Finally, the park rangers decide to do something about the problem. They have the garbage cans emptied at the end of each day.

Now what will happen to the raccoon family? Will the raccoons continue to look for food in the garbage cans and finally starve? No, the raccoons will learn that food is no longer available in the garbage cans. Although their environment has changed, they will get food in other ways. They may eat more of their natural food, such as insects and wild berries. They may also learn to feed at a nearby garbage dump.

How does learning take place? For most kinds of learning there are two important steps. The first step is to repeat the experience. This is called practice. For a dog to learn to walk on its hind legs, it must repeat the experience. In other words, it must practice. For a person to learn to play the piano, the experience must be repeated. The person must practice.

The second step in learning is reinforcement (rē-in fôrs′mənt). This lets the learner know whether the practice is correct. One kind of reinforcement is punishment. A mother lion teaching her cubs to hunt may slap them if they don't follow her lead.

Poodle in circus act

Mountain lion, cubs and turtle

Another type of reinforcement is reward. If your dog performs a trick, you may reward it with food or a pat on the head. Wild-animal trainers often reward their animals with food. Words of praise from the teacher reward a piano student who has practiced a musical piece.

Do you know?

Most kinds of learning require practice and reinforcement. However, there is a special kind of learning that occurs in some animals and depends on a single experience. This kind of learning is called imprinting. Imprinting was discovered by a biologist named Konrad Lorenz.

Lorenz studied various types of birds, including geese. Newly hatched geese will follow the first moving thing they see. Normally, this is their mother. However, they respond to whatever they first see as their mother. Lorenz kept some goose eggs in an incubator. The first moving thing that these incubator-hatched geese saw was Lorenz. Thus Lorenz became imprinted on the minds of the geese as their mother. They behaved toward Lorenz as they would have toward their real mother.

Learning in animals is sometimes the result of training by people. Look at the picture of the blind person and the dog guide. A dog guide must be taught to lead a person across streets and around objects.

Some kinds of learning are more difficult than others. And some kinds of learning take place only in humans. Learning that requires imagination and the making of mental pictures occurs only in humans. You use mental pictures to learn about the structure of matter. You make mental pictures of the invisible particles of matter called atoms. You also make mental pictures of the particles that make up an atom. As you can see, in such learning you form one mental picture after another. That is something only humans can do.

IDEAS TO REMEMBER

- ▶ Structural adaptations, such as protective coloration, help organisms to survive.
- ▶ Animals are born with certain instincts that aid survival.
- ▶ Migration involves the movement of animals to better feeding grounds or to breeding grounds.
- ▶ Many cold-blooded animals and some warm-blooded animals survive through the winter by hibernating.
- ▶ Learning is the result of experience. Most types of learning are aided by practice and reinforcement.

Reviewing the Chapter

SCIENCE WORDS

A. Write the letter of the term that best matches the definition. Not all the terms will be used.

1. Behavior in which an animal goes into a deep sleep
2. Adaptation in which an animal looks like some dangerous or poisonous animal
3. A process that results in a change of behavior because of experience
4. An animal with a fairly constant body temperature
5. Behavior that involves the movement of animals over a long distance
6. Adaptation in which an animal looks similar to something in its environment
7. Any behavior pattern that an animal is born with
8. A region where animals go to reproduce and to raise their young

a. protective resemblance
b. warm-blooded animal
c. hibernation
d. protective coloration
e. breeding grounds
f. migration
g. cold-blooded animal
h. mimicry
i. instinct
j. learning

UNDERSTANDING IDEAS

A. Write the terms below in two groups: behavioral adaptations; structural adaptations.

large canines   nest-building   webbed feet   hibernation
thick fur   pointed beak   migration   sharp quills

B. Study the graph. Then answer the questions that follow.

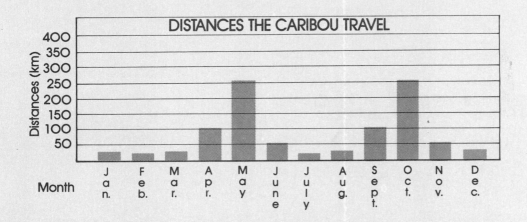

DISTANCES THE CARIBOU TRAVEL

1. During which months is the caribou most likely to be migrating from one region to another?
2. During which month or months does the caribou travel the farthest?
3. The caribou lives in northern Canada. In which general direction is it most likely to travel during the fall?

C. Write the term that does not belong in each group. Explain why the term does not belong.

1. bat's wings, frog's legs, lion's teeth, gibbon's arms
2. chameleon, kangaroo, snowshoe hare, snowy owl
3. eagle's beak, tiger's claws, cow's molars, musk ox's fur

USING IDEAS

1. Observe some of the animals in your community. Identify examples of protective coloration or protective resemblance.
2. How is your thumb a structural adaptation?

Chapter 4

Climate and Life

Imagine yourself traveling around the world taking pictures of wildlife in nature. Do you think you would ever see a polar bear standing by a palm tree? What about an alligator sunning itself next to a cactus? Would you see a chameleon on a block of ice with a penguin?

You wouldn't see those things together in nature. Polar bears and penguins live in cold arctic regions. Palm trees live where it is warm. Alligators live where it is both warm and wet. A cactus lives only where it is dry. Where do chameleons live?

There are regions on the earth where only certain animals and plants are found. In this chapter you will learn about these regions. You will also find out what types of plants and animals are found in each region.

BIOMES
What factors determine a biome?

Most living things are adapted for just one kind of climate. **Climate** is the average weather for a large region over a long period of time. Many factors affect climate. These include rainfall, temperature, wind, and sunlight. The type of climate in a region determines the plants and animals that can live there.

All the plants and animals that live in a region that has a particular climate make up a **biome** (bí'ōm). Climates and types of living things change from one biome to another. The map shows the locations of six major biomes. How many of these biomes can be found in North America?

Water and temperature are two factors of climate that are important to a biome. Much of the

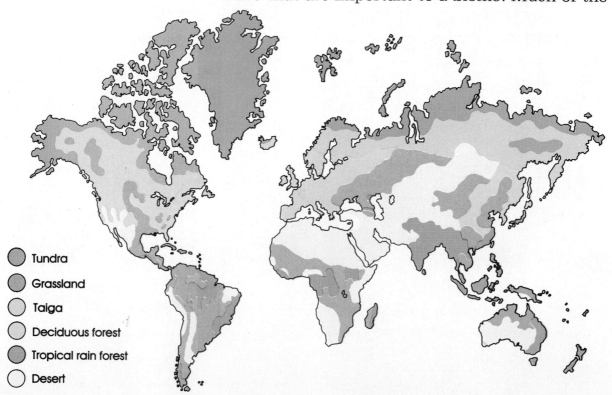

- Tundra
- Grassland
- Taiga
- Deciduous forest
- Tropical rain forest
- Desert

water comes from precipitation, such as rain and snow. Temperature is affected by the amount of sunlight the biome gets. A graph like the one shown gives the average monthly rainfall and average monthly temperature for a given place. Look at the graph. What is the average monthly rainfall for March? What is the average temperature for October?

The table below lists the six biomes shown on the map. The average yearly precipitation is given for each biome. The average temperature range for the year is also given. Which biome has the lowest average precipitation? Which one has the greatest range in temperature?

Some biomes are named after the most common types of plants that live in them. For example, what plants would you expect to find in the grassland biome? What plants would you find in the deciduous forest?

The same kind of biome can be found on different continents. For example, the tundra spreads across the northern parts of North America, Europe, and Asia. Tropical rain forests occur in South America, Africa, and Asia.

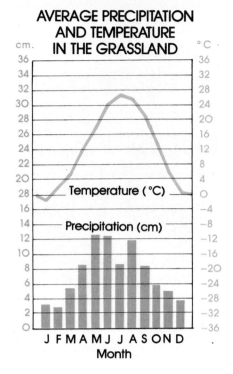

AVERAGE PRECIPITATION AND TEMPERATURE IN THE GRASSLAND

AVERAGE PRECIPITATION AND TEMPERATURE OF BIOMES		
Biome	Average precipitation (yearly)	Average temperature range (yearly)
Tundra	11 cm	−26°C to 4°C
Taiga	35 cm	−10°C to 14°C
Deciduous forest	115 cm	6°C to 28°C
Tropical rain forest	253 cm	25°C to 27°C
Grassland	90 cm	0°C to 25°C
Desert	16 cm	24°C to 32°C

How do temperature and precipitation vary among biomes?

PRECIPITATION (cm)

Month	Deciduous forest	Rain forest	Cold desert
Jan.	12	28	2
Feb.	10	27	3
March	13	33	2
April	9	28	1
May	10	20	1
June	8	21	1
July	10	16	0–1
Aug.	8	13	0–1
Sept.	7	13	0–1
Oct.	6	11	1
Nov.	9	17	2
Dec.	10	27	2

TEMPERATURE (°C)

Month	Deciduous forest	Rain forest	Cold desert
Jan.	6	26	−1
Feb.	6	25	2
March	10	27	6
April	16	27	8
May	21	27	12
June	26	27	14
July	28	27	20
Aug.	26	27	18
Sept.	22	27	14
Oct.	18	27	10
Nov.	10	27	3
Dec.	6	26	0

Materials 3 sheets of graph paper / 2 colored pencils (different colors)

Procedure

A. Set up a graph like the one shown on page 79 on each of three pieces of graph paper.

B. Label one graph *Cold desert,* label one *Deciduous forest,* and label one *Tropical rain forest.*

C. The figures for precipitation and temperature are listed in the tables. Use one colored pencil to make a bar graph of the monthly precipitation for each of the biomes. Use the second colored pencil to make a line graph of the monthly temperature for each of the biomes.

Conclusion

1. In which biome does the temperature vary little throughout the year?

2. The highest average temperature for a single month occurs in which biome? In which month does it occur?

3. Which biome has the least precipitation throughout the year?

4. In which biome does the most precipitation fall during a single month? What is the amount of precipitation?

Using science ideas

Find the average yearly precipitation and the average yearly temperature for each of these biomes. Compare the averages.

THE TUNDRA

What are the features of the tundra?

The **tundra** (tun'drə) is a large biome in the far north. It is the coldest of all the biomes. In the tundra the ground is always frozen. There are sudden changes between the seasons in the tundra. Summer lasts for only 6 to 8 weeks. There are long hours of daylight and no darkness. In the short summer, only the top layer of the earth thaws. But water from melting ice cannot seep into the frozen soil below. So many ponds and puddles form.

The plants of the tundra grow quickly in the summer, but they do not last long. Most of them are small. They include grasses, lichens, and mosses. There are some woody plants, but they grow no more than a few centimeters in height. There are no trees in the tundra. There is not

Lichens   Tundra

Arctic fox

enough liquid water deep in the ground for trees to survive. In addition, trees could not survive the strong winds of winter.

Millions of insects hatch in the ponds and puddles that form in the summer. The air is filled with swarms of blackflies, deerflies, and mosquitoes. These insects are a source of food for the many birds that nest in the tundra during the summer.

Eagles, hawks, and falcons live in the tundra during the summer. These birds migrate to other areas in the winter. Two kinds of birds that live in the tundra all year are the snowy owl and the ptarmigan (tär'mə gən). Musk oxen and caribou graze in large herds. Smaller mammals include arctic hares, arctic foxes, and lemmings.

Caribou

Collared lemming and young

Winter in the tundra is very harsh. There are many months of cold and darkness. Food is scarce. Many animals—such as caribou, gulls, and foxes—migrate in search of food. Some small animals, such as lemmings, burrow under the snow for protection. Musk oxen face the full might of the tundra winter. Their heavy coats enable these animals to withstand the cold and the wind.

82

THE TAIGA

What are the features of the taiga?

The **taiga** (tī′gə) is the largest biome. It is south of the tundra. This biome spreads across North America, northern Europe, and northern Asia.

The taiga is very cold during the long winter. But in the summer the forest lands are very popular. Many people enjoy summer fishing and other recreation in the clear lakes and streams of the taiga. *Taiga* is a Russian word that means "swamp forest." This name is used because the melting snow often creates swampy conditions in early summer.

The trees of the taiga are a very important resource. They provide huge amounts of lumber for buildings, furniture, and other items. Also, many of the trees are useful for making pulp from which paper is made. The trees in the taiga are conifers (kō′nə fərz). **Conifers** are trees that produce seeds in cones. Most conifers are evergreens and have needlelike leaves. Spruce, fir, and pine are the main trees in the taiga.

Taiga and pinecones

Wood duck

Mule deer

Wolverine

Many types of animals live in the taiga. Only a few grazing animals can live in this biome. This is because the many trees of the taiga shade so much of the ground that few grasses and other small plants can survive. Large animals, such as moose and deer, graze in small meadows and clearings. Beavers eat plants around ponds and streams. A few small animals, such as squirrels, live on the seeds they obtain from cones. There are many insects, which are eaten by birds. Some of these types of birds also use seeds from the conifers as food.

In winter, many of the taiga animals are less active. Insects hibernate. Squirrels and bears sleep much of the time. Other animals remain active throughout the winter. Lynxes, wolves, and wolverines hunt small animals, such as the snowshoe hare. Caribou and many kinds of birds migrate from the tundra to the taiga.

THE DECIDUOUS FOREST

What are the features of the deciduous forest?

Suppose you were traveling south from Canada into Michigan or Wisconsin. How would the scene change as you traveled? What types of trees would you find? You would probably notice that there were fewer conifer trees as you moved south. There would be more and more trees with broad leaves instead of needles. You would be in another biome—the **deciduous** (di sij'ü əs) **forest**. This biome is named after the broad-leaved trees that are most common there.

Deciduous trees are trees that lose their leaves at some time during the year. Most deciduous trees lose their leaves in the autumn months, just before winter.

Deciduous forest

Oak leaves

Box turtle

The deciduous forest biome includes several parts of the world. The eastern United States is in this biome. So are most of Europe and parts of Japan and Australia. There are not as many trees in this biome as there used to be. Most of the biome is now filled with people and cities. Also, much of the land in this biome has been cleared of trees so that it can be farmed.

The climate in the deciduous forest biome is moist, with rain in summer and snow in winter. The winter is cold and the summer is hot. There are four seasons in the deciduous forest biome.

Wild turkey

Blue grouse

Raccoons

Striped skunk feeding

Gray squirrels

In spring, many wildflowers bloom. In summer, the broad leaves of the trees shade the ground. Some light filters through the leaves, allowing shrubs to grow. Mosses and ferns grow in the deep shade of the forest floor.

There are many kinds of trees in the deciduous forest. Some of these are maple, oak, walnut, elm, and beech. Many of these trees produce fruits and nuts that are eaten by animals.

In autumn, the leaves change from green to red, gold, or brown. The leaves fall and cover the ground. They decay and help to enrich the soil.

The animals of the deciduous forest include deer, squirrels, chipmunks, raccoons, and skunks. There are many small birds. Larger birds, such as grouse and wild turkeys, are also common. Near ponds and streams you might find snakes, turtles, frogs, and toads.

In winter, many animals are less active. Some birds migrate from the taiga to pass the winter in the deciduous forest. Other birds migrate from the deciduous forest to warmer areas. Many reptiles and insects hibernate.

THE TROPICAL RAIN FOREST
What are the features of the tropical rain forest?

The biome that is the richest in plants and animals is the **tropical rain forest.** The plants and animals are present in huge numbers. And there are many thousands of kinds of plants and animals. Look again at the map on page 78. You can see that tropical rain forests are near the equator.

Most trees in the tropical rain forest have broad green leaves. The leaves stay green all year. The reason for this is that the climate does not vary. It is almost always hot and rainy. There is little change in temperature throughout the year.

Tropical rain forest

Orchid

Blue crowned motmot

Spider monkey

What is it like in the rain forest? Outdoors there, you would feel as if you had a roof over your head. The leaves of the tall trees actually form a kind of roof. This "roof" keeps out sunlight, so few plants grow on the forest floor.

Many strange and beautiful plants, such as orchids, grow on the tall trees. These plants are vines that climb toward the sunlight. Most of the plants have beautiful and colorful flowers that attract insects and birds.

Most animals of the tropical rain forest live in the trees. These animals include many kinds of insects, lizards, snakes, frogs, birds, and mammals, such as monkeys. All the animals have a good supply of food. Many feed on seeds and fruits

Tiger beetle feeding

from the trees. Some snakes, such as the huge pythons and anacondas, prey on the large animals of the forest.

The soil of the tropical rain forest is very poor. Almost all the nutrients are in the plants themselves. When a plant or animal dies, it decays quickly. The nutrients are immediately taken up by the growing plants.

Some parts of the tropical rain forest are being lost because of human activity. People cut down the trees and clear the land to make farms. They burn the dead trees. The ashes that are left have minerals that can be used by farm crops. But these minerals do not last long. After a few years the land no longer supports the growth of crops. Then the land is left, and the people clear more forest. How does this add to the problem?

Python

Toucan

Poison arrow frog

THE GRASSLAND

What are the features of the grassland?

Look at the map on page 78. What biome covers most of the central United States? It is the grassland biome. The **grassland biome** is also called the prairie.

Grassland

Wheat

The climate in the grassland biome is similar to the climate in the deciduous forest. But there is one important difference. It is in the amount of moisture. Most grasslands are found in the inland parts of continents, where there is less rain or snow than in places where deciduous forests are found.

The name *grassland biome* tells you what the common plants of the biome are. They are native grasses and grains. The grassland biome has few trees. There is not enough moisture to support their growth.

Pygmy owls

Black-tailed jack rabbit

Coyote

The grasslands are the most changed of all the biomes. Grasslands once supported large herds of grazing animals, such as bison. Now the grasslands are used in two major ways. In those areas with the highest rainfall, the native grasses have been plowed under. Grains—such as wheat, corn, oats, barley, and rye—are planted in their place. Most of the cereal grains used throughout the world are grown on the wetter grasslands.

The drier grasslands are not good for growing grain. Instead they are used as grazing lands for animals such as cattle and sheep. But many of the dry grasslands have been ruined by too much grazing. Too many animals grazing in an area kills the grasses, and the land changes into a desert.

Some common animals of the grasslands are jack rabbits, prairie dogs, squirrels, coyotes, and badgers. Insects are also common.

Many birds live in the grasslands. The birds have a good food supply. Some prey on the many insects. Other birds use the grasses, especially the seeds, for food. Large birds, such as hawks and owls, prey on smaller birds and small mammals.

Winter in the grasslands is cold, but there is not much snow. When it does snow, the open spaces and high wind cause the snow to drift. So there may be deep snow in some areas and bare ground in others.

Hawk

Do you know?

Some biomes occur on more than one continent. Certain animals are common to each biome. But some animals in a biome on one continent may not live naturally in that biome on another continent.

One example is the African clawed frog. It is native to Africa. But humans moved some of these frogs to southern California. Now it is common in California's Orange and San Diego counties.

The African clawed frog lives mainly in water, but it may travel on land. It is carnivorous and will eat anything it can catch.

THE DESERT
What are the features of the desert?

The **desert** is a region that receives little or no rain. In addition, the rain that does fall evaporates quickly. The largest desert biome in the world is the Sahara, in Africa. It receives almost no rain and has almost no plant life.

Some of the deserts in the United States are very different from the Sahara. The deserts of northern Nevada and northern Utah may get up to 25 cm of precipitation per year. This is enough to support the growth of shrubs, such as sagebrush. These deserts are called cold deserts because the winter temperatures are very low.

All deserts have one thing in common besides their dryness. There is always a wide range in temperature between day and night. Often the days are hot and the nights are cold.

Scorpion

Desert

Plants and animals of the desert have many adaptations that allow them to live there. Some plants, such as cactuses, store water that can be used during dry periods. Other desert plants have thick, leathery leaves. Little water is lost from such leaves. The roots of desert plants are shallow. But they extend very far in all directions.

All animals that live in the desert have adaptations that prevent water loss from their bodies. Reptiles, such as snakes and lizards, have tight, waterproof skins. Some animals, such as the kangaroo rat, can live without drinking any water. They get their moisture from the plants they eat. And they prevent water loss by staying underground during the day.

Insects and birds are common in the desert. The birds eat the insects. Lizards and scorpions also eat insects. Coyotes, hawks, and rattlesnakes prey on small animals, such as rabbits and mice.

Kangaroo rat

Collared lizard

Irrigation of the desert

Some deserts in Arizona and southern California have been changed into lush farms and resorts by bringing water to them. This is called irrigation. Many other deserts could be used for growing food if people could find ways to irrigate them.

How are these animals adapted to conditions where they live?

Materials reference books

Procedure

A. Six animals are pictured in this activity. Some are found in only one biome. Others live in more than one biome. Each is able to survive because it obtains the necessities of life from the region or regions where it lives.

B. Do the following for each animal.
1. Identify the biome or biomes in which the animal is found.
2. Identify any adaptations that help the animal survive the environmental conditions that occur where it is found.
3. Identify its chief sources of food. Also identify any adaptations it has for obtaining food.
4. Identify any adaptations the animal has for defense.

Conclusion

1. Which animal is adapted to the widest range of conditions?

2. Suppose each animal were transferred to a biome in which it is not normally found. What survival problems would be faced by the animal?

wolverine

striped skunk

desert iguana

giraffe

muskox

anaconda

AQUATIC HABITATS

What are the features of aquatic habitats?

The term *biome* is used only for land regions. Yet water covers most of the earth. And many plants and animals live in water. A body of water where organisms live is called an **aquatic** (ə-kwat'ik) **habitat.**

One type of aquatic habitat is the **freshwater habitat.** Ponds, lakes, and streams are freshwater habitats. Many kinds of plants are found in or near the water. Cattails may grow at the water's edge. The roots of water lilies anchor at the bottom. But their leaves and flowers float on top of the water. Other plants may live under the water.

Some animals that live in or near fresh water are insects, such as dragonflies and mosquitoes, frogs, toads, turtles, and snakes. Birds are very common.

Dragonfly

Mud turtle

Mosquito larvae   Pond

97

Shrimp (*top*), blue crab, and oysters

Lobster

Kelp

Another aquatic habitat is the **marine habitat.** The marine habitat includes all the water in the oceans and seas. This water is salt water. The marine habitat is a huge one, for the marine waters cover about 70 percent of the earth. Many kinds of fish live in marine waters. Crabs, shrimp, and lobsters also live in marine waters. The oceans and seas supply much of the world's food.

Most life in marine waters is found in shallow water or near the surface. There is a good reason for this. The source of all food in the oceans is the plants that carry out photosynthesis. To do this they need sunlight. But plants cannot get sunlight if they are deep in the water. Microscopic plants float on the surface. These plants belong to a group of organisms called **plankton** (plangk'tən). Other plants, such as kelp and other types of seaweed, are very large. These plants live on or near the surface of the water.

Some animals in the marine habitat feed on producers, which are living things that make their own food. Others feed on animals that eat producers. Therefore, every animal in a marine habitat depends on producers. The food chain formed by this relationship can be seen in the drawing.

In addition to sunlight, producers need nutrients in order to carry out photosynthesis. In shallow water, nutrients from decaying organisms are available to the producers. In deep water, nutrients on the bottom are a long way from the producers. But there are some areas where nutrients from the bottom are brought to the surface. In these areas, water from the bottom rises to the surface in a process called **upwelling.** In regions where there is upwelling, there are large numbers of living things.

There are areas within the marine habitat that have special features and special living things. These features are determined in part by the temperature of the water and the shape of the coast. Coral reefs are found in tropical waters,

Coral reef

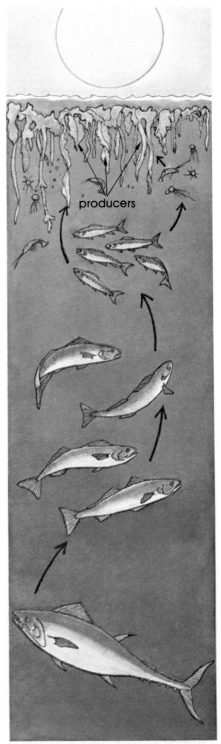

producers

Rocky coastline

Florida Keys

such as those near Florida. The Florida Keys are islands that have been built up by coral. Many beautiful tropical fish are found near coral reefs.

Along rocky coasts, such as those in California and New England, small pools form during low tide. Starfish, mussels, snails, and barnacles are often found in these pools.

A third type of aquatic habitat is the estuary (es'chü er ē). An **estuary** is a place where a fresh-water river flows into an ocean or a sea. The estuary is a good habitat for many forms of life. So the estuaries of the world are also important sources of food for people. That is why we must not pollute the streams that empty into them.

Tide pool

Estuary

100

What kind of biome do you live in? Find out the high and low temperatures and the average annual amount of precipitation for your town. You can find this information in an almanac or by contacting a local weather station. Then look at the table on page 79. In which biome does your town best fit according to the amount of precipitation and the temperature range? Read the description of this biome in this chapter. Does the description sound like the area in which you live? If it doesn't, what conditions make the area different?

IDEAS TO REMEMBER

▶ A biome is made up of all the living things that are found in a region that has a particular climate.

▶ Certain plants and animals are adapted to the climate of each biome.

▶ The six major biomes on the earth are the tundra, the taiga, the deciduous forest, the tropical rain forest, the grassland, and the desert.

▶ Certain communities of plants and animals live within each biome.

▶ Aquatic habitats are bodies of water in which certain kinds of plants and animals live.

▶ Aquatic habitats, especially the oceans and seas, are important sources of food for people.

Reviewing the Chapter

SCIENCE WORDS

A. Use all the terms below to complete the sentences.

deciduous forest   biome   grasslands
tropical rain forest   desert   taiga
aquatic habitat   tundra

       All the living things found in a region that has a particular climate make up a/an __1__. In the __2__, the soil is frozen and no large plants are found. In the __3__, however, conifers are an important resource. The __4__ is named after the broad-leaved trees that grow there. The __5__ is rich in plant and animal life, yet the soil there is poor. The __6__ receives little precipitation and can support only specialized plants, such as the cactus. Prairies, or __7__, are now often used to grow grain or to graze animals. A body of water where organisms live is called a/an __8__.

B. Unscramble each group of letters to find a science term from the chapter. Write a sentence using each term.
  1. gaita   **2.** klontnap   **3.** etamlic
  4. staryue   **5.** glinwuelp   **6.** nierfsco

UNDERSTANDING IDEAS

A. List the six biomes, starting with the biome that receives the least precipitation and ending with the one that receives the most. How does the vegetation change as the amount of precipitation changes?

B. Identify the biome in which each of the following groups of animals lives.

1. eagles, falcons, snowy owls, caribou
2. deer, raccoons, turkeys, frogs
3. wolves, lynxes, squirrels, moose
4. kangaroo rats, scorpions, rattlesnakes, lizards
5. monkeys, pythons, insects, toucans

C. The graph on the left shows the average monthly temperature in a certain biome. The graph on the right shows the average monthly precipitation in a certain biome.

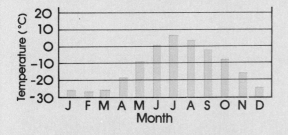 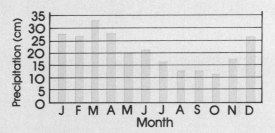

1. Which biome does the temperature graph apply to?
2. Which biome does the precipitation graph apply to?

D. Explain why most marine life is found in shallow water or near the surface of the ocean.

USING IDEAS

1. Desert plants usually grow apart rather than close together. Find out why this is so.
2. Find out about the problems that engineers faced in building the Trans-Alaska Pipeline.

Science in Careers

The general name for the science that studies living organisms is *biology*. However, there are many fields in biology.

Some *biologists* study cells. These people investigate the inner workings of cells and the chemistry of life at the level of the cell. The study of cells is called *cytology* (sī tol'ə jē). Some biologists study tissue. They are interested in identifying different kinds of tissue.

A *botanist* is a person who studies plants. Some botanists study plant growth. Botanists also attempt to develop new types, or strains, of plants. Botanists may develop strains of food plants that give higher yields. Or the new strains may be resistant to diseases.

A person who studies animals is called a *zoologist.* Some zoologists specialize in the study of animal be-

Zoologists

Botanist

havior. They try to identify the factors that control animal behavior. In some cases, they try to learn the meaning of an animal's movements or actions. They have learned that many animals communicate through their actions. There are many interesting fields in the life sciences.

People in Science

Eugenie Clark (1922–)

Dr. Clark is a professor of zoology at the University of Maryland. Her major interest is marine life. Much of her recent research has involved studies on the behavior of sharks. Her studies have indicated that sharks, like many other animals, can learn. For instance, some sharks can be trained to push a target to obtain food as a reward. Dr. Clark, along with other scientists, is also investigating the mating behavior and migration patterns of various kinds of sharks.

A scientist observing the feeding behavior of a shark

Developing Skills

WORD SKILLS

At the back of this book is a section called the Glossary and another section called the Index. A glossary lists the important terms in a book and their definitions. An index lists the main topics covered in a book and the pages on which information about the topics can be found. Subtopics and their page numbers are listed under some main topics.

Use the Glossary and Index of this book to answer the questions.

1. In what order are the terms and topics listed in the Glossary and Index?

2. What other helpful information is contained in the Glossary?

3. In the Index, what subtopics are listed under the main topic *Matter?*

4. Find the term *tissue* in the Glossary and write the definition. Now find this term in a dictionary and write the definitions. How does a glossary differ from a dictionary?

5. Suppose you wanted to obtain information on the topic of how cells reproduce. Which topics and subtopics would help you locate this information?

READING A MAP

A map is a representation of all or part of a region. The map on the next page shows where the mallard duck lives in eastern North America. This duck migrates from north to south in the fall. It migrates from south to north in the spring. It breeds during the summer months. Use the map to answer the questions.

1. If you live in Georgia, during what season will you most likely see a mallard duck?

2. While in Canada in October, you spot some migrating mallards. In which direction will the mallards probably be flying?

3. In which of the following places does the mallard *not* breed—Iowa, New Jersey, Tennessee, Canada?

4. A friend in northern Minnesota tells you that some mallards are living in a marsh near her home. What time of year is it?

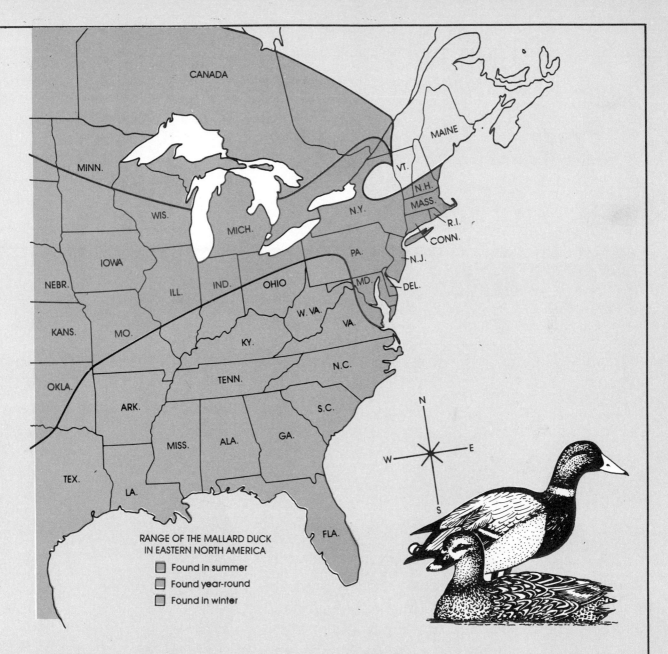

RANGE OF THE MALLARD DUCK
IN EASTERN NORTH AMERICA

- Found In summer
- Found year-round
- Found in winter

MAKING A MAP

Many animals do not migrate. Instead, they are found throughout their areas, or ranges, all year. Trace a map of North America. Use a field guide to find the ranges of the moose, the arctic fox, and the black-tailed jack rabbit. Use a different colored pencil to show on your map the range of each animal. Identify any regions where the ranges overlap.

UNIT TWO

Investigating Our Physical World

Our physical world is made up of everything around us. Everything in the world is made of matter. Scientists study how matter behaves and changes. Energy is an important part of our physical world. You cannot see energy. But you can observe the effects of energy.

In this unit you will study two aspects of our physical world—matter and energy. You will study matter and its changes. You will also study light energy, electrical energy, and how electricity affects your life every day.

Chapter 5

Matter and Atoms

Look at the bars of gold in the picture. Suppose you cut one of the bars in half. Then you cut one of the halves in half. Suppose you kept cutting each new half in half. How many times could you cut the gold in half? Would you finally have a piece of gold so small that it could not be made smaller? What is the smallest possible piece of gold?

Scientists believe that there is a smallest possible piece of gold. This piece would be so small you could not even see it. Such a piece could not be cut into smaller pieces and still be gold. This smallest possible piece is called an atom of gold. In this chapter you will learn about atoms and how some atoms are different from others. You will also learn about the basic kinds of matter.

MATTER AND MASS

How do scientists define matter?

Everything in the world is made of matter. Rocks, soil, buildings, and cars are all made of matter. Animals and plants are made of matter. You are made of matter. Even the invisible air around you is made of matter.

Before we can define matter, we must look at some characteristics of matter. Matter takes up space. It is easy to see that a rock or a building or a living thing takes up space. Does air take up space? If you have ever blown up a balloon, you know that it does. Which balloon in the picture takes up more space?

Matter also has mass. **Mass** is a measure of the amount of matter in an object. An object's mass can be measured by using a balance like the one in the picture. Which object has the greater mass? How do you know? Mass is measured in grams or in kilograms. The mass of a paper clip is about 1 g. The mass of this book is about 1 kg. We can now define **matter** as anything that has mass and takes up space.

The terms *mass* and *weight* are often thought to mean the same thing. But they do not have the same meaning. **Weight** is a measure of the force of gravity on an object. When we talk about weight, we usually mean the force of gravity between some object and the earth. The closer an object is to the earth, the more it weighs. So an object's weight is not always the same.

The mass of an object, however, is always the same. Mass is constant because the amount of matter in an object does not change. Look at the picture of the astronaut floating in the space shuttle. This astronaut is said to be *weightless.* Actually, he does weigh something. But he weighs less in space than he does on earth. This is because the force of gravity becomes weaker as one moves farther from the center of the earth. The astronaut's mass in space, though, is the same as his mass on the earth.

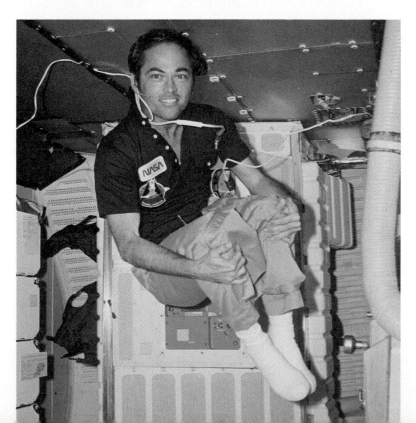

How is a balance used to determine mass?

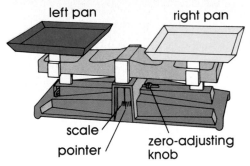

left pan   right pan

scale

pointer

zero-adjusting knob

Materials balance / set of metric masses / variety of objects

Procedure

A. Look at the drawing of the balance. Identify the main parts of the real balance by finding them in the drawing.

B. The balance is zeroed when the pointer lines up with the center mark on the scale. Zero the balance.

    1. Why must the balance be zeroed before it is used?

C. Place the object whose mass you are to find on the left pan. Add masses to the right pan until the balance is zeroed again. The mass of the object is equal to the combined mass of the masses.

    2. Record the mass of the object.

D. Repeat step **C** for the other objects assigned to you.

Conclusion

1. Which object had the greatest mass?
2. Which object had the least mass?

Using science ideas
How would the results be affected if this activity were done on the moon?

ATOMS

What are atoms, and what are they made up of?

All matter is made up of atoms. What do atoms look like? How small are they? How do they behave? Scientists are trying to find the answers to these and other questions about atoms. They have done many experiments with atoms. One of the machines that scientists use to study atoms is shown in the picture below.

The smallest speck of dust contains billions of atoms. The atoms are so small that they cannot be seen. But scientists can learn about atoms by experimenting with matter. In the past it was believed that atoms were small solid balls, like tiny BBs. Scientists no longer believe this.

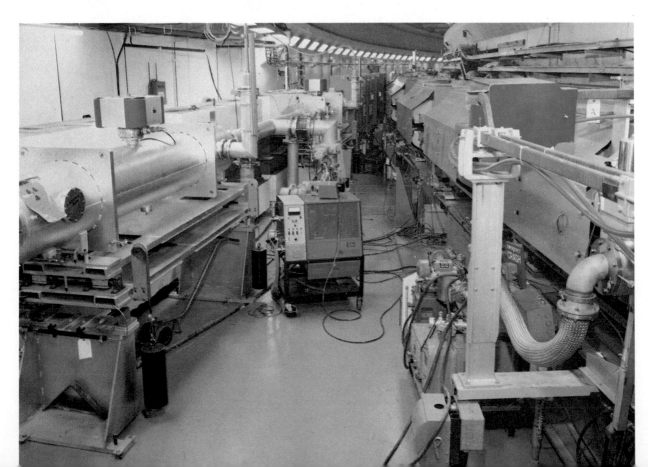

Scientists have made many models of atoms. The models show what scientists believe atoms are made up of. The models help the scientists understand how atoms behave. One of the models, called the Bohr model, is very useful. The drawings will help you understand this model.

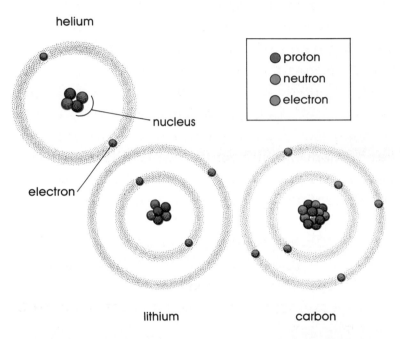

helium

| proton |
| neutron |
| electron |

nucleus

electron

lithium   carbon

The central part of an atom is called the **nucleus** (nü′klē əs). Two kinds of particles are found in the nucleus. They are called **protons** (prō′tonz) and **neutrons** (nü′tronz). Particles called **electrons** (i lek′tronz) move around the nucleus. Electrons move in paths called **orbits.** There is one electron for every proton in the nucleus.

There is space between the nucleus and the electrons. In fact, atoms are made up mostly of empty space! The simplest atom is the hydrogen (hī′drə jən) atom. It has 1 proton and 1 electron. If its nucleus were the size of an orange, the electron moving around it would be about 1 km away!

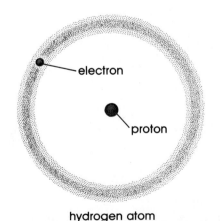

electron

proton

hydrogen atom

GROUPING THE ELEMENTS

What are the basic kinds of matter?

There are thousands of different kinds of matter on the earth. Are the atoms in all these different kinds of matter the same? No, there are many different kinds of atoms. Some matter is made up of only one kind of atom. A substance made up of only one kind of atom is called an **element** (el'ə-mənt). An **atom,** then, can be defined as the smallest particle of an element. Different elements are made up of different kinds of atoms.

There are 92 natural elements. In addition, scientists have been able to make 14 artificial elements. So right now there is a total of 106 known elements. This means that there are 106 different kinds of atoms known today. Some of the elements and some items made from these elements are shown here. Which of these items can you find around your home? Gold and aluminum are other elements. What are some items made from these elements?

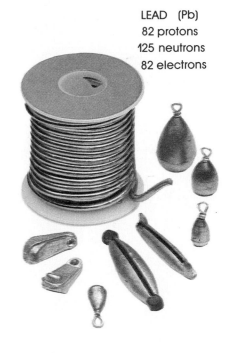

LEAD (Pb)
82 protons
125 neutrons
82 electrons

SILVER (Ag)
47 protons
61 neutrons
47 electrons

COPPER (Cu)
29 protons
35 neutrons
29 electrons

Atoms of different elements differ from one another. The most important difference between atoms is in the number of protons in the nucleus. The number of protons in the nucleus is called the **atomic number** of the atom. All atoms of any one element have the same atomic number.

You learned that the hydrogen atom is the simplest atom. There is 1 proton in a hydrogen nucleus. So hydrogen's atomic number is 1. An oxygen atom has 8 protons in the nucleus. So oxygen's atomic number is 8. A uranium atom has 92 protons in the nucleus. What is uranium's atomic number?

For each proton in the nucleus, there is one electron moving around the nucleus. How many electrons does an oxygen atom have? How many electrons does a uranium atom have? Look at the models of the boron and nitrogen atoms. What is the atomic number of boron? What is the atomic number of nitrogen?

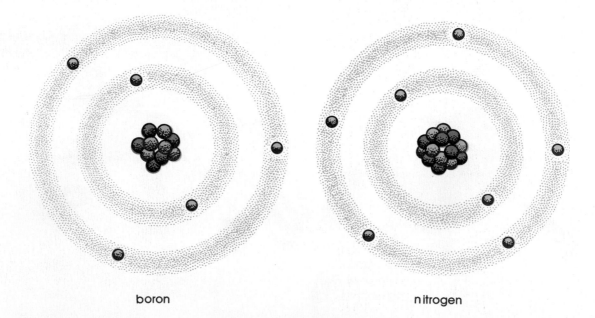

boron   nitrogen

Nearly all the mass of an atom is found in the nucleus. Protons and neutrons have almost the same mass. Elements with few protons and neutrons in the nucleus are said to be light elements. Hydrogen is the lightest element known. It has only one proton in its nucleus. Elements with many protons and neutrons are said to be heavy elements. Uranium has 92 protons and 146 neutrons. So uranium is a heavy element.

Electrons have much less mass than protons and neutrons have. Nearly 2,000 electrons equal the mass of one proton or neutron!

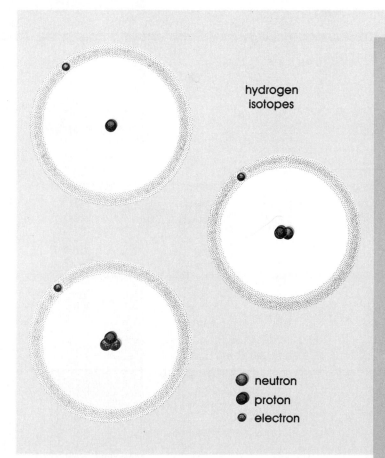

hydrogen isotopes

neutron
proton
electron

Do you know?

All atoms in any one element have the same number of protons in the nucleus. However, the number of neutrons in the nucleus is not always the same in all atoms of an element. Those atoms that have the same number of protons but different numbers of neutrons are called isotopes (ī'sə tōps) of the element. Isotopes occur naturally in most elements.

Isotopes are very useful to scientists. They can be traced by using special instruments. Because this is so, the behavior of elements can be studied. Some isotopes are especially useful in medicine. Some isotopes are used to identify areas of disease in the body.

Many facts about elements and their atoms are found in a chart called the **periodic table.** The table is shown below. The elements are listed in rows in the order of their atomic numbers. Find carbon in the table. What is carbon's atomic number? Each element also has a symbol. The symbol is usually one or two letters that stand for the name of the element. Look at the symbols for the elements in the table.

The periodic table can tell us other things about elements. For example, many elements fall into groups, or families. All elements in the same fam-

The periodic table

1	1 **H** Hydrogen								
2	3 **Li** Lithium	4 **Be** Beryllium							
3	11 **Na** Sodium	12 **Mg** Magnesium							
4	19 **K** Potassium	20 **Ca** Calcium	21 **Sc** Scandium	22 **Ti** Titanium	23 **V** Vanadium	24 **Cr** Chromium	25 **Mn** Manganese	26 **Fe** Iron	27 **Co** Cobalt
5	37 **Rb** Rubidium	38 **Sr** Strontium	39 **Y** Yttrium	40 **Zr** Zirconium	41 **Nb** Niobium	42 **Mo** Molybdenum	43 **Tc** Technetium	44 **Ru** Ruthenium	45 **Rh** Rhodium
6	55 **Cs** Cesium	56 **Ba** Barium	57 **La** Lanthanum †	72 **Hf** Hafnium	73 **Ta** Tantalum	74 **W** Tungsten	75 **Re** Rhenium	76 **Os** Osmium	77 **Ir** Iridium
7	87 **Fr** Francium	88 **Ra** Radium	89 **Ac** Actinium ‡	104 **Unq** Unnilquadium	105 **Unp** Unnilpentium	106 **Unh** Unnilhexium	107 *	108	

†	58 **Ce** Cerium	59 **Pr** Praseodymium	60 **Nd** Neodymium	61 **Pm** Promethium	62 **Sm** Samarium	63 **Eu** Europium	64 **Gd** Gadolinium	65 **Tb** Terbium
‡	90 **Th** Thorium	91 **Pa** Protactinium	92 **U** Uranium	93 **Np** Neptunium	94 **Pu** Plutonium	95 **Am** Americium	96 **Cm** Curium	97 **Bk** Berkelium

* No names have been given

ily are alike in some ways. Most elements in a family behave, or react, in the same way. They also have similar characteristics. But like the members of a human family, the elements in a family are not exactly alike. The families of elements are shown in the columns in the table.

Find the element fluorine (flü′ə rēn) in the periodic table. Fluorine and all the elements listed below it belong to the same family. These elements all behave in a similar way. All the elements in the fluorine family are poisonous gases. What elements belong to the helium family?

					1 H Hydrogen	2 He Helium
5 B Boron	6 C Carbon	7 N Nitrogen	8 O Oxygen	9 F Fluorine		10 Ne Neon
13 Al Aluminum	14 Si Silicon	15 P Phosphorus	16 S Sulfur	17 Cl Chlorine		18 Ar Argon

28 Ni Nickel	29 Cu Copper	30 Zn Zinc	31 Ga Gallium	32 Ge Germanium	33 As Arsenic	34 Se Selenium	35 Br Bromine	36 Kr Krypton
46 Pd Palladium	47 Ag Silver	48 Cd Cadmium	49 In Indium	50 Sn Tin	51 Sb Antimony	52 Te Tellurium	53 I Iodine	54 Xe Xenon
78 Pt Platinum	79 Au Gold	80 Hg Mercury	81 Tl Thallium	82 Pb Lead	83 Bi Bismuth	84 Po Polonium	85 At Astatine	86 Rn Radon

66 Dy Dysprosium	67 Ho Holmium	68 Er Erbium	69 Tm Thulium	70 Yb Ytterbium	71 Lu Lutetium
98 Cf Californium	99 Es Einsteinium	100 Fm Fermium	101 Md Mendelevium	102 No Nobelium	103 Lr Lawrencium

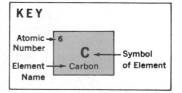

KEY

Atomic Number → 6 C ← Symbol of Element
Element Name → Carbon

- COMPOUNDS AND MOLECULES -

What is formed when atoms are chemically joined?

Most elements are not found pure in nature. Elements are usually found combined with one another. Two or more elements that are chemically joined form a substance called a **compound** (kom'pound).

Some compounds are shown in the pictures. Their names are given. Have you heard of any of these compounds? Some items made from these compounds are also shown. Find the elements in each compound in the periodic table on pages 120–121.

The simplest particle of many compounds is a molecule (mol'ə kyül). A **molecule** is a chemical unit made up of two or more atoms. A molecule of a compound contains two or more atoms that are chemically joined.

IRON OXIDE
(used in paint
 pigments and in inks)

made of: iron
           oxygen

POTASSIUM DICHROMATE
(used in glues and dyes)

made of: potassium
           chromium
           oxygen

COPPER NITRATE
(used in varnishes
 and enamel paints)

made of: copper
           nitrogen
           oxygen

NICKEL SULPHATE
(used in ceramics)

made of: nickel
           sulfur
           oxygen

As you have learned, the smallest particle of an element is an atom. In some elements, the atoms are chemically joined with atoms of the same kind. For example, the element oxygen is made up of pairs of oxygen atoms. The two oxygen atoms making up a pair are chemically joined. The paired atoms act as a chemical unit. Such a pair of oxygen atoms makes up an oxygen molecule. The element hydrogen is also made up of paired atoms. The paired hydrogen atoms act as a chemical unit. Two hydrogen atoms that are chemically joined make up a hydrogen molecule.

hydrogen molecule
formula: H_2

Not all atoms form molecules. The atoms of some elements act as single particles. That is, the atoms are not chemically joined with other atoms to form larger units. For example, helium is a gas made up of single helium atoms. The other elements in the helium family are also gases made up of single atoms. These gases usually do not combine with any other atoms.

A compound always contains at least two different kinds of atoms. Scientists use a formula to show the kinds and numbers of atoms in a molecule of a compound. The formula gives the symbol for each element and the number of atoms of each element.

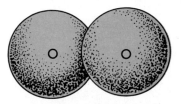

oxygen molecule
formula: O_2

You have probably heard of the compound carbon dioxide. The formula for carbon dioxide is CO_2. This means that each molecule of carbon dioxide contains 1 atom of carbon and 2 atoms of oxygen. The formula for glucose (glü′kōs), a kind of sugar, is $C_6H_{12}O_6$. What are the elements in glucose? How many atoms of each element are there in a molecule of glucose?

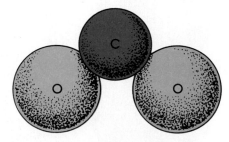

carbon dioxide molecule
formula: CO_2

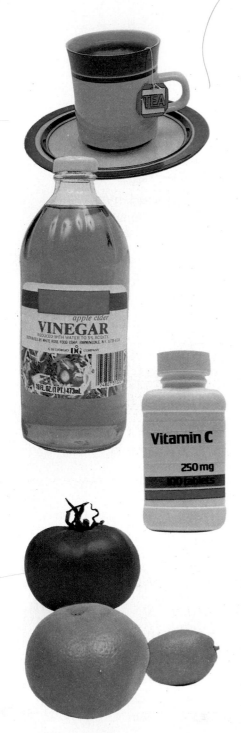

KINDS OF COMPOUNDS
How are compounds classified?

All compounds are formed by elements that are chemically joined. But all compounds are not alike. Compounds are classified into groups according to certain characteristics. Some compounds are called **acids.** All acids contain the element hydrogen (H). Acids have a sour taste. Vinegar and lemon juice are acids. The pictures show some other substances that contain acids. There are acids in many foods. But they are weak acids. Some acids are dangerous or even poisonous. Strong acids can burn skin and destroy other materials. **Never taste a substance to find out if it is an acid.**

Have you ever heard of hydrochloric (hī drə-klôr'ik) acid? It has many uses in chemistry. But hydrochloric acid can be very dangerous. The formula for hydrochloric acid is HCl. What elements make up hydrochloric acid? The table shows some other acids and their uses.

SOME COMMON ACIDS AND THEIR USES

Acid	Formula	Some uses	
Sulfuric	H_2SO_4	Car batteries	
Nitric	HNO_3	Fertilizers	
Carbonic	H_2CO_3	Soft drinks	
Acetic	$HC_2H_3O_2$	Plastics	

Bases make up another group of compounds. All bases contain the elements oxygen and hydrogen (OH). Bases have a bitter taste and feel slippery. The pictures show some items that contain bases. Some foods contain bases. But like acids, strong bases can be very dangerous or poisonous. **Do not taste or touch a substance to find out if it is a base.**

Many household cleaning products, such as ammonia and lye, contain strong bases. Lye is usually used in drain cleaners. Lye may contain the base sodium hydroxide. The formula for sodium hydroxide is NaOH. What elements are in sodium hydroxide? The table shows some common bases.

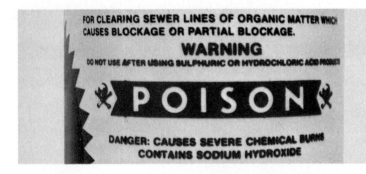

SOME COMMON BASES AND THEIR USES

Base	Formula	Some uses
Sodium hydroxide	NaOH	Making textiles and paper
Ammonium hydroxide	NH_4OH	Household cleansers and detergents
Potassium hydroxide	KOH	Making soap, bleaching
Calcium hydroxide	$Ca(OH)_2$	Plasters and cements

Scientists have ways to tell if a substance is an acid or a base. They use an indicator (in′də kā-tər). An **indicator** is a substance that changes color when it is added to an acid or a base. One indicator is litmus (lit′məs) paper. Litmus paper can be red or blue. Blue litmus paper turns red in an acid. Red litmus paper turns blue in a base. A substance that is neither an acid nor a base is said to be **neutral** (nü′trəl). Neutral substances cause no change in indicators. The picture shows an acid and a base being tested with litmus paper.

You have learned that acids and bases are two kinds of compounds. **Salts** make up a third group of compounds. A salt is made by chemically combining an acid and a base. But the salt has different characteristics than either the acid or the base. You are probably familiar with table salt. It is used to flavor food and it is needed in everyone's diet. The formula for table salt is NaCl. What elements make up table salt?

Can you identify some acids and bases?

Materials   5 small jars or cups / red and blue litmus paper / vinegar / lemon juice / ammonia / baking-soda solution / tap water / tape / safety goggles

Procedure
A. Put on safety goggles. Put about 5 mL of each liquid into separate jars. Label each jar.

   1. Which of the liquids do you think will turn red litmus paper blue? Which do you think will turn blue litmus paper red?

B. Test each liquid with red litmus paper. Use a new strip for each liquid.

   2. For each liquid, identify whether there was a change in the litmus paper or no change. Record your results.

C. Repeat step **B** using strips of blue litmus paper.

   3. For each liquid, identify whether there was a change in the litmus paper or no change. Record your results.

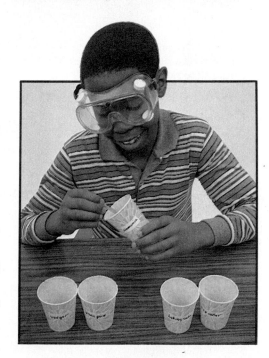

Conclusion
1. Which liquids are acids?

2. Which liquids are bases?

3. Are any of the liquids neutral? Which ones? How do you know they are neutral?

4. Of the liquids that you predicted would turn red litmus paper blue, how many actually did?

5. Of the liquids that you predicted would turn blue litmus paper red, how many actually did?

Using science ideas
Take some strips of litmus paper home. Test some liquids, such as milk, fruit juices, and cleaning fluids. Identify those substances that are acids, those that are bases, and those that are neutral. Use care when working with these substances.

Using calcium chloride

There are many kinds of salts. The kind of salt depends on the acid and the base that are used to make the salt. Stannous fluoride (stan'əs flü'ə-ríd), SnF_2, is a salt that is added to toothpaste to help prevent tooth decay. The salt calcium chloride (kal'sē əm klôr'íd), $CaCl_2$, is used to melt ice on roads and sidewalks.

Finding out

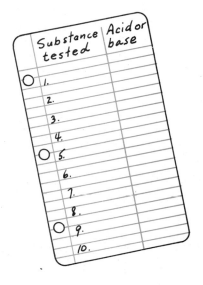

Can red cabbage juice be used as an indicator? Your teacher will give you some juice from red cabbage that has been boiled.

Bring in some materials from home that you would like to test. Test such materials as vinegar, fruit juices, tea, milk, bleach, window cleaner. Put a small amount of each material into a separate jar. Add several drops of cabbage juice to each jar. Record any color changes that occur. Red cabbage juice will turn blue-green in a base and deep red or violet in an acid.

Make a chart like the one shown. Write the name of each material in the first column. Write whether it is an acid or a base in the second column.

Did any of the materials you tested fail to cause the cabbage juice to change color? If so, how can you explain this?

IDEAS TO REMEMBER

► Matter is anything that has mass and takes up space.
► Matter is made up of tiny particles called atoms.
► Atoms are composed of particles called protons, neutrons, and electrons.
► Matter that contains only one kind of atom is an element.
► There are 92 natural elements on the earth.
► Elements are often combined to form compounds.
► There are many kinds of compounds, including acids, bases, and salts.

Reviewing the Chapter

SCIENCE WORDS

A. Use all the terms below to complete the sentences.

periodic table   nucleus   molecule   weight   mass
atomic number   neutrons   electrons   orbits   element

Anything that has __1__ and takes up space is matter. A measure of the force of gravity on matter is called __2__. All matter is made of atoms. The central part of an atom is called the __3__. It contains protons and __4__. Particles called __5__ travel in paths around this central part. These paths are called __6__. The number of protons in an atom is known as the __7__. A substance made of only one kind of atom is called a/an __8__. A chemical unit made up of two or more atoms is a/an __9__. Information about these substances can be found in a chart called the __10__.

B. Write the letter of the term that best matches the definition. Not all the terms will be used.

1. Two or more elements that are chemically joined
2. A substance that changes color in an acid or a base
3. A substance that tastes sour
4. A substance that turns red litmus paper blue
5. A substance made from an acid and a base
6. The smallest particle of an element

a. indicator
b. salt
c. acid
d. base
e. atom
f. compound
g. neutral

UNDERSTANDING IDEAS

A. Use the periodic table on pages 120 and 121 to find the number of protons and electrons in each of these elements:

1. calcium   **2.** aluminum   **3.** silicon   **4.** sodium

B. Use the tables of acids and bases to find the elements in each of these compounds:

1. acetic acid   **2.** sulfuric acid   **3.** ammonium hydroxide

C. Why does this parent keep household cleaners locked in the cabinet?

D. The force of gravity is slightly less on a mountaintop than at sea level. Compare the mass and weight of a person at both places.

USING IDEAS

1. Read the ingredients listed on several foods and household products in your home. Write the name of each product and the name of any acid, base, or salt that it contains. Be sure to tell whether each substance is an acid, a base, or a salt.
2. Make a model of an oxygen atom, using construction paper or clay.

Chapter 6

Chemical Changes in Matter

Look at the picture on this page. What kinds of matter can you identify? What features of the matter help you identify it? Features that can be used to identify matter are called properties.

How do you think the matter in the picture has changed? Do you think these changes were fast or slow? Do the properties of matter change when matter changes?

In this chapter you will find the answers to these questions. You will learn about the different ways that matter changes. You will also learn what parts of atoms are involved in changes in matter.

Wood carver

— PROPERTIES AND CHANGES —
In what ways does matter change?

There are two kinds of changes that matter can undergo. These are physical changes and chemical changes.

A **physical change** is a change in the size, shape, or state of matter. The same matter is present before and after a physical change.

Ice melting is a physical change. Water freezing is also a physical change. Sugar dissolving in water is a physical change. In each case the matter after the change is the same as the matter before the change.

What physical changes are shown in the pictures? What other examples of physical changes can you give?

Gold pellets

Liquid gold

Gold bars

In a physical change, the physical properties of matter are changed. A **physical property** is one that can be identified without causing a chemical change in the matter. Color, odor, shape, and hardness are some physical properties.

The house shown in the picture is red. Red color is a physical property of the house. Suppose you painted the house blue. The physical property of color would be changed. But the house would still be a house. What kind of change would this be?

A **chemical change** is one in which matter is changed into one or more different kinds of matter. Burning wood is a chemical change. When wood or other matter burns, it combines with oxygen in the air. The ashes, gas, and smoke that are formed are different from the original wood and oxygen.

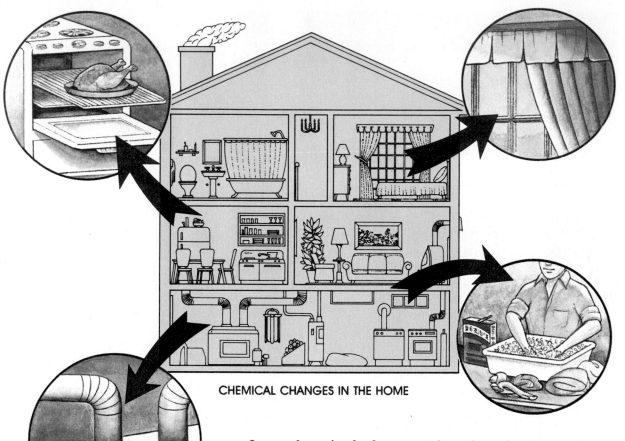

CHEMICAL CHANGES IN THE HOME

In a chemical change, the chemical properties of matter are changed. A **chemical property** is one that determines how an element or compound reacts with other elements or compounds. For example, gasoline will burn. This means it will react with oxygen in the air. So burning is a chemical property of gasoline. The elements sodium and chlorine will combine to form table salt. The ability of these elements to combine is a chemical property of each element.

Many chemical changes take place in your home. Cooking food involves a chemical change. Detergent removes soil from clothes. Colors fade from fabrics. Pipes rust. Use the picture to name other chemical changes in your home.

Can you identify a product of a chemical reaction?

Materials   wide-mouthed bottle / 1-hole rubber stopper / rubber tubing / 2 small pieces of glass or metal tubing / jar / limewater / baking powder / vinegar / safety goggles

Procedure
A. Put on your safety goggles. Set up your materials as shown. The jar should contain limewater. Limewater will turn milky white if carbon dioxide is added to it. Be sure the end of the glass or metal tube is in the limewater.

B. Add two spoonfuls of baking powder to the bottle.

C. Add about 25 mL of vinegar to the bottle, and quickly place the stopper in the bottle.
   1. What evidence do you see of a chemical reaction taking place?

D. Observe the limewater.
   2. Describe what happens to the limewater.

Conclusion
1. What is one product that is released when baking powder reacts with vinegar?
2. Why is this reaction an example of a chemical reaction?

Using science ideas
How could the limewater test be used to indicate that a chemical reaction is taking place inside your body?

CHEMICAL REACTIONS
What happens during a chemical change?

A chemical change is often called a **chemical reaction** (rē ak'shən). During a chemical reaction many different things may happen. The things that happen during a chemical reaction involve the movement of atoms and molecules. In other words, atoms and molecules react with one another during a chemical change.

One or more different kinds of matter are always formed in a chemical reaction. And the properties of the matter formed are different from those of the original matter.

Many chemical reactions release energy. Recall the example of the burning wood. What kinds of energy are released when something burns? The energy is in the form of heat and light.

Chemical reactions may be rapid or slow. Burning is a rapid reaction. The explosion of dynamite is also a rapid reaction. In a rapid reaction, much energy may be released in a very short time.

Energy from a chemical reaction

A dynamite explosion

Some reactions take place slowly. The rusting of iron is a slow reaction. The souring of milk is also a slow reaction. Energy is released in both of these reactions. But the energy is released so slowly that it is not noticed.

Look at the picture of the silver cup. The cup has turned black because the silver has reacted with air. This is called tarnishing. Tarnishing is a slow reaction. The liquid in the bowl is silver polish. It removes the tarnish. This is a rapid reaction.

There are many kinds of chemical reactions. In one kind of reaction, compounds are broken down into simpler compounds or into elements. As you know, a water molecule is made up of 2 atoms of hydrogen and 1 atom of oxygen. Water can be broken down into molecules of oxygen and hydrogen gas.

What happens when electricity passes through water?

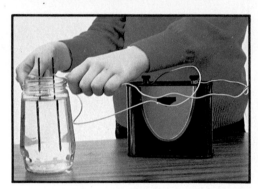

Materials   jar or clear plastic cup / wire stripper or knife / 2 pieces of bell wire, each 30 cm long / 2 pieces of pencil lead, each 6 cm long / sodium carbonate / 6-volt battery / pliers / spoon

Procedure
A. Use a knife or wire stripper to remove 3 cm of insulation from the ends of two pieces of bell wire. **Caution:** *Work carefully when using the knife or wire stripper.*

B. Wrap one bare end of each wire around each of two pieces of pencil lead. Pencil lead is a form of carbon. Pliers can be used to tighten the wires around the rods.

C. Nearly fill a jar with water. Add a spoonful of sodium carbonate to the water.

D. Fasten the free ends of the wires to the terminals of a battery. Hold the wires so that the carbon rods, not the copper wires, are in the water. Observe what happens.
  1. What collects on the rods in the water?

Conclusion
1. Neither the carbon nor the sodium carbonate is changed in this activity. What must have changed to form the bubbles? What kind of energy was used?
2. What difference did you see in the amount of gas that collected on the two rods?
3. The formula for water is H_2O. What gases, do you think, collected on the rods? Where did the gases come from?

In another kind of reaction, elements combine with other elements or with compounds to form more complex compounds. Oxygen and iron combine to form the compound called iron oxide. Iron oxide is the chemical name for rust.

In a chemical reaction, matter is always changed to one or more different kinds of matter. But the amount of matter present both before and after the reaction does not change.

Suppose you wanted to make a loaf of bread. You might start out with flour, sugar, milk, and yeast. These ingredients are changed into a loaf of bread. This is a chemical change. The oven supplies heat energy so that this change can take place. During baking, some moisture and gases are given off from the dough.

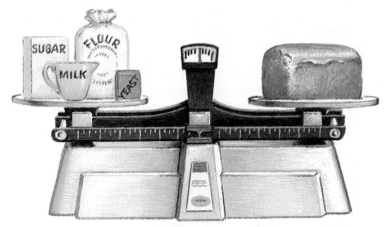

INGREDIENTS (flour, sugar, milk, yeast) + HEAT → BREAD + GASES + MOISTURE

In this reaction, flour, sugar, milk, and yeast are ingredients, or reactants. Bread, gases, and moisture are products. If you could collect all of the reactants and all of the products and put them on a balance, you would find that they have equal mass. You can see this in the drawing.

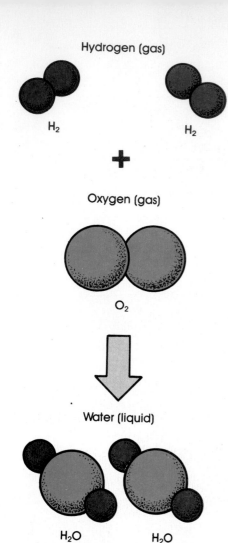

Hydrogen (gas)

H₂   H₂

+

Oxygen (gas)

O₂

Water (liquid)

H₂O   H₂O

As you can see by comparing the reactants and the products when you make bread, matter can be changed. But matter cannot be created or destroyed in any chemical reaction. This fact is called the **law of conservation of matter.**

The law of conservation of matter applies to all chemical reactions. For example, suppose you wanted to make two molecules of water. To do this you would have to combine two hydrogen molecules with one oxygen molecule. This chemical reaction is shown here. At room temperature, hydrogen and oxygen are gases and water is a liquid. You can see that matter is changed in this chemical reaction. But, as in any chemical reaction, the products have come from the reactants.

There is one other important law that relates to chemical reactions. This is the law of conservation of energy. The **law of conservation of energy** states that energy is neither created nor destroyed during a chemical reaction. Like matter, however, energy can change form.

Finding out

How can you demonstrate the law of conservation of matter? Use a funnel to carefully pour a spoonful of baking soda into a bottle. Use a second funnel to pour some vinegar into a balloon. Attach the balloon to the bottle without letting any of the vinegar pour into the bottle. Use a balance to find the mass of this setup. Record the mass. Now lift the end of the balloon so that the vinegar pours into the bottle. Does a chemical reaction take place? Find the mass of the setup again. Has matter been conserved?

CHEMICAL BONDS

What holds the atoms in a compound together?

In a chemical reaction, compounds may be formed. You know that compounds are formed when atoms of different elements combine. But what holds the atoms together? The atoms are held together by forces called **chemical bonds.**

Chemical bonds are formed when atoms are attracted to other atoms. Some atoms attract many different atoms. Carbon and oxygen atoms easily react with other atoms. Because of this, carbon and oxygen can form many kinds of compounds. Some atoms, such as those of helium, do not attract any other atoms. So helium does not form chemical bonds.

What are chemical bonds? Scientists have learned that the forces that attract atoms involve electrons. Remember, electrons are found in orbits outside the nucleus of an atom. Some of these electrons are involved in forming bonds.

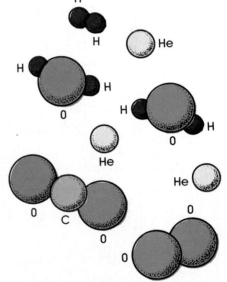

some atoms bond, forming molecules

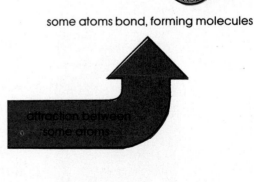

attraction between some atoms

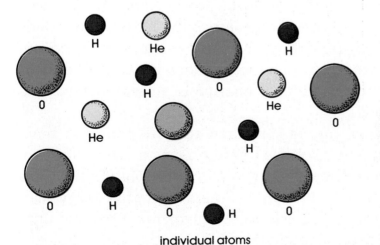

individual atoms

Making a compound is something like building a model with plastic blocks. The blocks are like the atoms in a compound. The plastic blocks hook on to one another. The way the blocks are held together may be compared to the way atoms are bonded together. By hooking the blocks together, you can build many different objects. If you want to change an object, you must take the blocks apart. Then you can combine them in a different way. You still have the same blocks. They are just arranged differently. In a similar way, atoms can be rearranged to form different compounds.

Breaking the bonds that hold atoms together involves energy. Making new bonds also involves energy. When bonds are broken and new bonds are made, energy is either released or used up. The energy in chemical bonds is called **chemical energy.** Chemical energy is stored in chemical bonds.

Now you can understand why chemical reactions may release energy. During a chemical reaction some bonds are broken. New bonds are formed. If the reaction releases more energy than it uses up, energy will be given off. Heat and light are usually produced.

— OTHER CHANGES IN MATTER —

What kinds of changes involve the nuclei of atoms?

As you know, chemical reactions involve the breaking and forming of bonds between atoms. Bonds involve electrons. The nuclei (nü′klē ī) of atoms are not involved in chemical reactions. (The word *nuclei* is the plural of *nucleus.*) But sometimes the nuclei of atoms can be changed. A reaction involving the nuclei of atoms is called a **nuclear** (nü′klē ər) **reaction.** In a nuclear reaction, elements are changed into different elements.

Much energy is stored in the nuclei of atoms. In fact, every nucleus can be thought of as a tiny package of energy. Only recently have scientists found ways to "open" these packages and release the energy. The energy in the nucleus is called **nuclear energy.** Nuclear energy is released during a nuclear reaction.

In one kind of nuclear reaction, large nuclei break apart. Each nucleus splits into two or more smaller nuclei. The splitting of a nucleus into smaller parts is called **nuclear fission** (fish′ən).

NUCLEAR FISSION

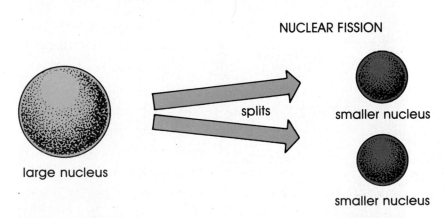

large nucleus   splits   smaller nucleus

smaller nucleus

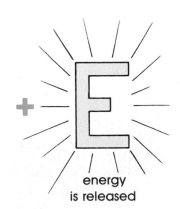

+ energy is released

Nuclear submarine

The fission of many atoms in a short period of time releases a large amount of energy. The energy from fission has many uses. The submarine in the picture runs on energy from nuclear fission. A nuclear power plant produces electric power from the energy of nuclear fission. In these cases, the reactions are controlled. So the energy is released slowly.

Nuclear power plant

Where does the huge amount of energy that is released by nuclear fission come from? The answer can be found by comparing the mass of matter before fission with the mass after fission. Unlike the result of a chemical reaction, there is less mass after fission than before fission. A small amount of mass is changed into energy during a fission reaction.

In a second kind of nuclear reaction, two or more small nuclei combine, or fuse. The combining of nuclei is called **nuclear fusion** (fyü'zhən). When fusion occurs, a larger nucleus is formed. Two hydrogen nuclei can be fused to form a helium nucleus. The mass of the two hydrogen nuclei that fuse is greater than the mass of the helium nucleus that forms. As in nuclear fission, the "missing" mass is changed into energy.

NUCLEAR FUSION

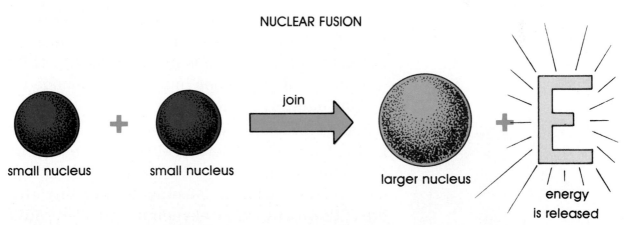

small nucleus   small nucleus   join   larger nucleus   energy is released

High temperatures and pressures are needed to start nuclear fusion. Once fusion starts, this reaction releases even more energy than fission does. Many scientists believe that fusion can be used to produce electrical energy in the future. But first they must learn how to control the reaction.

For hundreds of years, people have wondered how the sun produces energy. The answer is by nuclear fusion. The sun is made up mostly of hydrogen. As the hydrogen in the sun is changed to helium, energy is released.

Many kinds of nuclear reactions take place naturally. The nuclei of certain elements break down into simpler nuclei. During such reactions, elements change into other elements. Elements that break down into other elements are called **radioactive** (rā dē ō ak′tiv) **elements.**

Uranium is a radioactive element. The element uranium breaks down and changes into the element lead. Most natural radioactive elements break down slowly. So the energy is released over a long period of time.

Uranium ore

Do you know?

As you know, it is possible to get energy from gasoline. But did you realize that you could also get energy from water? Obviously, water cannot be used to power your family car. But water is a source of a fuel called deuterium (dü tir'ē əm), which can be used in nuclear fusion.

If nuclear fusion is ever a major source of energy on earth, large amounts of fuel will be needed. Water, which covers three fourths of the earth, can provide one of these fuels. Do you think it would be wise to use water in this way? Explain your answer.

IDEAS TO REMEMBER

▶ When matter changes, the properties of matter change.
▶ A chemical change is also called a chemical reaction.
▶ Matter and energy are neither created nor destroyed in a chemical reaction.
▶ Atoms in a compound are held together by chemical bonds.
▶ A change in the nuclei of atoms is called a nuclear reaction.
▶ The nuclear reactions called fission and fusion supply large amounts of energy.
▶ In a nuclear reaction, mass is changed to energy.

Reviewing the Chapter

SCIENCE WORDS

A. Write the letter of the term that best matches the definition. Not all the terms will be used.

1. A property that determines how an element or compound reacts with other elements or compounds
2. Forces that hold atoms together in compounds
3. The combining of atomic nuclei
4. A change in the size, state, or shape of matter
5. The splitting of a nucleus into smaller nuclei
6. A property such as color, odor, or hardness
7. A change in which different kinds of matter are formed

a. nuclear fusion
b. physical property
c. chemical bonds
d. nuclear energy
e. chemical change
f. nuclear fission
g. chemical property
h. physical change

B. Copy the sentences below. Use science terms from the chapter to complete the sentences.

1. The _____ stored in chemical bonds can be released during a chemical change.
2. Any reaction involving the nuclei of atoms is a/an _____.
3. Elements that break down into other elements are called _____.
4. A property that can be identified without causing a chemical change in matter is a/an _____.
5. A chemical change is sometimes called a/an _____.

UNDERSTANDING IDEAS

A. Write these three headings: (1) *Nuclear reaction,* (2) *Chemical reaction,* (3) *Physical change.* Write each of the following terms under the correct heading.

decaying leaves
mixing oil and vinegar
combining of small nuclei
breakdown of an element
   into another element

rusting of iron
digesting food
sifting gold from sand
changing hydrogen to
   helium

B. Energy may be released as a result of chemical reactions and nuclear reactions.
   1. Compare chemical and nuclear reactions as to where the energy is stored before it is released.
   2. How do the laws of conservation of mass and energy apply to chemical reactions? How do they apply to nuclear reactions?

C. Study the following diagram.

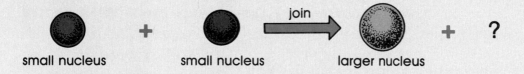

small nucleus   small nucleus   larger nucleus

   1. What kind of reaction is shown in the diagram?
   2. What else is produced as a result of this reaction?

USING IDEAS

1. Use your library to find out how you can use physical properties to identify such minerals as quartz, mica, and garnet.
2. Describe two physical changes and two chemical changes that can occur in your body.

Chapter 7

Light Energy

The beams of light in the picture are similar but not identical. What is the difference between the beams shining from the left and right corners of the building? Obviously, the beams of light are of different colors. But what is light? How does it help us to see objects that are not producing light? Why does light come in different colors? What happens to light when it strikes matter? In this chapter you will learn about the nature and behavior of light. You will also find the answers to the questions just raised.

THE NATURE OF LIGHT
What are the characteristics of light?

Light is energy that you can see. Light travels through space in the form of waves. There are several other forms of energy that travel as waves. Among them are radio waves and X rays. Light, X rays, and other forms of energy that travel as waves are examples of **radiant** (rā′dē-ənt) **energy**. Light, then, is just one member of the family of radiant energy. Except for light, all forms of radiant energy are invisible.

The sun gives off many kinds of radiant energy. Other objects also give off radiant energy. Light bulbs, toasters, and people as well give off radiant energy. In many cases the energy that is given off is invisible.

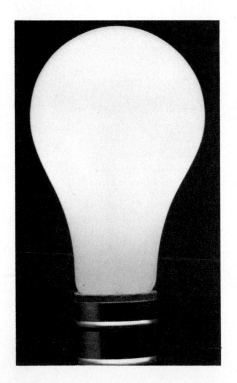

Light and other forms of radiant energy travel through space at the same speed. This speed, called the speed of light, is about 300,000 kilometers per second (km/s). This means that every

Waves

second, a light wave travels about 300,000 km. In one second, a wave of light could travel around the earth seven times.

Light waves travel much faster than other kinds of waves, such as sound waves. Scientists haven't found anything that travels faster than the speed of light.

To understand how light travels, you must understand waves and how they move. Waves of light can be compared to waves of water.

Imagine you are in a boat on the ocean. You can feel the boat rise and fall with each passing wave. As the boat rises, for a moment it is on the top, or **crest,** of a wave. As the wave passes, the boat drops to the bottom, or **trough** (trôf), of the wave.

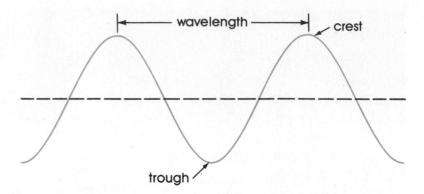

Like the ocean water, light travels in waves. Look at the drawing representing light waves. The highest point on a wave is the crest. The lowest point is the trough.

The distance between the crest of one wave and the crest of the next wave is called the **wavelength**. Waves of radiant energy that have short wavelengths have more energy than those with long wavelengths. Use a metric ruler to measure the wavelength of each wave in the drawing below. Which wave has more energy?

Another characteristic of waves is frequency (frē′kwən sē). **Frequency** is the number of waves that pass a point in a certain period of time. Waves of radiant energy with high frequencies have more energy than do those with low frequencies.

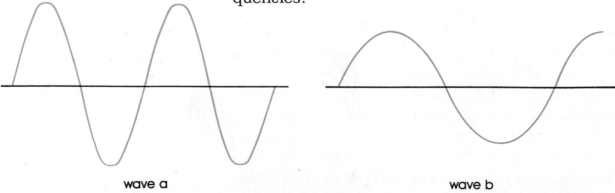

wave a   wave b

There are two kinds of radiant energy that have frequencies close to the frequencies of light. These are infrared (in frə red') waves and ultraviolet (ul trə vī'ə lit) waves. **Infrared waves** are lower in frequency than light waves. **Ultraviolet waves** are higher in frequency than light waves. Which waves, infrared or ultraviolet, have more energy?

Infrared waves have less energy than ultraviolet waves. Infrared waves are easily absorbed by matter and changed into heat. The people in the picture are absorbing infrared waves from the sun. Perhaps you have seen infrared lamps in a

restaurant. The lamps are used to keep food warm. Heat lamps also give off infrared waves.

People can also absorb ultraviolet waves from the sun. As you know, ultraviolet waves have more energy than infrared waves have. Too many ultraviolet waves, then, can be dangerous for people. Such waves can cause sunburn. They can also injure body cells and may cause skin cancer. Fortunately, the upper atmosphere screens out most of the ultraviolet waves from the sun before they reach the surface of the earth.

There is a very important difference between light waves and other kinds of waves, such as sound waves. Sound waves can travel only through matter. So sound waves can travel

Meerkats under heat lamp

158

through air and through water and even through many solids. However, sound waves cannot travel through outer space. Outer space is, for the most part, a vacuum (vak′yüm). A **vacuum** is any space that contains little or no matter. Waves of radiant energy can travel through a vacuum.

Astronauts on the moon's surface can see and photograph each other even though there is no air on the moon. However, the astronauts communicate with each other by using radio waves. Why can't astronauts on the moon's surface communicate simply by using sound waves?

THE BEHAVIOR OF LIGHT

What happens to light when it strikes matter?

Scientists have learned much about light by studying how it behaves. They have found that light waves travel in straight lines. You cannot see an object that is around the corner from you. The reason you cannot see such an object is that light waves do not bend around corners.

light waves

Light waves can change direction. When light waves strike an object, some of the waves bounce off. But the paths of the waves to the object are straight lines. And the paths of the waves away from the object are also straight lines.

Scientists have also found that light travels out in all directions from a source. For example, suppose you place a lighted lamp in the center of a room. Light will travel out from the lamp in all directions. No matter where in the room you are, some light waves will reach you.

Three things may happen when light waves strike matter. Some of the light waves may pass through the matter. We say that this light is **transmitted.** Some of the light waves may bounce off the matter. This light is **reflected.** Some of the light waves may be trapped by the matter. This light is **absorbed.**

What actually happens when light waves strike matter depends on the kind of matter the light strikes. As you can see in the top drawing, a mirror reflects light. In the second drawing you can see that a clear glass window transmits most of the light it receives. And in the third drawing you can see that the leaves of a plant absorb much of the light they receive.

Most light waves from the sun are transmitted through the earth's atmosphere. When this light strikes the surface of the earth, some of it is reflected and some of it is absorbed. What is happening to light striking matter in the picture below?

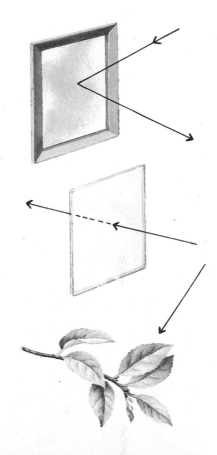

You can see through matter such as clear glass because it transmits light without scattering it. Matter through which light can pass without being scattered is said to be **transparent.** Other kinds of matter scatter light waves that pass through it. Matter that scatters light that passes through it is said to be **translucent** (trans lü′- sənt). Objects look blurry when viewed through a translucent material, such as frosted glass. Matter through which light cannot pass is said to be **opaque** (ō pāk′). A brick is opaque. In the pictures, which of the materials held by the girl is transparent? Which is translucent? Which is opaque?

Matter that is transparent may also reflect a little light. So you may be able to see yourself in a window. Both translucent matter and opaque matter also reflect some light. In addition, all kinds of matter absorb some of the light that falls on them. So both a window and a brick will absorb some light. Which, do you think, absorbs more?

Do light waves travel in straight lines?

Materials cardboard toilet-tissue tube / cardboard / waxed paper / aluminum foil / table lamp / scissors / masking tape / pin

Procedure

A. Stand a toilet-tissue tube in the center of a piece of cardboard. Trace around the tube on the cardboard. Cut out this circle.

B. Place a piece of waxed paper over one end of the tube. Be careful not to crush the tube as you tape this paper to the tube. Tape a piece of aluminum foil over the other end of the tube.

C. With a pin, carefully make a small hole in the center of the aluminum foil.

D. Carefully push the tube through the hole in the cardboard.

E. Darken your classroom. Stand facing a lighted lamp. Hold the piece of cardboard with the tube in it about 50 cm from the lamp. The aluminum-foil end of the tube should face the lamp.

F. Move the cardboard closer to or farther away from the lamp until you can see the image of the bulb clearly on the waxed paper.
  1. How is the image on the paper different from the bulb itself?
  2. Make a sketch of the bulb, the tube, and the image. Indicate the paths of the light waves from the top and bottom of the bulb to the top and bottom of the image.

Conclusion

1. Describe the paths of the light waves from the top and bottom of the bulb to the top and bottom of the image.
2. Do light waves travel in straight lines?

163

SEEING COLORS

Why are there different colors of light?

As you know, there are several forms of visible light. Your eyes distinguish the different forms as different colors. How does one color of light differ from another? The different colors of light have different frequencies. Red light has the lowest frequency. Violet light has the highest frequency. White light is actually a mixture of various waves of light having different frequencies.

White light can be separated into the colors that make it up by passing it through a prism (priz'əm). A **prism** is a specially shaped transparent object that is used to separate light. As white light passes through a prism, it is separated into bands of color. Together the bands of color are called the **spectrum** (spek'trəm). A spectrum formed by one prism is shown here. What are the colors of the spectrum?

Prism forming the spectrum

Do you know?

Sometimes you can see the spectrum in the sky. It is called a rainbow. A rainbow can form when tiny raindrops are in the air. Waves of sunlight are bent as they enter the drops, much as light is bent as it enters a prism. The sunlight is separated into the colors of the spectrum. Some of the light is then reflected from the raindrops to your eyes. As a result, you see a rainbow.

Your eyes are special organs for detecting light. Your eyes can distinguish the different colors of light. But why do different objects have different colors?

An object has color because it is either producing light or reflecting light. An object that is producing light will be the color of the light that it is giving off. For example, neon gas produces red light when electricity is passed through the gas. If copper is burned in a flame, green light will be produced. If a material gives off all colors of light, what color will you see?

The color of an object that is producing light can be changed. This is done by covering the object with a colored transparent material. The bulb in a green traffic light produces white light. But green glass or plastic is placed in front of the bulb. The glass or plastic absorbs all colors except green. It lets the green light pass through. So the traffic light looks green.

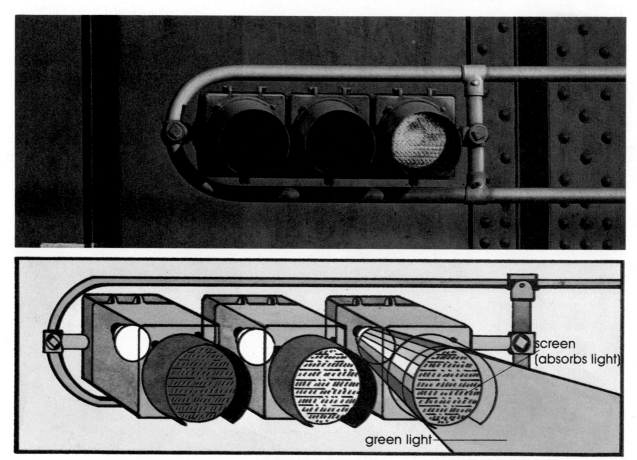

As you know, objects can reflect light. The color an object reflects is the color that you see. The petals of a red rose are reflecting red light and absorbing the other colors that fall on it. What color of light is reflected by a lemon?

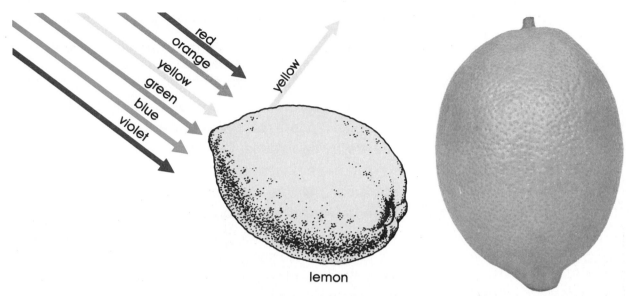

lemon

If an object reflects all colors equally, it will appear white. If an object absorbs most of the light falling on it, it will appear black. Such an object is reflecting very little light.

The absence of light is darkness. In a room where there is absolutely no light, you will not be able to see at all. Even in a dark room, however, there is usually some light. But you know that things are difficult to see in the dark. Why is it difficult to tell the color of an object in a dark room?

— REFLECTION AND MIRRORS —

What happens to light that strikes a smooth surface?

Did you know that a mirror is made from sand? Obviously a mirror does not reflect light in the same way sand does. But do you know why?

You have learned that light waves travel in straight lines. As you can see below, light that is reflected from the smooth surface of a mirror has the same pattern as light that strikes the mirror. As you can also see, light that strikes a rough surface like sand is scattered in many directions. Even though a mirror is made from sand, a mirror reflects light differently than sand does.

Since light reflected from a mirror has the same pattern as the light that strikes the mirror, reflections called images can be seen in a mirror. An image in a mirror appears to be the same distance behind the mirror as the object is in front of the mirror. However, the image is reversed from left to right.

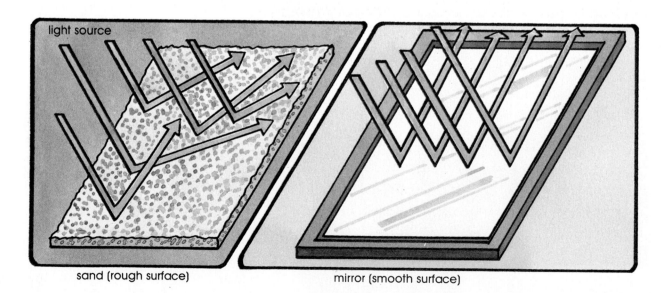

sand (rough surface)   mirror (smooth surface)

Most mirrors have flat surfaces. A mirror with a flat surface is called a plane mirror. But some mirrors have curved surfaces. A mirror in which the reflecting surface curves outward is called a **convex** (kon veks') **mirror.** A convex mirror is shaped like the back of a spoon's bowl. A convex mirror makes things look smaller. However, the mirror reflects light from a large area. The side-view mirrors on trucks are usually convex mirrors. Such a mirror provides a wide field of vision behind the truck so that the driver can see the traffic.

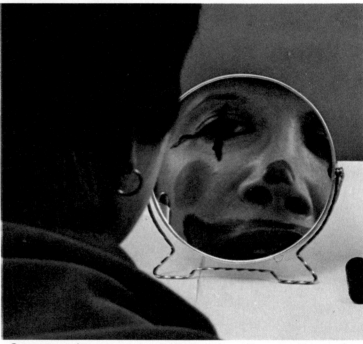

Convex mirror

Concave mirror

A mirror in which the reflecting surface curves inward is called a **concave** (kon kāv') **mirror.** A concave mirror is shaped like the inside of a spoon's bowl. Concave mirrors produce enlarged images. Shaving mirrors and makeup mirrors are concave mirrors.

BENDING LIGHT WAVES

How can you change the path of light waves?

A light wave that travels from one transparent material to another can change direction. This happens because the speed of light changes slightly as light moves from one material to another. Such a change in the direction of a light wave is called **refraction** (ri frak′shən). Look at the picture of the pencil in the water. The light waves moving from the water to the air change direction, causing the pencil to look bent.

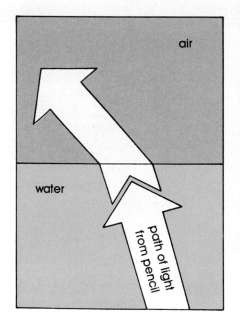

An important tool for controlling light is a lens (lenz). A **lens** is a transparent material having at least one curved surface. Most lenses are made of glass or plastic. Your eyes contain lenses made of living matter. All lenses are alike in one way. Light travels more slowly through a lens than through air. So light passing through a lens changes direction, or is refracted (ri frak′tid).

There are two basic kinds of lenses—convex lenses and concave lenses. A **convex lens** is thicker in the middle than it is at the edge. A **concave lens** is thinner in the middle than at the edge. Both kinds of lenses are shown in the drawing.

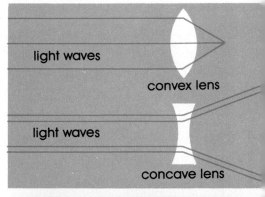

A convex lens bends together waves of light that pass through it. So a convex lens can be used to focus light to a point. A convex lens can be used to form an image on a screen. For example, a convex lens in a movie projector is used to focus light on the screen. Telescopes and magnifying glasses also contain convex lenses. As you can see, a convex lens in a magnifying glass can be used to make things appear larger.

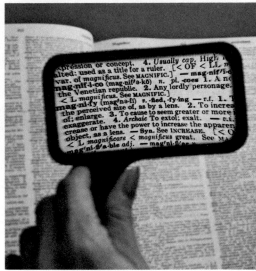

A concave lens spreads out light waves that pass through it. Concave lenses are used to correct an eye problem called nearsightedness. In this eye defect, light waves focus in front of the retina. A nearsighted person has trouble seeing things clearly that are not close by. Concave lenses help to focus light waves on the retina.

Finding out

How can you change the direction of light waves?
You can demonstrate the refraction of light. Put a coin in the bottom of an empty cup. Stand away from the cup so that you can just see the edge of the coin. Have a friend slowly pour water into the cup until the cup is full. Keep your eye on the edge of the coin. What do you observe? Try to explain your observation.

What are some properties of a convex lens?

Materials magnifying glass (convex lens) / book / sheet of white paper / lamp

Procedure

A. Place a magnifying glass over a page of type in a book. While looking through the magnifying glass, slowly lift it to about 4 cm above the page.

    1. Describe what happens.

    2. What do you think will happen if you move the magnifying glass away from the paper? Try it.

B. Darken the room. Stand about 1.5 m from a lamp, with your back to it. Hold a sheet of white paper in one hand and the magnifying glass in the other.

C. Hold the magnifying glass about 5 cm in front of the paper. Look at the paper. (Do not look through the magnifying glass.) Move the magnifying glass slowly back and forth until an image forms on the paper.

    3. Describe the image that you see.

D. Experiment with the paper and magnifying glass to produce a larger image. Then try to produce a smaller image.

    4. How did you produce larger and smaller images?

Conclusion

Identify two properties of a convex lens.

Using science ideas

The lenses in your eyes are convex lenses. Why don't you see things upside down?

1.5 m

MODERN USES OF LIGHT

How is light being put to work in new ways?

Much of our work and play occurs under the natural light of the sun. Artificial light from bulbs and lamps allows many activities to continue after sunset. Headlights and taillights on cars and trucks make night driving safer. The electric lights in your home make it possible for you to read and study at night. Many baseball games are played at night, "under the lights." People have learned to produce light so that they can see when sunlight is not available.

Today, light is being used for other purposes also. Look at the beam of colored light in the picture. It is the artificial light of a laser (lā′zər). A **laser** is a device that strengthens light. A laser can produce a very powerful, very thin beam of light. A laser beam spreads out very little as it moves. The light of a laser is also very pure. This means that it is made up of light waves of a single color. In ordinary light of a certain color, say blue, other colors are also present. The color of laser light depends on the kind of laser being used.

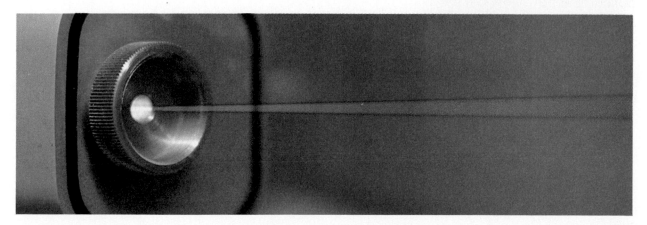

Laser used in welding

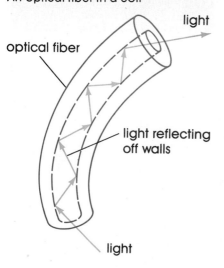
An optical fiber in a coil

optical fiber

light

light reflecting off walls

light

A laser beam is sometimes referred to as concentrated light. A laser beam can be powerful enough to burn through metal. So laser beams can be used to drill holes in machine parts or to cut metal into shapes. Laser beams can also be used to weld metal parts together.

Laser beams are now being used in medicine. Very thin laser beams can be used to destroy diseased tissue. Laser beams are being used to treat an eye disorder in which the retina becomes detached. An eye surgeon can use a laser beam to "weld" the retina back into place.

Laser light is now being used to carry voice signals. The light travels through a very thin glass or plastic tube called an optical fiber. The light reflects, or bounces, along the inner walls of the fiber, as shown in the drawing. In the future, most telephone calls may be carried by light waves traveling through optical fibers. In fiber optics communications, thousands of telephone calls can be carried at the same time by a beam of laser light.

Laser light is artificially produced. But people are also finding new uses for the natural light of the sun. Solar cells convert the energy of sunlight to electrical energy. Such solar cells are used on spacecraft.

Sunlight is also used to heat buildings. Solar panels collect the sunlight. The energy is stored as heat. The heat is used to warm the air, which is then pumped throughout the building. Solar energy may supply a large part of the world's energy needs in the future.

Solar panels on a house

IDEAS TO REMEMBER

▶ Light is a form of radiant energy.
▶ Light may be reflected, transmitted, or absorbed by matter.
▶ Different colors of light have different frequencies.
▶ Mirrors and lenses can be used to change the paths of light waves.
▶ A laser can produce concentrated light.

Reviewing the Chapter

SCIENCE WORDS

A. Copy the sentences below. Use science terms from the chapter to complete the sentences.

1. Light is a visible form of _____ .
2. A change in the direction of light as it passes from one material to another is called _____ .
3. Light that is trapped by matter is said to be _____ .
4. Light that passes through matter is said to be _____ .
5. Light that bounces off matter is said to be _____ .
6. Matter that allows light to pass through without being scattered is said to be _____ .
7. Matter that scatters light that passes through it is said to be _____ .
8. Matter through which light cannot pass is said to be _____ .

B. Write the letter of the term that best matches the definition. Not all the terms will be used.

1. A device that can produce concentrated light
2. The distance between the crest of one wave and the crest of the next
3. The bands of color that make up white light
4. A lens that bends together waves of light
5. The number of waves that pass a point in a period of time

    a. concave lens
    b. frequency
    c. laser
    d. wavelength
    e. spectrum
    f. convex lens

UNDERSTANDING IDEAS

A. What is a lens? Identify the concave lens and the convex lens in the drawing. How does each type of lens change the path of light waves passing through it? Name three objects that contain lenses.

B. Explain why a banana appears yellow. Why does a yellow traffic light appear yellow?

C. Identify each material as *opaque, translucent,* or *transparent.*

1. gold   **2.** wood   **3.** waxed paper
4. air   **5.** ice   **6.** magnifying glass

D. Write the term that does not belong in each group. Explain your answers.

1. transmit, reflect, absorb, decay
2. space, infrared waves, X rays, ultraviolet waves
3. prism, lens, mirror, window
4. crest, wavelength, laser, frequency

USING IDEAS

1. Use your library to find out about animals that give off light. Choose one such animal, and explain how it uses its light to survive.
2. Attach a rope to a doorknob. Produce waves in the rope by flicking it. How can you produce high-frequency waves? How can you produce low-frequency waves? How does wavelength change as you change the frequency?

Chapter 8

Using Electricity

Electricity is an important part of your life. You use it to light your home. You may cook your food with electricity. It allows you to speak to friends across town. Electricity even helps to entertain you. Without it, there would be no radios, televisions, computers, or electronic games. In this chapter you will study the nature of electricity. You will also learn how electricity is used to run many of the machines that we use every day.

178

— ELECTRONS AND ELECTRICITY —

How is electricity related to the movement of electrons?

You are probably familiar with electric charges building up on things. For example, charges build up on clothes in a dryer. The clothes cling to each other. Charges can build up in your hair when you comb it. The hairs will repel each other. Electric charges that build up on an object are called static electricity. The buildup of such charges involves the transfer of electrons from one object to another.

Another type of electricity is called current electricity. In this type of electricity, electrons flow from one place to another. The electricity flows along a path made of matter such as metal wire. Matter through which electricity can flow is called a conductor. Current electricity is the type of electricity used in your home and school.

There are two types of current electricity—direct current and alternating (ôl'tər nā ting) current. In **direct current (dc)** the electrons always flow in one direction. This is the type of current produced by a battery. Where is direct current used around your home?

In **alternating current (ac)** the electrons flow in two directions. First they flow in one direction. Then they flow in the opposite direction. As you can see in the pictures on page 181, power companies produce alternating current. This is the type of current you use in your home. Power companies produce this type of current for two reasons. It is cheaper to produce than direct current. It is easier to send over a long distance.

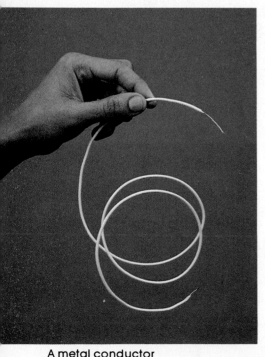

A metal conductor

Power plant producing ac   Power lines carrying ac   Appliance using ac

All electric currents produce magnetism. If you coil wire around a nail and connect the wire to a battery, the nail will act as a magnet. Such a magnet is called an electromagnet. Electromagnets are used to change sound to electric current in telephones. Radios and televisions also contain electromagnets.

Finding out

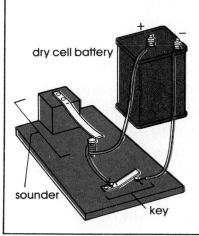

dry cell battery

sounder

key

How can you make a telegraph?   One device that uses electromagnets is a telegraph. To make a telegraph, nail a block that measures 7 cm on each side to a board. Nail a metal strip to the block as shown. Hammer a roofing nail to the board so that its head is just below the metal strip. This part of your telegraph is called the sounder. Nail a second metal strip to the board as shown. Bend up the end of this strip. Hammer another nail under the end of this metal strip. This part of your telegraph is called the key. Now wire the telegraph as shown. Press the key to make the sounder click. What part of your telegraph is an electromagnet?

CIRCUITS
What is an electric circuit?

Current electricity can·flow only when it can follow a complete path. Look at the picture of the bulb connected to the battery. The electricity flows from the battery, through one wire, to the bulb. It continues through the bulb to the other wire and back to the battery. This path is called a circuit.

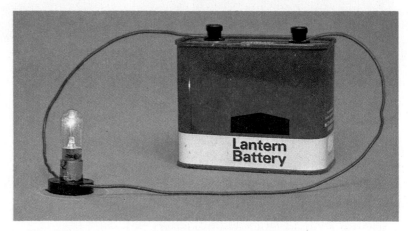

series circuit

parallel circuit

Two kinds of circuits are shown in the drawing. In a series circuit there is only one path for electricity to follow. If that path is broken, electricity will not flow. In a parallel circuit there is more than one path for electricity to follow. And a break in one path does not interfere with the flow of electricity through the other paths.

Most of the circuits in your home are parallel circuits. This allows you to use only the lights or other electrical appliances you need. If your home contained only series circuits, all the electrical items on each such circuit would be on or off at the same time.

Complex appliances, such as televisions, contain many circuits. The current in these circuits must be controlled if the appliances are to run properly. The pictures show three examples of circuits in appliances. Refer to the pictures as you read about each circuit.

  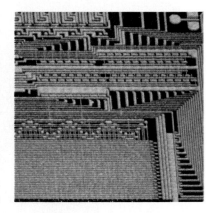

The picture on the left shows a circuit that uses tubes to control current. Until far into the 1950s, radios, televisions, and other electrical devices contained tubes. Tubes took up much space, produced a lot of heat, and burned out often.

In the late 1950s, tubes were replaced by transistors (tran zis'tərz), shown in the center picture. As you can see, transistors are much smaller than tubes. The transistors are connected to all other parts of the circuit with flat wires. Such a circuit is called a **printed circuit.** The use of transistors greatly reduced the size of a typical circuit. This in turn reduced the size and weight of radios and other such things.

During the 1970s, another advance was made. It allowed a whole circuit, with all the parts needed to control the current, to be put on one silicon chip. A chip, shown on the right, can be smaller than a fingernail. Yet all the parts and connections for the circuit are on the chip. This type of circuit is called an **integrated** (in'tə grā-tid) **circuit.**

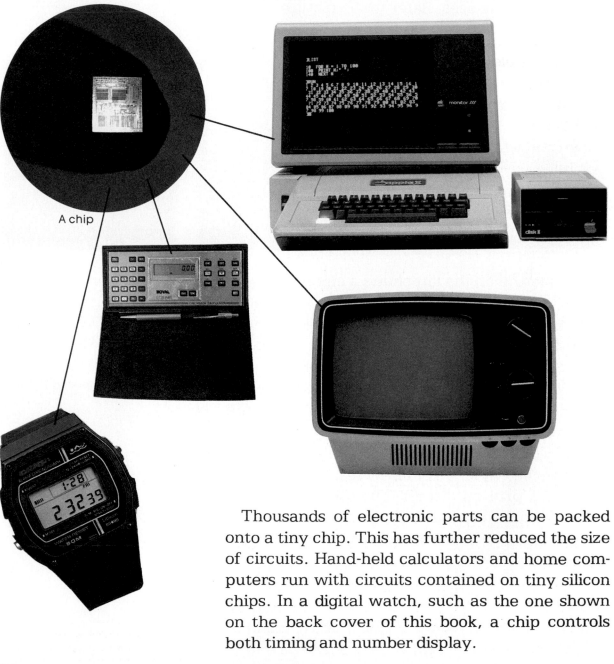

A chip

Thousands of electronic parts can be packed onto a tiny chip. This has further reduced the size of circuits. Hand-held calculators and home computers run with circuits contained on tiny silicon chips. In a digital watch, such as the one shown on the back cover of this book, a chip controls both timing and number display.

-ELECTRICITY AND THE TELEPHONE-
How does a telephone work?

Energy can often be transferred from place to place in the form of electricity. For example, sound can be changed to electricity by a telephone. The electricity then produces sound in another telephone. Before we learn how this occurs, it is necessary to learn something about sound.

Think about the strings of a guitar when they are strummed. The strings vibrate, or move back and forth very quickly. As you can see in the top drawing, the strings come in contact with particles of air as they vibrate. Each string pushes out against nearby air particles, causing them to crowd together. As a string springs back, it leaves a space with few air particles.

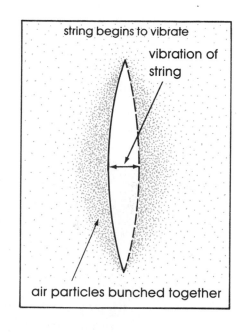

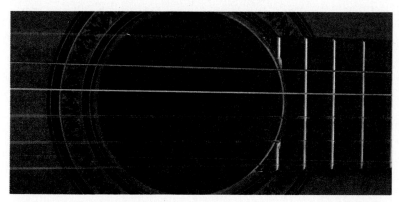

The bottom drawing shows how the push on the air, started by the vibrating strings, is transferred outward by the air particles. This happens because the air particles that are bunched together push against other air particles and then rebound. Each time a string vibrates, it bunches up the air particles again. So a series of vibra-

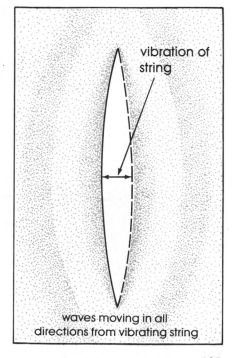

tions, or a wave, is produced in the air. Such waves are called sound waves. Sound waves move out in all directions from a source.

Sound waves can only move through matter. It is not possible to produce sound waves if there are no particles of matter to vibrate. In fact, sound waves travel more quickly through solids than through liquids. This is because the particles are closer together in solids.

Sound waves allow you to talk with other people. However, sound waves weaken as they travel through the air. So unless the people you are talking with are nearby, the sound waves may fade out before reaching them. To speak with someone who is far away, you use a telephone.

Sound waves do not travel through the wires that connect telephones. Instead, the sound waves are changed into an electric current in a telephone. The current moves through wires. The current is changed back into sound waves at the telephone that is receiving the current. Refer to the drawing as you read about how a telephone works.

A telephone contains a transmitter (trans-mit′ər) and a receiver. You talk into the **transmitter** and listen through the **receiver.** The

disc

transmitter

transmitter contains a small disc. When you talk into the phone, sound waves strike this disc. The disc begins to vibrate. These vibrations have the same pattern as the sound waves that are striking the disc. The vibrations cause the electric current in the telephone to vary. This means that the strength of the current changes as the vibrations change. The pattern of the current is the same as the pattern of the sound waves. If the loudness or the pitch of the sound waves changes, the pattern of the current will change. The current moves through the telephone wires.

The current reaches the receiver of another phone. The receiver contains an electromagnet and a metal disc. The current moves through the wires of the electromagnet. Remember that the strength of the current varies. So the strength of the electromagnet also varies. The electromagnet attracts the metal disc. Since the strength of the attraction varies, the disc begins to move back and forth. As the disc vibrates, it produces sound waves. The pattern of the sound waves is the same as the pattern of the current. So the pattern of sound waves that has entered the transmitter is reproduced by the receiver. This enables a person to hear exactly what you said.

receiver

disc

electromagnet

Some telephone signals must travel long distances. In such cases the current may first be changed to radio waves. These waves are then beamed from place to place. They may even be beamed up to a satellite. The waves are then beamed down to a receiving station. At the station the waves are changed back to electric current. The current then moves through wires to the receiver of a telephone. Today you can talk by telephone with people almost anywhere in the world.

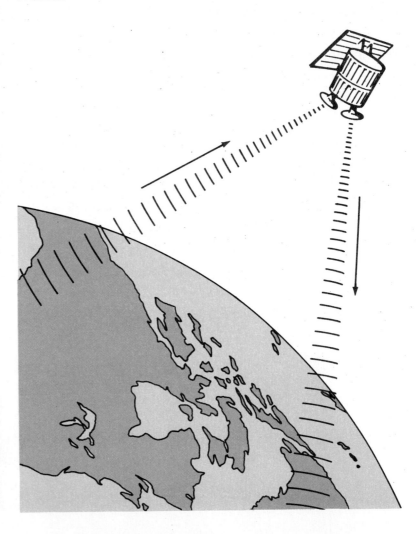

Radio wave relay tower

How does a telephone receiver work?

Materials small metal can with both ends removed / balloon / paper clip / metal file / 6-volt battery / insulated wire / scissors / nail / ruler / 2 rubber bands / tape

Procedure

A. Do this activity with a partner. Stretch a piece of balloon across one end of a metal can. Use rubber bands to hold it in place.

B. Tape a paper clip to the center of the balloon.

C. Cut a piece of wire about 60 cm long. Remove 3 cm of the outside covering from each end. Wrap one end of the wire about 10 turns around a metal file. Connect the other end to a battery.

D. Cut a piece of wire about 80 cm long. Remove 3 cm of the outside covering from each end. Wrap the wire around a nail, leaving 30 cm of wire at each end. Connect one end of the wire to the battery.

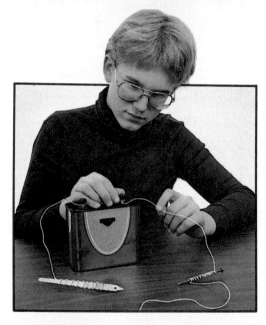

E. Have your partner hold the open end of the can near one ear. While holding the nail near the paper clip, scrape the file with the end of the wire that is wrapped around the nail.
   1. Describe what happens.

Conclusion

1. Does a telephone use an open circuit or a closed circuit?

2. Compare this telephone receiver with the drawing of the telephone receiver on page 187. How are they alike?

1 sound waves striking microphone

2 cutting tool producing groove in disk

3 metal copies made from disc

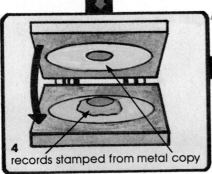

4 records stamped from metal copy

COPYING SOUND WAVES

How can sound waves be recorded?

Sound waves can be copied and saved for future use. A phonograph record, for example, contains a copy of sound waves. The sound waves are reproduced when the record is played.

To make a record, a plastic disc is used to copy the sound waves. (1) The sound waves that are to be recorded strike a receiver called a microphone. The microphone changes the sound waves into electric current. As in a telephone, the strength of the current varies. The pattern of the current is the same as the pattern of the sound waves.

(2) The current flows into a special cutting tool. As this tool receives the current, it cuts a groove in the spinning plastic disc. As the current varies, the groove that is being produced varies. (3) The disc is used to make a master disc. (4) Phonograph records are produced from the master disc.

(5) To play a record, a fine needle is placed in the groove of the record. As the record turns, the movement causes the needle to vibrate. The vi-

5 reproducing sound from record

brations are changed into electric current by the record player. The current is sent to a loud-speaker. An electromagnet in the speaker turns the current into sound waves. You hear the sound that is produced.

Sound waves can also be copied with a tape recorder. Small pieces of metal are present on the tape in a recorder. The sound waves to be recorded strike a microphone. An electric current is produced. The current has the same pattern as the sound waves. The current passes through the wires of an electromagnet. As the current varies, the strength of the electromagnet varies.

The electromagnet causes the metal pieces on the tape to become arranged in a magnetic pattern. The pattern is the same as the pattern of the current. So the tape holds a copy of the sound waves that produced the current.

When a tape is played, the magnetic pattern it holds is changed into an electric current with the same pattern. The current flows through a speaker. The speaker turns the current into sound waves that you can hear.

Playing back the recording

Recording on tape

How is a needle used to produce sound from a record?

Materials   sheet of paper / straight pin / tape / record player / old phonograph record

Procedure

A. Put a record on a record player and turn it on.

B. Gently hold a pin in the groove of the record.
   1. What happens?

C. Make a cone out of a piece of paper. Use tape to hold the cone together.

D. Stick the pin through the small end of the cone. The pin should extend through the paper.

E. Gently hold the pin in the groove of the record.
   2. Do you notice any difference in sound when using the cone?

Conclusion

1. What happens to the pin in the groove as the record turns?

2. How does the pin produce sound?

192

RADIO AND TELEVISION

How are radio and television signals sent and received?

When you turn on a radio, you hear sound. However, the radio is not receiving electric current from a radio station. What does the radio receive that causes it to make sound?

You have learned that light, radio waves, and other forms of radiant energy travel as waves. Such waves differ from sound waves. But radio waves can be used to send sound signals. A radio is able to receive these radio waves. In the radio the waves are changed into sound. Refer to the drawing on page 194 as you read to find out how radio waves are produced and received.

(1) In a radio station a microphone is used to change sound waves into electric current. The strength of the current varies with changes in the sound waves. So the pattern of the current is the same as the pattern of the sound waves.

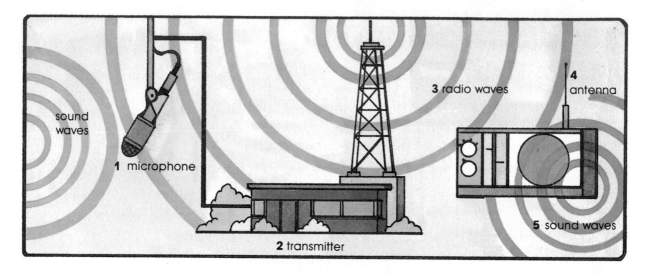

1 microphone

sound waves

2 transmitter

3 radio waves

4 antenna

5 sound waves

(2) A radio station also has a device called a radio transmitter. This **radio transmitter** produces radio waves. (3) The electric current is used to produce a pattern in the radio waves. So the radio waves carry the pattern of the sound waves that produced the current. The radio waves are sent out by the transmitter.

(4) A radio has an antenna that can receive the waves. As the waves are received, they are changed into an electric current. The current contains the same pattern as the pattern of the radio waves. The current is sent to a speaker. (5) The speaker changes the current into sound waves. You hear the sound waves as music or speech.

A television station also sends out radio waves that carry sound signals. In addition, the station sends out waves that carry picture signals. A television camera is used to produce the picture signals. The waves that carry the signals are called television waves.

The radio and television waves can be received by an antenna. The waves are changed into separate currents. Sound is produced in the television speaker in much the same way as in a radio speaker.

The current that carries the picture signal is used to produce a stream of electrons. The electrons strike the back of the television screen. The screen contains thousands of dots. These dots glow when struck by electrons. Different dots glow in different colors. So a color image is produced on the screen. Each second, 30 images are placed on the screen. This is so fast that a moving picture appears before your eyes.

Sending radio and television signals involves changing sound and light to electricity. The electricity is changed to radio and television waves. When received, these waves are changed back to electricity. The electricity is then used to produce sound and light.

STORING AND USING INFORMATION

How can electricity be used to store information?

We live in an information age. Each year, discoveries are made in science, history, and other fields. These discoveries are recorded for the future. Stores must keep track of the goods they sell so that more can be ordered. Schools keep records of students' grades, attendance, and courses completed. How is all this information stored? How can so much information be used?

There are a number of ways to store information, or data. There are also devices that can help us use information. How do the things in the pictures help us use and store information?

A **computer** is a device that can store and use information. A computer in a bank can receive information on people's accounts. The computer can also make changes in the accounts as people put money in or take it out. Computers can solve problems, record sales, and do many other jobs.

A desk-top computer

How can computers store and handle information? A computer stores information in **memory circuits.** These circuits are on chips in many modern computers. As you put information into the computer, the memory circuits become used up. However, the information is lost when the computer is off. To store information permanently, the computer can transfer information to tapes or to memory disks. The tapes or disks put the information back into the computer when needed.

Computers also contain circuits that can process information. These circuits calculate, solve problems, and do whatever special jobs the computer was designed to do.

In many computers, the problem-solving circuits are contained on a chip. Such a chip is called a microprocessor (mī krō pros'es ər). A **microprocessor** is a computer on a chip. Computers found in schools and homes contain such chips.

An ant carrying a microprocessor

A computer is given instructions to follow when it is used. Instructions are given in a language that the computer can understand. Many small computers use a language called BASIC. The set of instructions that tells the computer what to do is called a **program.**

The student in the pictures is using a computer. Refer to the pictures as you read about what is happening.

In the first picture the student has read what the program is about. The student has been told by the computer to press a key to go to the next step.

In the second picture the computer has placed a question on the screen. The question was in the computer's memory circuits. The student has responded by spelling out the answer. The answer can be seen on the screen.

In the third picture the computer has checked the answer. The computer has informed the student that the answer is right. Now the computer will put another question on the screen.

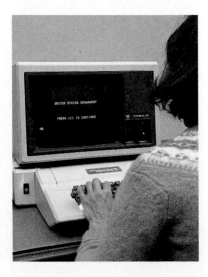

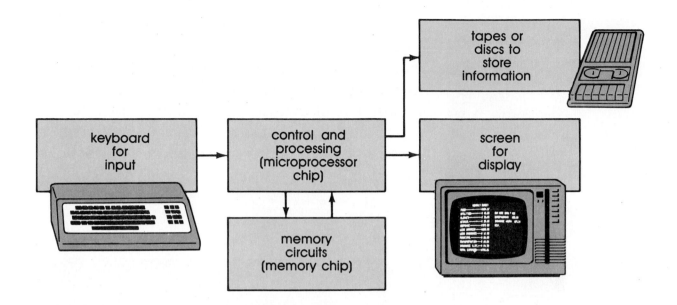

Microprocessors are used in other devices besides computers. A calculator is controlled by a microprocessor. It is the microprocessor in a calculator that follows instructions. A person using a calculator enters some numbers and instructions. For example, let us say the person enters 2 + 2 and then presses the equals sign (=). The calculator receives these numbers and the instruction to add them. In a short time, the calculator adds the numbers and shows the answer.

Microprocessors are used in many other ways. They are used in cars and electronic games. In cars they may tell drivers about such conditions as fuel level, oil level, and even whether the door is closed. In electronic games they make different sound and light patterns. As you play such a game, the microprocessor reacts to your actions by changing the patterns.

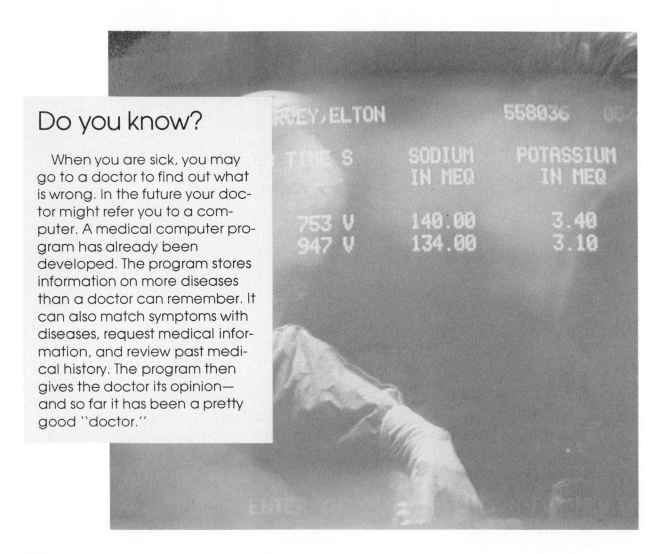

Do you know?

When you are sick, you may go to a doctor to find out what is wrong. In the future your doctor might refer you to a computer. A medical computer program has already been developed. The program stores information on more diseases than a doctor can remember. It can also match symptoms with diseases, request medical information, and review past medical history. The program then gives the doctor its opinion—and so far it has been a pretty good "doctor."

Home video game

Computers and microprocessors have changed our lives. Computers help us store and recall large amounts of information. Computers also help us use this information to solve problems. New uses for computers and microprocessors will be found every year. They will continue to play an important role in our lives.

IDEAS TO REMEMBER

▶ Electricity is the movement of electrons.
▶ An electric current flows in a path called a circuit.
▶ In a telephone, sound waves are changed to electric current and then back to sound waves.
▶ Sound waves may be copied on records or tapes.
▶ Radiant energy can be used to transmit sound and light signals.
▶ Computers help us to store and use information.

Reviewing the Chapter

SCIENCE WORDS

A. Write the letter of the term that best matches the definition. Not all the terms will be used.

1. The kind of chip that contains problem-solving circuits
2. The part of a telephone that changes sound waves to electric current
3. A circuit containing transistors that are attached by flat wires
4. Current in which the electrons always flow in one direction
5. A set of instructions that tells a computer what to do
6. The part of a telephone that changes electric current to sound waves
7. A circuit in which all parts and connections are contained on a chip
8. Current in which the electrons flow first in one direction and then in the opposite direction
9. A device that uses small pieces of metal to copy sound waves
10. A computer circuit in which information is stored

a. printed circuit
b. receiver
c. memory circuit
d. microprocessor
e. program
f. short circuit
g. alternating current
h. transmitter
i. tape recorder
j. direct current
k. integrated circuit

UNDERSTANDING IDEAS

A. Study the computer flow chart shown. Match the letters in the chart with the correct part and function listed below.

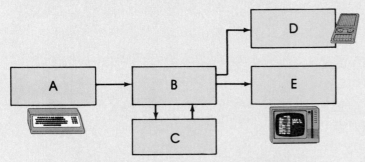

1. Memory circuits (memory chip)
2. Tapes or disks to store information
3. Control and processing (microprocessor chip)
4. Screen for display
5. Keyboard for input

B. Describe how electronic circuits have changed.

C. A cause makes things happen. An effect is what happens. For each pair of sentences, write which is the cause and which is the effect.

1. **a.** Electric current is produced and flows to a speaker.
   b. The needle on a record vibrates as the record turns.
2. **a.** The electric current in a telephone begins to vary.
   b. Sound waves strike the disc in the transmitter.
3. **a.** Memory circuits become used up.
   b. The keyboard is used to put data into a computer.

USING IDEAS

1. Find out some of the terms used in the computer language known as BASIC. What will a computer do when it receives each instruction?
2. How do AM radio and FM radio differ?

Science in Careers

The study of matter and energy falls under two general areas in science. These are *chemistry* and *physics.* Both the *chemist* and the *physicist* are interested in the nature and behavior of matter. Both study the relationships between energy and matter, but they may investigate different aspects.

Chemists are usually more concerned with the physical and chemical properties of elements and compounds. *Analytical chemists* determine the kinds of matter present in particular samples. They may also determine the amount of each element or compound in a sample. *Organic chemists* study the compounds of carbon. Areas of their work often overlap areas of biology.

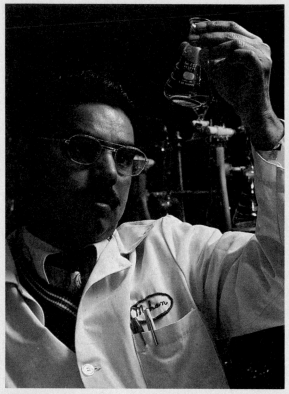

Analytical chemist

Biochemist

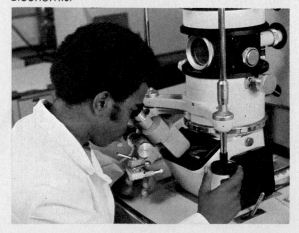

Physical chemists study the energy changes that occur in chemical reactions.

Physicists may be interested in matter on a very large or very small scale. Some physicists study the nature of light and electricity. Others investigate the structure and behavior of particles that are smaller than atoms. And many physicists study the relationships between energy and matter. Perhaps this type of work would interest you.

People in Science

Dolphus E. Milligan (1928–1973)

Dr. Milligan was a chemist. He studied what happens to molecules as they break apart during chemical reactions. Using an instrument called a spectroscope, Dr. Milligan was able to identify a number of short-lived chemical units called reaction intermediates. The reaction intermediates exist only for a brief period of time during chemical reactions. However, they play important roles in how matter rearranges during chemical reactions.

A spectrometer being used to investigate chemical reactions

Developing Skills

WORD SKILLS

Prefixes and suffixes are word parts that change the meanings of the base words to which they are added. A prefix is added to the beginning of a base word. A suffix is added to the end of a base word. The tables show how prefixes and suffixes are used to change the meanings of words.

Use the tables for help in determining the meaning of each of the following words. If you do not know the meaning of the base word, look it up in a dictionary.

1. atomic
2. poisonous
3. elemental
4. nonacid
5. unreactive
6. compression
7. ultraviolet
8. superconductor
9. fissionable
10. extraterrestrial

Prefix	Meaning	Example
extra-	beyond	extraordinary
non-	not	nontoxic
super-	above, most	superabundant
ultra-	beyond	ultrasonic
un-	not, opposite of	unfair

Suffix	Meaning	Example
-able	that can be	obtainable
-al	of, having the nature of	ornamental
-ic	having to do with	metallic
-ion	act or process of	expression
-ous	full of	joyous

READING A BAR GRAPH

A bar graph can be used to compare information. This bar graph compares the amount of electrical energy used by various electrical appliances in 10 hours. This electrical energy is measured in units called kilowatt-hours. Use the bar graph to answer the questions.

1. Which uses more energy in 10 hours, a toaster or an iron?
2. How much energy in 10 hours, does a radio use?
3. How much energy does a refrigerator use in 10 hours?
4. In 10 hours, how much more energy does an iron use than a television?
5. In 10 hours, how much more energy does a clothes washer use than a lamp?
6. Do you think a freezer uses more or less than 3 kilowatt-hours of electricity in 10 hours?

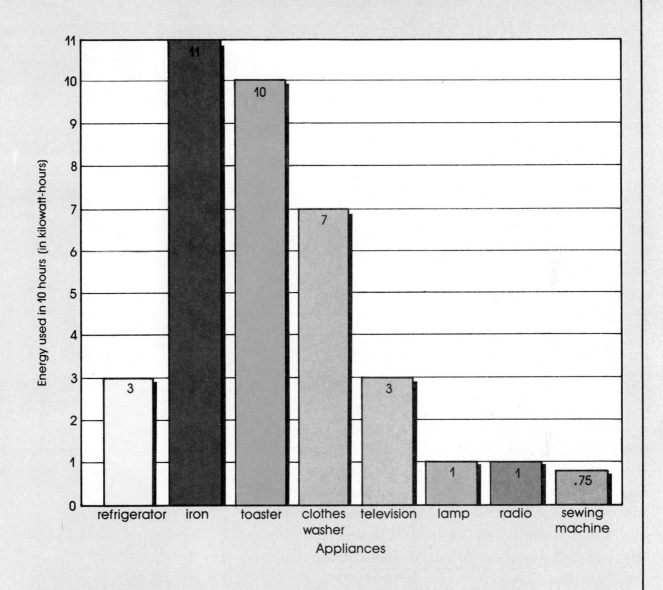

MAKING A BAR GRAPH

This chart shows data for the changes in the number of computers used in the United States from 1960 to 1976. Make a bar graph that compares the number of computers in use each year.

Year	Computers in use
1960	10,000
1965	20,000
1970	70,000
1975	200,000
1976	250,000

UNIT THREE

Investigating the Earth and Space

We live on the earth. The earth supplies many materials that we need. How would you describe the earth? What are some of its features? The features of the earth can change. These changes may be rapid or slow. The air around the earth can change too. The changes cause conditions that we call weather. Many of these changes can be predicted.

People have been interested in space beyond the earth for thousands of years. They have developed many ways to study space.

In this unit you will study the earth and its resources. You will also learn about changes in the earth itself and about the earth's weather. Finally you will learn about exploring beyond the earth into space.

Chapter 9

The Earth's Resources

Think of the different kinds of matter you use every day. You use food and clothing. You use your home for shelter. You use fuel to travel to school and to heat your home. Where does all this matter come from? How do you get more matter when it is used up?

Most of the matter and energy that people use comes from materials of the earth. The earth is the source of food for all living things. Most building materials come from the earth. Also most of the energy that is used to heat homes, run machines, and produce electricity comes from materials of the earth. What kind of matter is being taken from the earth in this picture?

In this chapter you will learn about the materials we get from the earth. You will also learn why we must use these materials wisely.

A RENEWABLE RESOURCE

evergreen forest

trees being cut for lumber

– LIVING RENEWABLE RESOURCES –
How are living resources renewed?

The materials we use from the earth are called natural resources (ri sôr′siz). A **natural resource** is a valuable material that is found in nature and used by people to meet their needs. Some natural resources are air, water, plants and animals, metals, and soil. What are some others?

Some resources are renewable (ri nü′ə bəl). A **renewable resource** is one that is replaced naturally. Plants and animals are renewable because they grow and reproduce. But this does not mean the supplies of plants and animals will never run out. There may not always be enough to replace those that are used.

Trees are a natural resource. At one time trees were abundant. People used much wood for building homes and for fuel. They thought they would never run out of trees. But they were wrong. They used the trees faster than new trees could

area cleared of trees

area replanted with young trees

grow. So trees became scarce in many places. Today, large numbers of trees are grown on tree farms. Special methods are used so that the trees will grow faster. Now trees that are used up can be replaced faster with new trees.

Animals are also renewable. They replace themselves by reproducing. Animals are widely used by people. They are used for food, for their hides, and for other materials they contain. At one time, some birds and other animals were killed only for sport. Birds were also killed for

Snow geese and sandhill cranes in wildlife refuge

their feathers. People once thought the supply of animals would never run out. Now some kinds of animals no longer exist. How can we save other kinds of animals? Many kinds of animals are raised on farms and ranches. Some wild animals are protected in refuges (ref'yüj iz). The numbers of many such protected animals are now increasing.

Living resources can be renewed. But as the earth's population increases, the resources are used faster. So they must be renewed even faster. In addition, the living resources that we now have must be used more carefully.

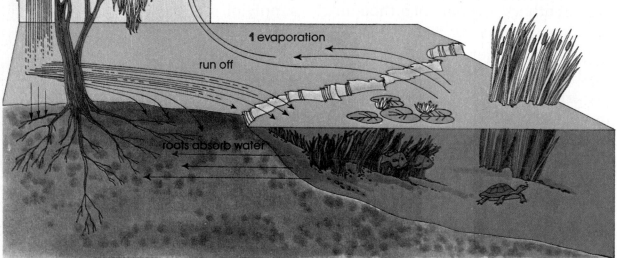

How are nonliving resources renewed?

Nonliving things do not grow or reproduce. Yet some nonliving resources are renewable. Three of these nonliving resources are water, air, and soil.

Water is needed by all living things. It is found in many places on the earth. Water is found in lakes, ponds, streams, rivers, and oceans. It is also found under the ground and in the air.

The supply of water is renewed in a natural cycle called the water cycle. Trace the path of water in the drawing. (1) Water evaporates from the surfaces of ponds, lakes, and oceans. The water vapor rises into the air. (2) As it rises, the water vapor cools and changes into liquid water. (3) Water falls back to the earth in the form of rain, snow, sleet, or hail. Some of this water falls into bodies of water. Other water soaks into the ground. The water is then available for use by plants and animals again.

2 water vapor changes to liquid water

3 rain

leaves release water

1 evaporation

run off

roots absorb water

THE WATER CYCLE

How oxygen and carbon dioxide are renewed

Air contains many kinds of gases. Oxygen and carbon dioxide are two gases found in air. They are needed by living things. How are these gases renewed after they are used? The drawing shows that oxygen and carbon dioxide in the air are renewed by living things.

Most living things use oxygen to obtain energy from food. During this process, carbon dioxide is given off as a waste product. Green plants use carbon dioxide and give off oxygen when they make food. What would happen if there were no green plants? The carbon dioxide in the air would build up to a very high level. Also, the amount of oxygen would decrease greatly.

Soil is another renewable resource. Soil provides minerals that plants need to grow. When soil is rich in these minerals, it is said to be **fertile.** Plants remove these minerals from the soil as they grow. Then as plants die and decay, the minerals are returned to the soil. In this way soil can remain fertile. The man in the picture is adding dead plant material to the soil.

—NONRENEWABLE RESOURCES—

What resources cannot be renewed?

As you know, certain resources can be renewed. But this is not true of all resources. Some of our most important resources are nonrenewable (non ri nü′ə bəl). A **nonrenewable resource** is one that exists in a limited amount. A nonrenewable resource cannot be replaced. Once it has been used, no more of the resource can be formed. Rocks from the earth's crust are nonrenewable resources. Limestone, sandstone, granite, and slate are important building materials. Minerals are also examples of nonrenewable resources.

Granite building

Granite quarry

A **mineral** is any pure hard material that is found in the earth's crust. Examples of some useful minerals are quartz, mica, salt, and sulfur. Quartz is used to make glass. Mica is used in electronic equipment. Salt, as you know, has many uses. Salt is mined in many places on the earth. Salt is also collected by evaporation from sea water.

Sulfur is used in matches, fertilizers, medicines, and paper pulp. Much sulfur is found in Texas and Louisiana and under the Gulf of Mexico. It is mined by pumping hot water deep into the mines. The hot water melts the sulfur. The melted sulfur is then forced to the surface.

Metals are among the most useful of the nonrenewable resources. Metals must be separated from the materials they are found with in the ground. These materials are called ores. An **ore** is rock or mineral from which useful metal can be obtained.

halite (salt)

mica

quartz

salt mine

quarry

SOME MINERALS IN THE EARTH'S CRUST

sulfur mine   sulfur

Finding out

Where are some deposits of nonrenewable resources found?   Pretend that you are an international miner. You have been given a list of places in the world where deposits of certain nonrenewable resources might be found. But before you can do anything, you must determine where each deposit is located. Use an atlas or a globe to do this. Then make a list that shows each deposit and the country it is found in. If the deposit is found in the United States or Canada, indicate the state, territory, or province in which it is found. Then plan a trip with the shortest possible route that will let you visit each deposit.

Potential Resource Deposits

RESOURCE DEPOSIT	LONGITUDE	LATITUDE
1. coal	76 W	41 N
2. iron ore	93 W	47 N
3. uranium	108 W	34 N
4. copper	24 E	8 S
5. nickel	100 W	56 N
6. gold	84 W	48 N
7. natural gas	116 W	34 N
8. uranium	2 E	46 N
9. silver	112 W	32 N
10. oil	102 W	32 N

Ores are obtained by mining. Some ores are mined from open pits, such as the one shown in the picture. Other ores are taken from mines deep under the ground. In some ores, the metals are not chemically combined with other materials. These metals are in pure form. Such metals are called **native metals.** Gold, silver, and copper are often found as native metals.

Iron mine

Iron ore

Some ores are called high-grade ores. These ores contain much metal. Low-grade ores have small amounts of metal. Supplies of high-grade ores have decreased. So now low-grade ores must be mined.

Iron is our most important metal. About 100 million metric tons of iron are used in the United States each year.

The map below shows some places where certain minerals and metals are found in North America. Which of these resources can be found nearest to where you live? Which can be found in Mexico? Where can zinc be found?

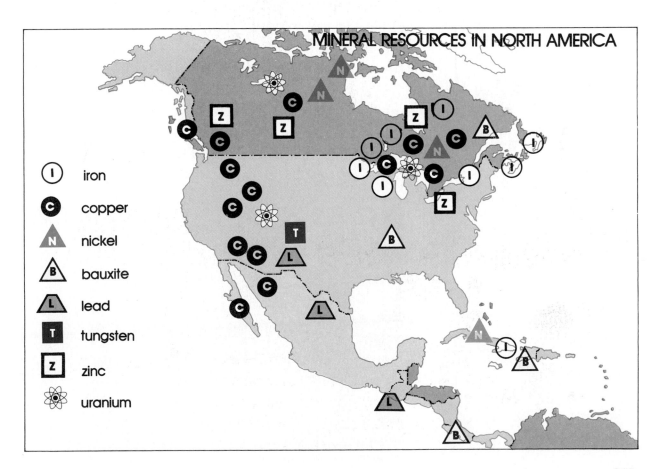

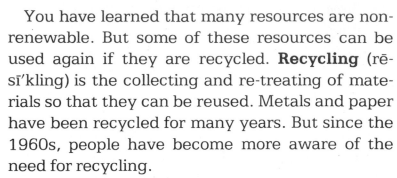

RECYCLING

How can nonrenewable resources be reused?

You have learned that many resources are non-renewable. But some of these resources can be used again if they are recycled. **Recycling** (rē-sī′kling) is the collecting and re-treating of materials so that they can be reused. Metals and paper have been recycled for many years. But since the 1960s, people have become more aware of the need for recycling.

Junked cars are a good source of iron and steel. These metals are melted down and formed into useful items again. Aluminum and tin cans are recycled to make new cans. Other products are also made from recycled cans. Items such as those in the pictures may be made from recycled aluminum.

Glass can be recycled too. Some glass bottles may be cleaned and used again. Items made of glass can also be ground up. Ground glass is sometimes used in making roads. And it can be melted to make new glass items.

Collecting aluminum cans for recycling

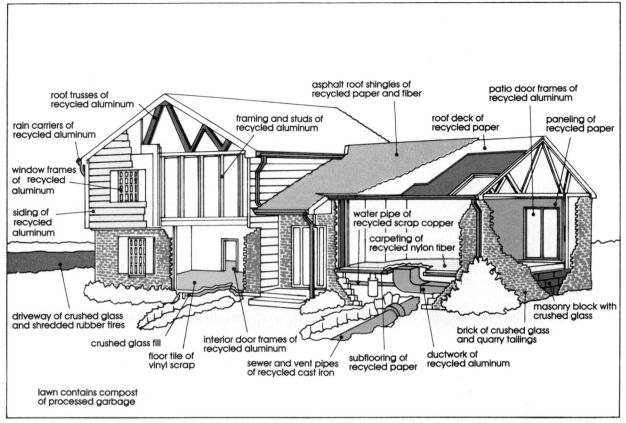

Labels on the diagram:

roof trusses of recycled aluminum

rain carriers of recycled aluminum

window frames of recycled aluminum

siding of recycled aluminum

asphalt roof shingles of recycled paper and fiber

framing and studs of recycled aluminum

roof deck of recycled paper

patio door frames of recycled aluminum

paneling of recycled paper

water pipe of recycled scrap copper

carpeting of recycled nylon fiber

masonry block with crushed glass

driveway of crushed glass and shredded rubber tires

crushed glass fill

floor tile of vinyl scrap

interior door frames of recycled aluminum

sewer and vent pipes of recycled cast iron

subflooring of recycled paper

ductwork of recycled aluminum

brick of crushed glass and quarry tailings

lawn contains compost of processed garbage

House made almost entirely from recycled materials

Recycled paper is often used in making new paper products. It is also used in insulation and plasterboard. Items such as those in the pictures may be made from recycled paper. Look at the drawing. What materials in this house are made from recycled aluminum?

Many towns have set up centers to collect waste materials. In such centers, glass, metal, and paper are separated. These materials are then sold to companies that recycle them. The small recycling centers are important. But they collect only a small amount of the materials that can be recycled. Today, less than one tenth of the materials that can be reused are being recycled.

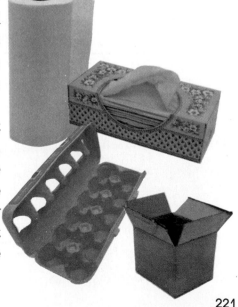

How much useful matter is wasted in your class?

Materials 5 large plastic trash bags / bathroom scale

Procedure

A. Make a chart like the one shown.

B. Collect the matter that is thrown out in your class in one day. Decide which matter could be recycled and which could not. Do not include food scraps for recycling.

C. Put the recyclable material into a plastic garbage bag.
  1. Check off in the chart the kinds of items that were placed in the bag.
  2. Weigh the bag and record the weight.

D. Repeat steps **B** and **C** every day for five days.

Conclusion

1. What kinds of matter are thrown away in your class every day?
2. Which materials could be recycled?
3. What was the total weight of recyclable materials thrown out in one week?
4. How could the amount of waste thrown out be reduced?

Using science ideas

Repeat this activity by using matter thrown out in other places in the school, such as the art room and the gym.

Date	Waste paper	Bottles	Cans	Other matter	Weight

FOSSIL FUEL RESOURCES

How are fossil fuels used?

Other important resources from the earth are the fossil fuels. **Fossil fuels** are fuels such as coal, oil, and natural gas that were formed from the bodies of dead plants and animals. This process occurred millions of years ago.

Fossil fuels are used in two main ways. They are burned for the heat energy they contain, and they are used as feedstocks. A **feedstock** is a raw material from which other materials are made. These drawings show some of the products made from fossil fuel feedstocks. Which of these items can you find in your home?

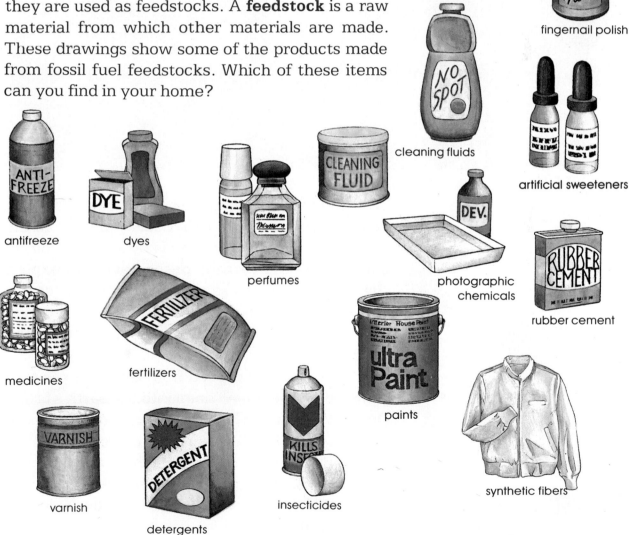

plastics

fingernail polish

cleaning fluids

artificial sweeteners

antifreeze

dyes

perfumes

photographic chemicals

rubber cement

medicines

fertilizers

paints

varnish

detergents

insecticides

synthetic fibers

Strip mining for coal

Fossil fuels have many uses. But they must first be removed from the earth. Coal is taken from the earth in two ways. One way is by strip mining. In a strip mine the earth is pushed away to expose the coal, which is close to the surface. The coal is then removed by huge machines. Coal is obtained also from shaft mines, which extend deep into the earth.

Oil and gas are removed from the earth through wells. Wells are drilled deep into the earth's crust. Once the oil or gas has been reached, pumps are used to bring it to the surface. Oil removed from the earth is called crude oil. To be made into useful products, crude oil must be refined. The products made from crude oil include gasoline, jet fuel, and heating oil.

The crust beneath the oceans is also a rich source of fossil fuels, especially oil. In fact, fossil fuels are the most important resource now being taken from beneath the ocean floor. There is oil beneath every ocean of the world. It is found in shallow areas near the shores.

Offshore oil wells

Offshore wells provide more than 20 percent of the oil used in the world. Offshore wells are drilled from platforms on the surface of the water. The drawing shows how an oil well is drilled from a platform on the surface of the water. In the United States there are several offshore wells. They are in the Gulf of Mexico and off the coast of southern California. There are new wells being drilled along the East Coast.

The ocean floor may also be a rich source of natural gas. It is believed that certain areas off the East Coast of the United States may hold much natural gas. Finding out exactly where this gas is located is costly. Once it has been found, it could increase our supplies of fossil fuels.

225

No one knows the amounts of fossil fuels that are still in the earth. The map shows areas where coal, oil, and natural gas are now found in North America. It also shows oil and gas wells off the coasts. What fossil fuels can be found nearest your town?

Fossil fuels are rapidly being used up. Some fossil fuels may be forming today. But the process takes millions of years. In addition, the conditions of the earth are no longer what they were when the fossil fuels first formed. Since these fuels cannot be replaced, they are nonrenewable resources. They must be used wisely. What can be done to conserve, or avoid wasting, fossil fuels?

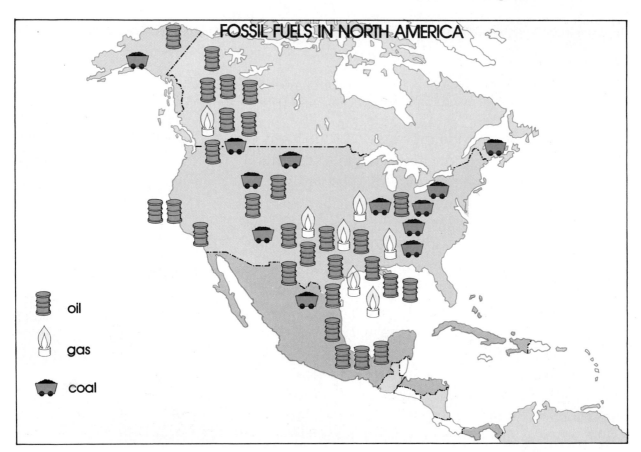

FOSSIL FUELS IN NORTH AMERICA

oil
gas
coal

-RESOURCES FROM THE OCEANS-
What resources do we get from the oceans?

Oceans cover more than 70 percent of the earth's surface. The oceans contain valuable resources. The water in the oceans is salt water. The salt in the oceans is mostly sodium chloride. Seawater also contains salts made of bromine, magnesium, sulfur, and calcium. In fact, seawater contains all the elements that make up the earth's crust.

Salt can be separated from seawater. This is done in a process called **desalination** (dē sal ə-nā'shən). This process is useful for two reasons. First, it removes salt from seawater. The salt may then be used for different purposes. Second, it makes fresh water, which is used for drinking and for watering crops.

Desalination plant

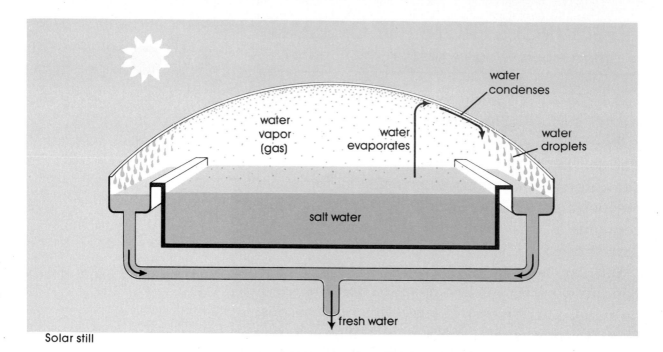

water condenses

water vapor (gas)

water evaporates

water droplets

salt water

fresh water

Solar still

One device that is used to separate salt from seawater is a **solar still.** Look at the drawing of the solar still. Energy from the sun evaporates the seawater. The water changes to water vapor, and the salt remains. The water vapor can be cooled to form liquid water again. This water is fresh water, free of salt, that could be used for drinking.

As the numbers of people in the world increase and water supplies become polluted, greater supplies of fresh water are needed. Many cities that need water are near oceans. These cities can benefit most from the desalination of seawater. But the desalination process is quite costly.

Desalination provides about 29 percent of all the salt used in the world. Other minerals, such as bromine and magnesium, are taken from the salt. Bromine is used in making medicines. Magnesium is often mixed with aluminum to make a light, strong metal.

How does a solar still work?

Materials   table salt / paper cup / plastic spoon / large plate / saucer / metric ruler / large clear bowl

Procedure

A. Half fill a paper cup with warm water. Add two spoonfuls of salt. Stir well.

B. Put a saucer on top of a large plate. Place them where sunlight will fall on them.

C. Pour salt water from the cup into the saucer until the water is about 3 mm deep.

D. Place a large clear bowl upside down over the saucer and plate.

E. Observe your solar still the next day.
  1. What do you observe in the large plate and on the bowl?

Conclusion

1. What happened to the water in the saucer?
2. Do you think the water in the large plate is fresh water or salt water? Give reasons for your answer.
3. Where did the energy come from to operate the solar still?

Using science ideas

Imagine that you are stranded on a desert island with no source of fresh water. All you have is a parachute, a few metal containers, and plastic bags holding food supplies. Describe how you would obtain fresh water.

Some important ores have been found on the ocean floor. These are found in round lumps called **nodules** (noj′ülz). Nodules contain large amounts of valuable minerals. Many nodules are made up of black manganese (mang′gə nēs) ore. Manganese is added to steel to make it easier to form and shape.

Nodules have also been found to contain small amounts of copper, nickel, and cobalt. Copper is used to make electric wiring and plumbing pipe. Nickel is used in making stainless steel. Cobalt is added to certain materials to give them strength. The pictures show nodules from the ocean floor. Scientists are trying to find ways to collect nodules without upsetting the balance of life in the oceans.

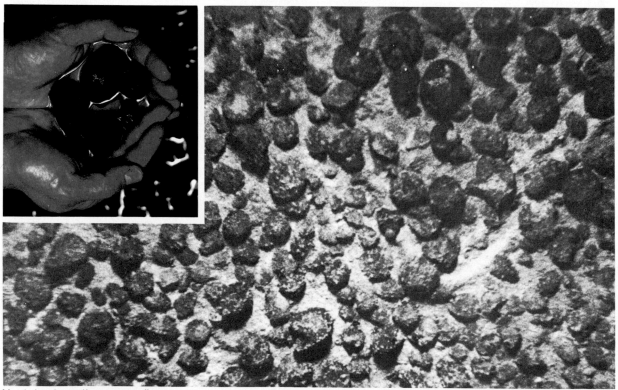

Nodules from the ocean floor

Food is another resource obtained from the oceans. The oceans have been a source of food for thousands of years. But fishing cannot supply all the food needed by the growing numbers of people. In the future, fishing may be replaced by mariculture (mar'ə kul chər). **Mariculture** is the farming of the oceans for food.

Do you know?

Oysters are shellfish that can be grown by mariculture. How are oysters farmed? There are several ways. One way is to use a network of strings attached to rafts. Several scallop shells are hung from each string. Each shell has many small oysters clinging to it. The oysters feed on food placed in the water around them. They grow large and meaty with this method. They are also protected from their natural enemies, such as the starfish. In 2 to 4 years, an oyster farmer can harvest large, tasty oysters to sell. The pictures show an oyster farm and some mature oysters.

Today, scientists are testing different ways of farming the oceans. One way is to raise fish and shellfish in bays and inlets. In these areas the fish are protected from strong waves and from natural enemies. Large amounts of fish can be grown in this way. This type of farming means that there is always a supply of fish.

Drying algae

Another product being farmed in the oceans is algae. In some countries, such as China and Japan, algae are used as food for people and animals. In addition, algae can be dried and made into a powder. This powder can be added to other foods. It is a good source of protein. Studies are being done on growing algae in large quantities.

IDEAS TO REMEMBER

▶ A natural resource is a valuable material that is found in nature and used by people to meet their needs.

▶ Living resources and some nonliving resources—such as air, water, and soil—are renewable resources.

▶ Some resources, such as minerals and metals, are nonrenewable resources.

▶ A mineral is any useful material that is found in the earth's crust.

▶ An ore is rock or mineral that contains useful metal.

▶ Recycling is the collecting and re-treating of materials so that they can be reused.

▶ Fossil fuels are fuels such as coal, oil, and natural gas that were formed from the bodies of dead plants and animals.

▶ Fossil fuels are used as sources of heat energy and also as feedstocks.

▶ A feedstock is a raw material from which other materials are made.

▶ The oceans are rich in resources such as minerals and foods.

Reviewing the Chapter

SCIENCE WORDS

A. Write the letter of the term that best matches the definition. Not all the terms will be used.

1. Any useful material that is found in the earth's crust
2. Any resource that exists in a limited amount
3. The collecting and re-treating of materials so that they can be reused
4. The separation of salt from seawater
5. Any raw material from which other materials are made
6. Lumps taken from the ocean floor that contain valuable materials
7. Rock or mineral from which useful metal can be obtained
8. Any resource that is replaced naturally
9. A resource such as coal, oil, or natural gas
10. Farming the oceans

a. feedstock
b. fossil fuel
c. mineral
d. fertile
e. ore
f. hematite
g. nonrenewable resource
h. mariculture
i. nodules
j. recycling
k. desalination
l. renewable resource

B. Unscramble each group of letters to find a science term from the chapter. Write a sentence using each term.

1. tieelrf   2. reo   3. dlseuon
4. lsat   5. olca   6. mlairne

UNDERSTANDING IDEAS

A. Do the following.

1. Explain the difference between a renewable natural resource and a nonrenewable natural resource. Give two examples of each.

2. Write the page number of each picture in this chapter that shows a natural resource or a method of obtaining a natural resource. Write **M** by the page number for each natural resource picture that shows a mineral. Write **O** by the number of each mineral picture that shows an ore.

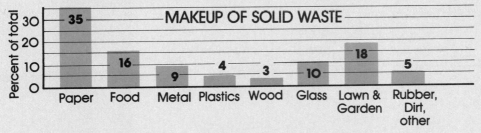

B. The graph shows the composition of solid waste disposed of by an average town. Suppose that the town is producing 1 million kg of solid waste a year.

1. Determine the amount of paper, the amount of metal, and the amount of glass that is thrown out each year.

2. Suppose the town recycles 30% of its waste paper. How much paper is recycled yearly?

3. Suppose the town recycles 10% of its waste metal and receives $0.10/kg. How much does the town earn yearly?

USING IDEAS

The map on page 219 shows where some metals and minerals are mined in North America. What are some important minerals and metals that North American countries import?

Chapter 10

Changes in the Earth's Crust

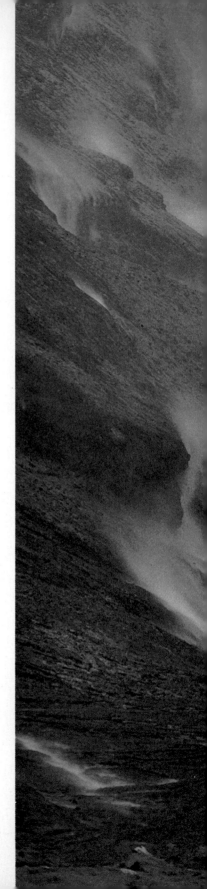

The earth seems to be a peaceful planet most of the time. Day and night follow each other, the air temperature rises and falls, and storms come and go. Such changes usually do not upset people's lives very much. At times, however, violent changes occur. An earthquake may rumble across the earth, changing the shape of the land. A sleepy volcano may erupt, burying the ground for kilometers around with ash. Events like these affect both people and the earth itself. In this chapter you will learn how movements of the top layers of the earth can cause earthquakes. You will also learn how such movements form volcanoes and other types of mountains.

THE FLOATING CRUST
How does the crust of the earth move?

Suppose the southern Atlantic Ocean did not exist. And suppose the west coast of Africa were pulled up against the east coast of South America. If this happened, the edges of these continents would fit together, like the pieces of a puzzle. But is it by chance that these continents seem to fit together?

In 1912 a man named Alfred Wegener (vā′gə-nər) said that it was not chance. Wegener said that all the continents were once part of a single land mass. But long ago this mass broke up. The pieces moved apart. Wegener suggested that the continents were still moving. Wegener's idea

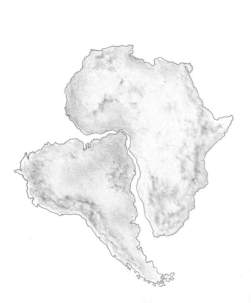

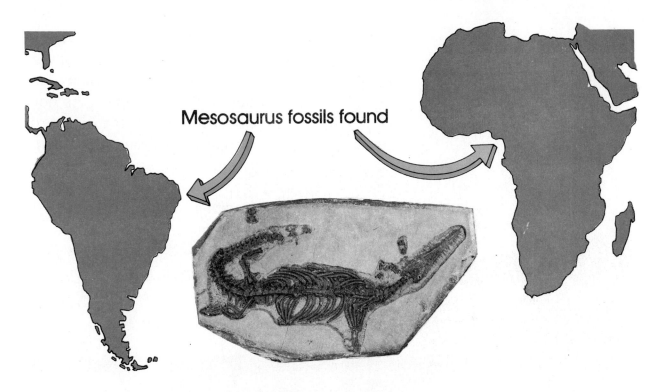

Mesosaurus fossils found

was called the theory of **continental** (kon tə-nen′təl) **drift.** A **theory** (thē′ər ē) is an idea that is used to explain observed facts.

Wegener presented some evidence to support his theory. He pointed out that rock layers and fossils from the edges of South America and Africa are very much alike. Also, certain land areas far from the poles showed evidence of having been covered by ice in the past. Such areas, then, must have been closer to one of the poles at some time. These findings could be explained by the theory of continental drift.

Some scientists supported Wegener's theory. However, most scientists did not believe that continents could move. What force could move such land masses? What were the continents floating on? Since Wegener's theory could not answer such questions, the theory was ignored.

Then, in the 1960s, scientists made a surprising find about the Atlantic Ocean. Hot liquid rock was flowing up through cracks in the ocean floor. The rock hardened, forming new ocean floor. As new floor formed, it pushed the older floor outward. Scientists called this process **sea-floor spreading.**

Look at the drawing that shows sea-floor spreading. You can see where hot liquid rock rises to the ocean floor. Notice how the rock spreads out in both directions after it reaches the ocean floor. This is what pushes the older ocean floor material outward. What do you think is happening to the Atlantic Ocean as a result of sea-floor spreading?

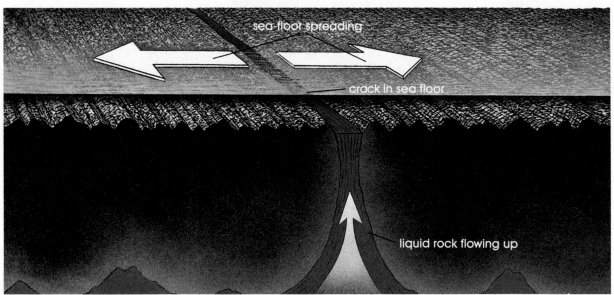

Sea-floor spreading

The Atlantic Ocean is becoming wider by the process of sea-floor spreading. If this is true, then North and South America are drifting away from Europe and Africa. The continents are moving apart, as Wegener suggested.

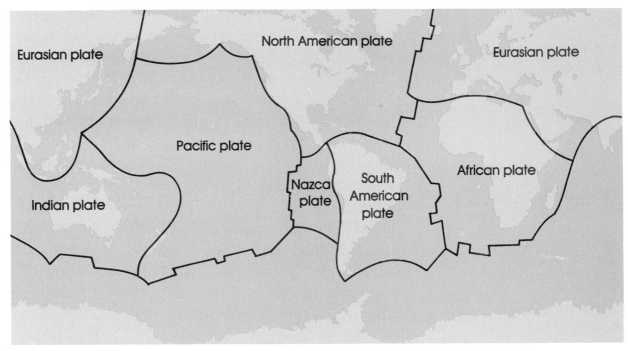

Major earth plates

The evidence of sea-floor spreading has led scientists to propose a new theory. It is called the **plate tectonic** (tek ton'ik) **theory.** The theory states that the crust of the earth is made up of about 20 sections called **plates.** The major plates are shown in the drawing. Each plate is thought to be about 100 km thick. As you can see, continents are located on some of the plates. Oceans are located on some of the plates. How are the major plates of the crust named?

The layer of earth below the crust is the mantle. The upper mantle is made of hot rock. This rock is like melted plastic. The plates of the crust seem to be floating in the upper mantle. Movements of the rock of the mantle may cause the plates to move. As plates move, they carry with them the oceans and continents above them.

The theory that the continents were once joined in a single land mass is now widely accepted. That land mass is called Pangaea. Scientists believe that the land mass broke up about 150 million years ago. Since that time the continents have drifted to their present positions. Where will they be years from now? The drawing shows one way the continents may appear in the future. Compare the positions of the continents today with their possible positions in the future. What changes can you point out?

As plates move, they may collide with, pull away from, or slip past each other. As you will see, the movements of plates can cause major changes in the earth's crust.

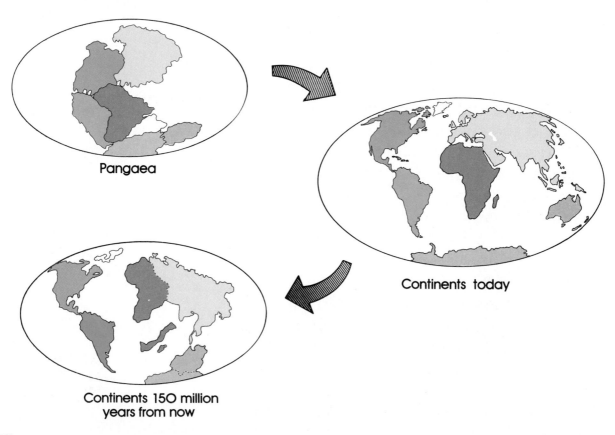

Pangaea

Continents today

Continents 150 million
years from now

Were the continents once joined in a single land mass?

Materials scissors / glue / cardboard / tracing paper or sheet of continent shapes

Procedure

A. Trace the continents shown in this activity and cut them out. Or cut the shapes of the continents from the sheet provided by your teacher.

B. Fit the east coast of South America next to the west coast of Africa.

C. Fit the other continents next to South America and Africa to form a single land mass.
  1. Do the continents fit together well to form a single land mass?

D. When you have made your land mass, glue it to a piece of cardboard.
  2. Which continents seem to fit together well?

Conclusion

What evidence is there that the continents were once joined in a single land mass?

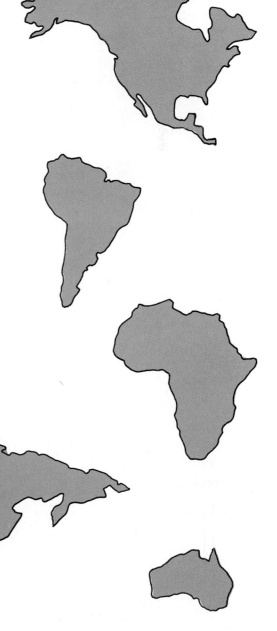

EARTHQUAKES
What causes earthquakes?

Press the palms of your hands together tightly. Now try to rub one palm over the other. Your palms will suddenly slip past each other. Two sections of the earth's crust can slip past each other in much the same way. When this happens, an earthquake occurs. An **earthquake** is a movement of the earth's crust. It results from blocks of rock slipping past each other.

What can cause blocks of rock to move past each other? Look at the drawing showing where most of the world's earthquakes occur. Does this give you a hint? Notice that most earthquakes occur along the boundaries between plates. It is the movements of plates that cause earthquakes.

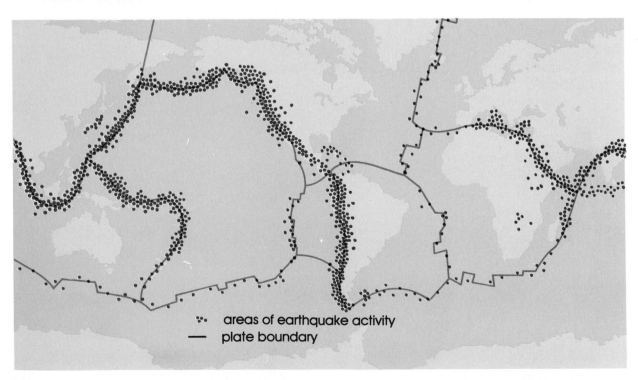

••• areas of earthquake activity
—— plate boundary

Cracks in the earth's crust where blocks of rock have moved are called **faults.** Most faults lie beneath the surface of the crust, but some are visible. For example, part of the San Andreas Fault can be seen in California. Can you point out the fault in the picture?

As two plates collide or slip past each other, blocks of rock along a fault may grind together. The sides of the blocks of rock may become locked. As plate movement continues, strain builds up along the fault. Eventually the strain becomes so great that the blocks of rock slip past each other. An earthquake takes place. The earthquake relieves the strain on the rocks. A strong earthquake can cause smaller quakes along other faults in the crust of a plate. These quakes can occur far from the boundary between the plates.

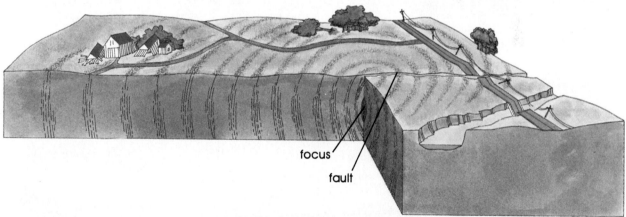

focus

fault

The place where the blocks of rock slip is called the **focus** of the earthquake. When an earthquake occurs, vibrations, or waves, move out in all directions from the focus. Traveling through rock, the vibrations can shake cities, destroy buildings, and topple bridges.

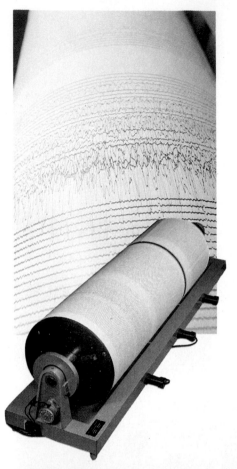

Earthquake waves can be recorded by instruments called **seismographs** (sīz'mə grafs). The scientist in the picture is studying a record of earthquake waves. Scientists can locate the focus of an earthquake from such a record. A seismograph also helps scientists measure the strength of an earthquake. The strength is stated as a number between 1 and 10. The higher the number, the more powerful the earthquake. The scale for measuring the strength of earthquakes is called the Richter (rik'tər) scale.

Studies are being done to find ways to predict earthquakes. It seems that certain signs may occur before an earthquake takes place. For example, the number of minor earthquakes, called tremors, may increase. Animals may show strange behavior before a quake strikes. For example, snakes and rats may leave their dens. Fish may leap from the water. Scientists hope that these and other signs will help them accurately predict when and where earthquakes will occur.

Earthquake damage

Can you find the location of an earthquake?

Materials   drawing compass / tracing paper

Procedure

A. The seismographs at three different stations recorded an earthquake. The data about the location of the earthquake is as follows: (1) It was 1,275 km from San Francisco. (2) It was 1,500 km from El Paso. (3) It was 960 km from Seattle.

B. Trace the map of the United States. Mark and label on the map the three cities listed.

C. On a piece of paper, mark the distance that represents 1,275 km. Set your compass to this distance. Draw a circle on your map with San Francisco at the center.

D. Repeat step **C** using the data for El Paso.

E. Repeat step **C** using the data for Seattle.

Conclusion

In what state did the earthquake occur?

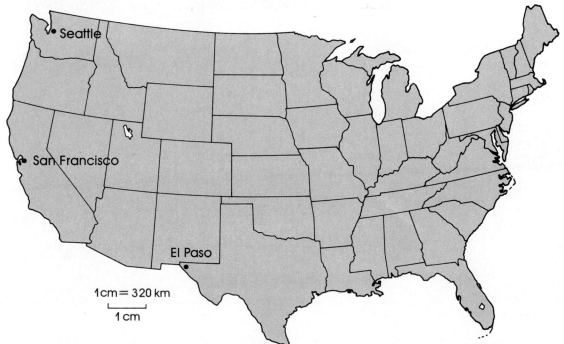

1cm = 320 km

1 cm

VOLCANOES
What causes volcanoes?

In the spring of 1980 something happened in the continental United States for the first time in 66 years. A **volcano** erupted. Mount St. Helens began spewing out ash, steam, and pieces of rock. It then exploded with such force that the top 400 m of the volcano were blown into the air. The blast leveled trees up to 24 km from the volcano. Land around the volcano was buried with ash, in some places to a depth of 150 m.

Mount St. Helens, Washington, eruption and damage

volcano

crust

magma pool

What is a volcano? What causes a volcano to erupt? A volcano begins many kilometers under the earth's crust. In certain places under the crust, the extreme heat causes rock to melt. This melted rock is called **magma** (mag′mə).

Magma is under great pressure from the weight of the rock layers above it. Imagine squeezing a tube of toothpaste with the cap on and then suddenly removing the cap. A ribbon of toothpaste would spurt from the tube. A volcano acts something like that. If magma pushes up through cracks in the crust, it may spurt out of the earth. The magma is called **lava** when it reaches the surface. If the pressure is great enough, lava, ash, and rocks will be blown from the volcano. This is what happened at Mount St. Helens.

Do you know?

Earthquakes and volcanoes can cause great damage. Earthquakes and volcanoes that occur at sea also produce sea waves called tsunamis (tsü-nä'mēz). A tsunami travels out from the quake at speeds up to 500 km/h. The wave may be only 1 m high in the ocean. But as it enters shallow water near a coastline, it builds in height. A wall of water up to 30 m high can hit the land. The huge wave can smash homes and drown people.

Tsunamis may come ashore far from the place where they were produced. The Alaska earthquake of 1964 produced tsunamis that hit Hawaii and Japan. Today, scientists can predict where and when tsunamis will hit land. They do this by using readings from seismographs.

A volcano can occur in any place where there is a deep crack in the earth's crust. However, most volcanoes are found in certain areas. One such area is the belt called the Ring of Fire, which encircles the Pacific Ocean. Why is Ring of Fire a good name for this area?

Look at the drawing that shows where most volcanoes are located. As you can see, most volcanoes occur at the boundaries between plates. Can you identify the Ring of Fire in the drawing?

Why do most volcanoes occur at plate boundaries? As you know, several kinds of movement can take place where plates meet. Two plates can spread apart at their boundary. This is what is happening along the floor of the Atlantic Ocean. You have learned that liquid rock is flowing up through cracks in the crust. This causes the ocean floor to spread. This liquid rock is magma. So volcanic activity is occurring along the boundary as the plates pull apart. Such volcanic activity is frequent along cracks in the ocean floor. However, it usually does not produce mountainlike volcanoes. So this type of volcanic activity is usually not noticed.

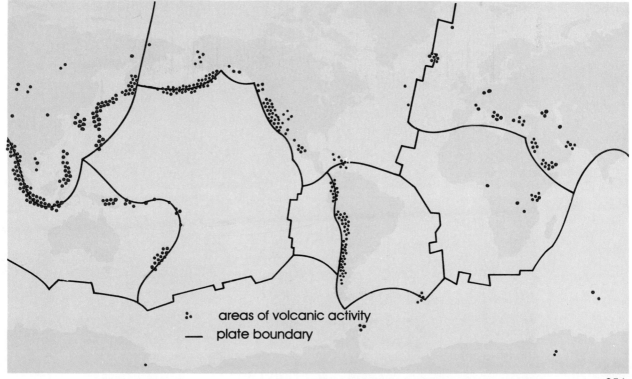

:. areas of volcanic activity
— plate boundary

Volcanic activity also occurs where plates collide. Where two ocean-carrying plates collide, one may sink under the other. Melting of parts of the sinking plate occurs. Some of the melted rock is forced to the surface. Chains of volcanic islands are formed in this way.

As a plate carrying an ocean sinks under a plate carrying a continent, parts of the ocean plate melt. Volcanoes are produced along the edge of the continent in places where magma is pushed toward the surface. Mount St. Helens was formed in this way.

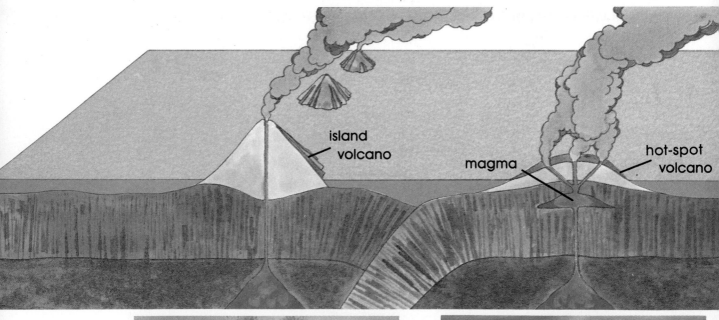

island volcano

magma

hot-spot volcano

Island volcano

Hot-spot volcano

Some volcanoes occur in the middle of plates. In this type of volcano, a chamber of magma forms. A volcano builds as the magma moves toward the surface. Such a volcano is called a hot-spot volcano.

Scientists are studying ways to predict when volcanoes will erupt. A volcano may rumble and smoke for a while before it erupts. Such signs usually give people time to leave the danger zone. However, scientists have not been able to predict the exact timing or strength of a volcanic eruption.

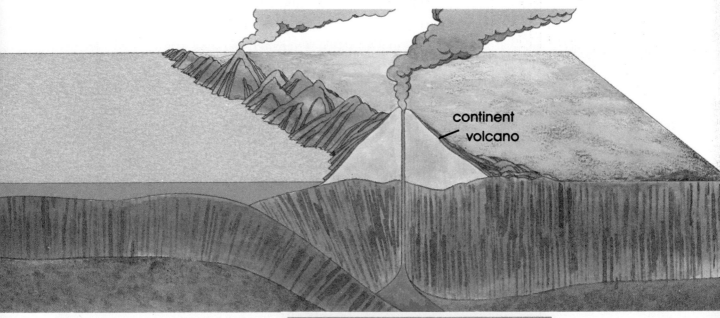

Continent volcano

MOUNTAIN BUILDING
How are mountains formed?

Huge mountain ranges are found in a number of places on the earth. The Himalayas in Asia rise more than 8,000 m above sea level. The Rocky Mountains in the western United States and Canada rise more than 6,000 m. How are mountain ranges formed?

Scientists think that a mountain range is formed when plates collide. When two plates carrying continents collide, the crust of each plate folds. As the plates push into each other, their crusts are forced higher and higher. Large mountain ranges are formed in this way. The Himalayas were formed when the plate carrying India rammed into the plate carrying Asia.

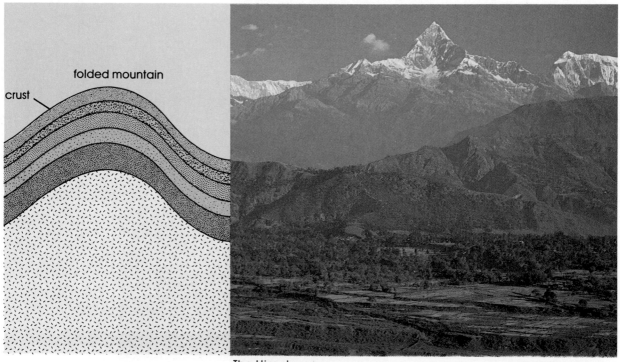

The Himalayas

A mountain range is also formed when an ocean plate sinks beneath a plate carrying a continent. When this happens, the ocean plate pushes against the crust of the plate carrying the continent. The land is forced up, and mountains form. Mountains that form through collisions between plates are called **folded mountains.** Volcanoes also form near plate boundaries.

Not all mountains form directly from collisions between plates. Sometimes mountains form along faults in the crust. Blocks of crust on one side of a fault move up while blocks of crust on the other side move down. Mountains formed in this way are called **fault-block mountains.** The Tetons of western North America are fault-block mountains. Scientists are not sure what forces the blocks of crust to move up and down.

fault block mountains

The Teton Range

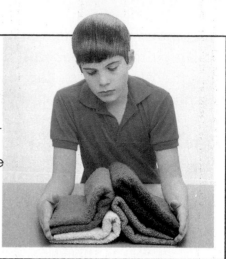
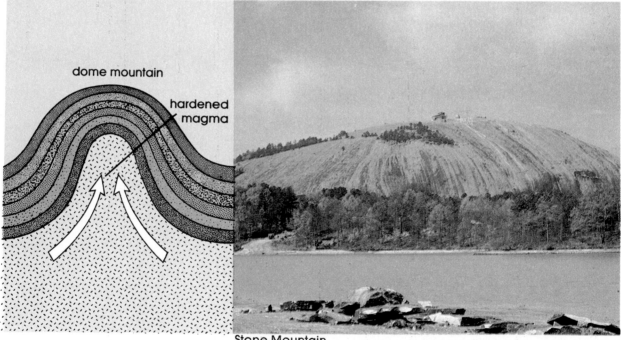

Stone Mountain

Sometimes magma is forced up under the crust but does not break through the surface. Instead, the magma pushes the crust up, forming a mountain with a rounded top and a wide base. The magma eventually hardens under the crust. This type of mountain is called a **dome mountain**.

The Rocky Mountains

The Appalachian Mountains

Mountains change slowly over the years. Much of this change is due to weathering by wind and rain. Because of this weathering, older mountain ranges are lower and have more rounded tops than do younger ranges. Which mountain range shown here is older?

IDEAS TO REMEMBER

▶ The earth's crust is made up of plates that move over the mantle.

▶ Earthquakes can occur when plates collide with, pull away from, or slip past each other.

▶ Volcanoes are produced when magma pushes up through cracks in the crust. Most volcanoes occur near plate boundaries.

▶ Most mountain ranges form from collisions between plates. Fault-block mountains and dome mountains seem to form in other ways.

Reviewing the Chapter

SCIENCE WORDS

A. Use all the terms below to complete the sentences.

folded mountains   seismographs   faults   dome mountain
plate tectonic theory   earthquake   plate   volcanoes

The __1__ states that the crust of the earth is broken into sections. Each section is called a/an __2__. When sections of the crust suddenly slip past each other, a/an __3__ occurs. Cracks in the crust along which rocks have moved are called __4__. When sections of the crust slip, waves moving out from the focus can be recorded by __5__.

Magma sometimes pushes through the surface along plate boundaries, forming __6__. If magma pushes the surface up and then hardens underneath, a/an __7__ forms. When two plates collide, the crust may be forced up, forming __8__.

B. Copy the sentences below. Use science terms from the chapter to complete the sentences.

1. The process in which hot liquid rock flows up and hardens to form new ocean floor is called ____.
2. The place where rocks slip is called the ____ of an earthquake.
3. Magma that reaches the surface is called ____.
4. When blocks of rock on opposite sides of a fault move vertically, ____ form.
5. The theory of ____ was an early idea that the continents move.

UNDERSTANDING IDEAS

A. Look at the following diagrams. Which one shows folded mountains? Which shows fault-block mountains? Which shows dome mountains?

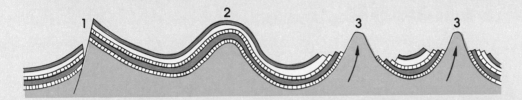

B. Earthquakes and volcanoes usually occur in the same kind of region of the earth. Explain why this is so.

C. A cause makes things happen. An effect is what happens. For each pair of sentences, write which is the cause and which is the effect.
1. **a.** Folded mountains form.
   b. Two plates collide.
2. **a.** Part of a plate sinks and melts.
   b. Volcanoes are produced.
3. **a.** Sections of rock slip past each other.
   b. Waves move out from the focus.
4. **a.** Low mountains with rounded tops occur.
   b. Wind and rain erode the land.
5. **a.** Certain facts are observed.
   b. A theory is proposed.

USING IDEAS

1. Collect pictures of various mountain ranges. Find out how each was formed. Locate the mountain ranges on a globe.
2. Find out about the New Madrid, Missouri, earthquake of 1811. How do scientists explain this earthquake?

Chapter 11

Forecasting the Weather

Weather has interested people for thousands of years. The first scientific book on weather was written by Aristotle in 350 B.C. Aristotle thought weather could be predicted by observing conditions in the nearby atmosphere.

Look at the picture. Suppose you had to predict the weather for this city. What would you say about the conditions pictured here?

Today, predicting the weather involves more than simply observing local weather conditions. Weather scientists collect information about the atmosphere over the whole earth. Using that information, they can predict the weather. In this chapter you will learn how information about weather is gathered. You will also learn how weather changes can be predicted.

— WEATHER INSTRUMENTS —
How do we get information about the weather?

Weather affects our lives in many ways. Many of our activities depend on the weather. What activities can you think of that are affected by weather? The weather helps you decide what type of clothes to wear. A baseball game may be canceled because of rain. School may be closed because of a snowstorm. You may decide to go to the beach because the day is sunny and warm. How have the people in these pictures adapted to different kinds of weather?

The study of weather is called **meteorology** (mē tē ə rol′ə jē). A scientist who studies weather is called a **meteorologist** (mē tē ə rol′ə jist). Meteorologists make weather forecasts. A **forecast** is a statement of what the weather will probably be like in the next few days. A forecast indicates what is most likely to happen. Why are weather forecasts important?

To make forecasts, meteorologists observe weather conditions carefully. They use special instruments to measure temperature, air pressure, wind speed and direction, and other conditions. The picture and drawing show some of these instruments. What weather instruments do you use at home?

Wind is an important weather condition. Winds and storms are caused by the movements of air masses. Wind speed and direction may affect what the weather will be like. A **wind vane** shows wind direction. An **anemometer** (an ə-mom'ə tər) tells wind speed. Look at the drawing. The cups catch the wind, making the arms spin. As the arms spin, the wind speed can be measured. The stronger the wind blows, the faster the arms spin.

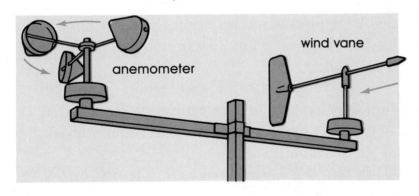

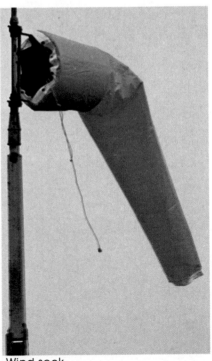

Wind sock

A **wind sock** can show both the wind speed and direction. The wind sock rotates on a pole and so shows the direction of the wind. Also, if the sock is blowing straight out, it shows that the wind is strong. If the sock is limp, there is very little wind. Wind socks are often found at small airports. They are used to determine the direction in which planes should take off or land.

Another weather condition is relative humidity. **Relative humidity** is the amount of water vapor in the air compared with the most the air can hold at that temperature. Warm air can hold more water vapor than cool air can hold. Would the relative humidity be higher on a warm, cloudy day or on a clear, cool day?

Relative humidity is stated as a percent. Suppose the relative humidity is 50 percent. This means that the air contains half the amount of water vapor that it can hold.

Relative humidity is measured with a **wet-and-dry-bulb thermometer.** This instrument has two thermometers. One has a wet bulb, and one has a dry bulb. The difference between the temperatures is found. Then a chart is used to determine the relative humidity. Look at the wet-and-dry-bulb thermometer in the drawing. Find the difference in temperature between the thermometers. Use the chart on page 265 to determine the relative humidity.

People feel uncomfortable when the relative humidity and the temperature are high. What is the weather like for the people in the pictures?

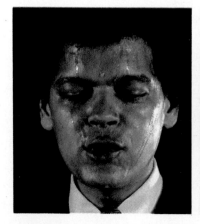

wet-and-dry-bulb thermometer

How can you measure relative humidity?

Materials   2 Celsius thermometers / cardboard / rubber bands / wide cotton shoelace / scissors

Procedure
A. Put two Celsius thermometers side by side on a piece of cardboard. Use rubber bands to hold them in place.
B. Cut a small length of cotton shoelace. Cut one end open.
C. Soak the piece of shoelace in water. Slip the opened end over the bulb of one of the thermometers. You have made a wet-and-dry-bulb thermometer.
D. Fan the thermometers for 2 minutes. Record the temperature reading of each thermometer.
1. Find the difference between the two temperatures. Use that number and the dry-bulb temperature to find the relative humidity in the table.
2. Determine the relative humidity each day at the same time for a week. (Be sure to wet the shoelace each time.)

Conclusion
Make a graph of the relative humidity for the days on which you took temperature readings.

RELATIVE HUMIDITY
(percent)

Dry-bulb temp. (°C)	Difference between wet-bulb and dry-bulb temp. (°C)								
	1	2	3	4	5	6	7	8	9
15	90	80	71	61	53	44	36	27	20
16	90	81	71	63	54	46	38	30	23
17	90	81	72	64	55	47	40	32	25
18	91	82	73	65	57	49	41	34	27
19	91	82	74	65	58	50	43	36	29
20	91	83	74	66	59	51	44	37	31
21	91	83	75	67	60	53	46	39	32
22	92	83	76	68	61	54	47	40	34
23	92	84	76	69	62	55	48	42	36
24	92	84	77	69	62	56	49	43	37
25	92	84	77	70	63	57	50	44	39
26	92	85	78	71	64	58	51	46	40
27	92	85	78	71	65	58	52	47	41

Relative humidity

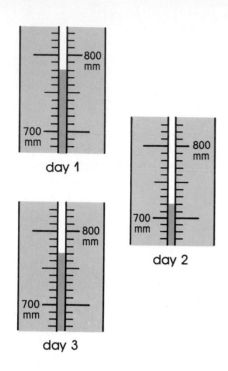

day 1

day 2

day 3

Air pushes on all surfaces that it touches. This push is called **air pressure.** Warm air puts less pressure on the earth than cool air does. So warm air tends to form low-pressure areas. Cool air forms high-pressure areas. Low-pressure areas often bring cloudy weather. High-pressure areas often bring fair weather.

Air pressure is measured with a **barometer** (bə-rom′ə tər). Barometric (bar ə met′rik) readings are usually given in millimeters or in inches. A "falling barometer" usually means that warm, moist low-pressure air is moving in. A "rising barometer" usually means that cool, dry high-pressure air is moving in. Look at the barometric readings in the drawing. What changes in weather probably took place over the days shown?

Finding out

At what temperature will water vapor come out of the air? The temperature at which the water vapor in air begins to condense is called the dew point. You can determine the dew point of the air in your classroom. You will need a shiny metal can, a thermometer, and some ice. Half-fill the can with water. Add one or two ice cubes to the water. Stir the water with a stirring rod. As you stir, watch for water to condense on the outside of the can. As soon as condensation begins, measure the temperature of the water. This temperature is the dew point. Measure and record the dew point at the same time each day for one week. A rise in the dew point means that the amount of water vapor in the air has increased. A drop in the dew point means that the amount of water vapor in the air has decreased.

— COLLECTING WEATHER DATA —

How is weather data gathered?

As you have learned, many kinds of instruments are used to measure weather. Where and how is weather data gathered? Most data is gathered from weather stations. There are several thousand land weather stations around the world. The data they collect includes temperature, air pressure, wind speed and direction, humidity, and rainfall. The data is sent to weather centers, where weather forecasts are prepared.

Many weather stations around the world send up weather balloons every day. Weather balloons carry instruments that measure the weather conditions at different levels of the atmosphere.

Weather balloon

Some balloons burst after a short time. The instruments are carried back to the earth by parachutes. Other balloons stay at certain heights for several months. During this time these balloons send back weather data.

In addition to the instruments already mentioned, some weather stations use radar. Radar can detect stormy areas. A storm appears as a cloudy area on a screen. The screen looks much like a television screen. The speed and direction of a moving storm can be determined by radar.

Satellites (sat'ə līts) also collect weather data. Satellites orbit the earth and send signals back to the earth, where the signals are changed into pictures. Such pictures show cloud cover and areas of ice and snow. Satellite pictures are very helpful in following the paths of storms. Look at the satellite picture. Compare it with the drawing. Where is a major storm located? What is the weather like over southern Florida? What is the weather like over southern Texas?

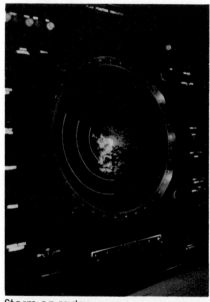
Storm on radar

Weather satellite picture

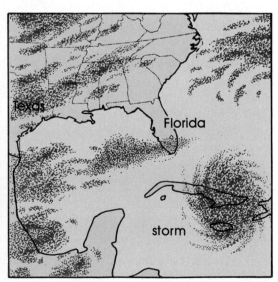

Weather satellite   Weather plane

As you know, much of the earth is covered by water. In ocean regions there are no weather stations. So weather data is collected by ships and planes. Some planes can transmit weather data to satellites. Ships transmit data to ground weather stations. Weather balloons are sometimes launched from ships. Ships also release **buoys** (boiz), objects that float on the water. Buoys contain instruments that record and transmit weather data to satellites.

In recent years, computers have become useful in weather forecasting. Information about the movement and behavior of the atmosphere is fed into a computer. Using this information the computer can predict changes in the atmosphere. The picture shows a meteorologist using a computer to forecast the weather.

WEATHER MAPS

What is a weather map, and how is it used?

Meteorologists use weather maps to help them predict weather changes for different regions. A **weather map** is a map on which the weather conditions over a large area are recorded. These maps are prepared by computers at the National Weather Service.

There are several types of weather maps. A weather map may show the temperature in different areas. Sometimes lines are drawn connecting areas that have the same temperature. These lines are called **isotherms** (ī′sə thėrmz). What are the temperature readings for the isotherms shown on the map at left?

Lines are used to connect places on a weather map that have the same air pressure. Each line is called an **isobar** (ī′sə bär). The air pressure is shown at the ends of each isobar. The air pressure is usually given in units called millibars. What air-pressure readings are shown at the ends of the isobars on the map on page 271? What would the air pressure be near Chicago, based on the map?

You have probably seen the symbols *H* and *L* on a weather map. These symbols indicate a high-pressure area and a low-pressure area. Remember, an area of high pressure usually brings fair weather. An area of low pressure usually brings cloudy weather. Find the highs and lows on the map. Meteorologists study the movements of these pressure areas. The information helps them predict weather changes.

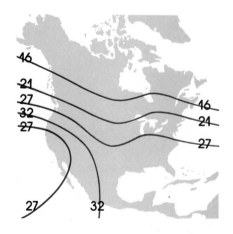

A weather map may also show the locations of air masses, cold fronts, and warm fronts. Wind speed and direction, rain or snow, cloud cover, and fog conditions may also be shown.

Study the symbols used on a weather map. Then study the weather map in the drawing. What type of front is moving up the East Coast of the United States? What is the temperature near Galveston, Texas? What is the weather like in Seattle, Washington?

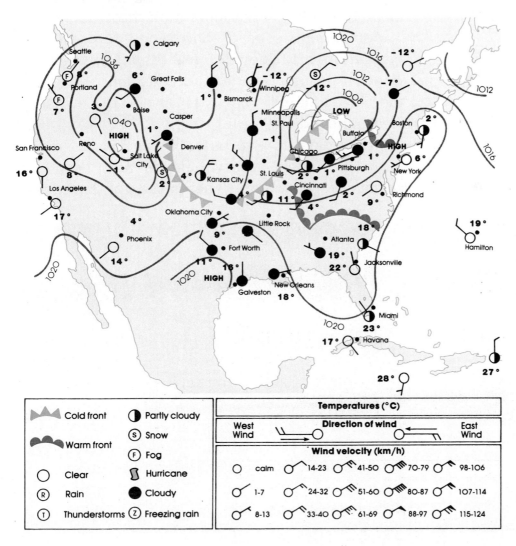

	Temperatures (°C)		
⋀⋀ Cold front	◑ Partly cloudy		
⌒⌒ Warm front	Ⓢ Snow	West Wind / Direction of wind / East Wind	
○ Clear	Ⓕ Fog		
Ⓡ Rain	⦚ Hurricane	Wind velocity (km/h)	
● Cloudy			
Ⓣ Thunderstorms	Ⓩ Freezing rain		

WEATHER FORECASTS

How are weather forecasts made, and how accurate are they?

The National Weather Service is the government agency that prepares weather forecasts. It has been in operation for more than 100 years. During that time, it has had a good record for predicting weather. In fact, today its short-range forecasts are quite accurate. By "short-range" we mean forecasts for not more than three days.

Meteorologists base short-range forecasts on measurements. They also use the information on weather maps. You have already learned about the instruments that are used to measure weather conditions.

Meteorologists also use observations to make forecasts. They observe clouds and how the clouds are changing. They observe the move-

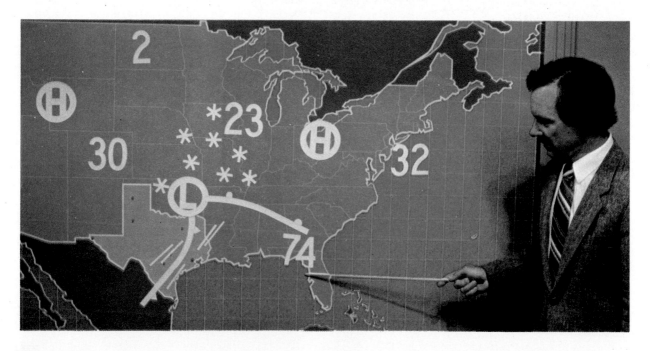

ments of air masses. They observe **visibility** (viz-ə bil'ə tē), which is how far an average person can see under present conditions. What are some conditions that might affect visibility?

Look at the picture on the left. What kind of weather condition produces such low visibility? Look at the picture on the right. How might the weather change in the area shown?

In addition to weather maps and observations, computers are often used to help make weather forecasts. But computer forecasts are not always correct. Sometimes weather conditions change rapidly. Also there may not be enough information about certain areas. The more information that is available, the more accurate the forecast will be.

For the next few days, check the daily weather forecasts and weather maps. Use the newspaper and television. Keep a record of how accurate these forecasts are.

How are some weather predictions made?

Procedure

Study the chart. Then use information from the chart to make weather predictions for the four situations below.

Wind direction	Air pressure at sea level (mm)	Kind of weather to be expected
SW to NW	764.54 to 767.08, steady	Fair, with little temperature change for one or two days
SW to NW	764.54 to 767.08, rising fast	Fair, followed by rain within two days
SW to NW	767.08 or above, steady	Continued fair, with little temperature change
E to NE	764.54 or above, falling fast	Rain probable in summer within 24 hours; in winter, rain or snow and windy
SE to NE	762.00 or below, falling slowly	Steady rain for one or two days
SE to NE	762.00 or below, falling fast	Rain and high wind, clearing within 36 hours
S to SW	762.00 or below, rising slowly	Clearing within a few hours, fair for several days
S to E	756.92 or below, falling fast	Severe storm soon, clearing within 24 hours; colder in winter
Going to W	745.00 or below, rising fast	Clearing and colder
E to N	756.92 or below, falling fast	Severe northeast gale, heavy rain; in winter, heavy snow and cold wave

1. South winds; air pressure 755.22, falling fast
2. Northwest winds; air pressure 764.87, rising fast
3. Southwest winds; air pressure 767.32, steady
4. East to north winds; air pressure 756.81, falling fast

Conclusion

1. What two instruments would be needed to make weather predictions with this chart?
2. What kind of weather can be expected with rising air pressure? With falling air pressure?
3. What are some ways to predict weather?

Weather is the day-to-day change in conditions of the atmosphere. But climate is the average weather for a large region over a long period of time. A scientist who studies climate is called a climatologist (klī mə tol'ə jist). A **climatologist** studies worldwide weather conditions over a long period of time. What type of climate is shown in the picture?

Climatologists use records of past weather to make long-range weather forecasts. A long-range forecast is really a scientific estimate. Long-range forecasts are not very accurate. Usually, forecasts are made for no more than 30 days. Look at the drawing below. It shows a 30-day precipitation forecast. What is the precipitation forecast for your area?

As we have said, long-range forecasts are made by studying past weather patterns. As better and more complete records of weather are kept, better long-range forecasts will probably result. At present, however, it is difficult to forecast weather far into the future.

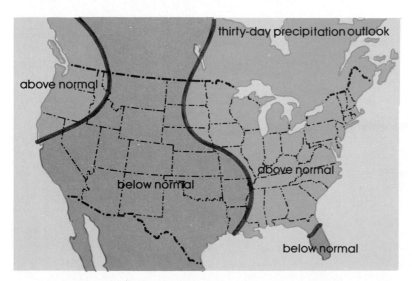

STORMS

What are some violent changes in weather?

The weather for a region usually follows a regular pattern. For example, in the Southwestern states the weather is often hot and dry. In some parts of Minnesota, there is usually snow on the ground by Christmas. But from time to time an area may have unusual weather conditions. A sudden, unexpected storm may occur and then quickly disappear. Or a storm may affect a region for an extended period of time. Such changes in weather are often violent.

One common violent change in weather is a **thunderstorm** (thun'dər stôrm). Thunderstorms are most common during late spring and summer. Two conditions are needed for a thunderstorm to occur. First, there must be rapidly rising currents of warm air. These currents usually result from the warm ground heating the air above it. A rising current of air is called an **updraft** (up'draft). Updrafts are shown forming in the drawing on the

thunderhead forming

updrafts

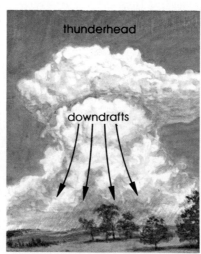

thunderhead

downdrafts

left. Second, the updrafts must contain much water vapor. When both of these conditions are present, a thunderstorm begins to form.

Air currents cool rapidly as they rise. As air cools, condensation (kon den sā'shən) takes place. Condensation is the process by which a gas changes to a liquid or a solid. In the air, condensation of water vapor causes tiny drops of liquid water or ice crystals to form. As a result, a cloud forms. As the air continues to rise, the cloud builds up higher and higher. A huge dark cloud, called a thunderhead, forms. The thunderstorm forms inside the thunderhead.

Look at the drawing of the thunderhead on page 276. The arrows on the drawing show how the air currents move upward. As rising currents inside the cloud continue to cool, more and more water vapor condenses. Sometimes many layers of ice form on ice crystals. The crystals get larger and larger, forming hailstones. Finally, rain or hail begins to fall. A current of cool air actually comes down with the rain or hail. A falling air current is called a **downdraft** (doun'draft). Either an updraft or a downdraft may be very violent.

Rapidly rising air causes electrical charges to build up inside the cloud. These charges can jump from one cloud to another. They can also jump between a cloud and the earth. Lightning is the movement of these charges. Lightning heats the air and causes it to expand rapidly. After a lightning flash, the air cools and contracts. The expansion and contraction of the air cause vibrations that you hear as thunder. Lightning resulting from thunderstorms can be very dangerous.

Hailstones

A **tornado** is a very violent windstorm. Tornadoes usually last only a short time. Some may last only 20 minutes. But longer-lasting tornadoes also occur. An average tornado travels 25 km. The width of its path is about 0.5 km. Winds may be as high as 500 km/h.

Over 400 tornadoes are reported in the United States each year. Tornadoes occur in every state in the nation. But they occur most often in the Midwest and in the South Central states.

Do you know?

At some time, a severe thunderstorm watch or a tornado watch has probably been declared in your area. A tornado or thunderstorm watch means there is a strong possibility that such a storm will occur in the area. Local radio and television stations report such watches. During a watch, people should be alert for a storm. If one is sighted, its location is reported to the local weather service office. This office will then issue a storm warning. A watch means a storm may occur. A warning means that a storm has been sighted. When a warning is issued for an area, people should seek shelter.

Tornadoes are most likely to occur in late spring and early summer. No one knows exactly what causes tornadoes. They form within thunderheads but only under certain conditions. First there must be a layer of warm, humid air close to the ground. Above that is a layer of cold, dry air. The layer of cold air keeps the warm air from rising. Then a rapidly moving cold front moves into the region. It acts like a wedge, lifting the warm, humid air. So the warm air is trapped between

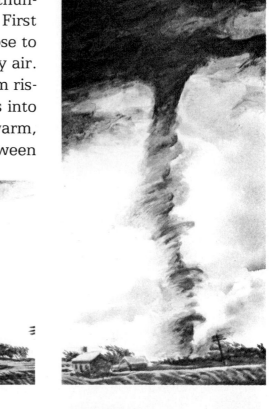

the two layers of colder air. Some of the warm air breaks through the cold air above and rushes upward. More air follows, forming the twisting mass of air that is a tornado funnel. The funnel is usually dark in color because of the dirt that is carried by the rising air.

Many tornadoes never touch the ground. But serious damage results where a tornado does touch the earth's surface. A tornado may tear roofs off buildings and uproot trees. Cars, animals, and people have been swept up by tornadoes. The damage a tornado causes is severe. But the area that is damaged is usually limited.

Tornado damage

A **hurricane** (hėr'ə kān) is a storm that develops over the ocean in a tropical area. A hurricane is a large body of warm, moist air.

Hurricanes form more slowly than tornadoes and are not as violent. Like a tornado, a hurricane is a rotating mass of air. But a hurricane affects a much larger area than a tornado. The width of a hurricane is usually about 650 km. The winds of a hurricane are at least 119 km/h. In the center is a calm region about 30 km wide. This region is called the eye of the storm. The strongest winds of a hurricane are around the eye. These winds may be 200 to 240 km/h. Hurricanes move more slowly than tornadoes. But they last longer, and the high winds and rain can do much damage.

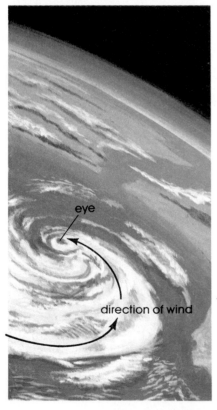

Hurricane

People can avoid a hurricane more easily than they can avoid a tornado. There is usually enough warning of an approaching hurricane. So people can leave the danger area. Many lives can be saved in this way.

IDEAS TO REMEMBER

- ▶ The study of weather is called meteorology.
- ▶ A forecast is a statement of what the weather will probably be like in the next few days.
- ▶ Weather forecasts are based on measurements of conditions such as wind speed and direction, relative humidity, and air pressure.
- ▶ Weather data is gathered at weather stations and from weather balloons, satellites, ships, and planes.
- ▶ A weather map is a map on which weather conditions over a large area are recorded.
- ▶ Meteorologists study weather maps in order to make forecasts.
- ▶ Short-range weather forecasts are generally accurate; long-range forecasts are less accurate.
- ▶ Storms such as thunderstorms, tornadoes, and hurricanes are examples of violent weather conditions.

Reviewing the Chapter

SCIENCE WORDS

A. Copy the sentences below. Use science terms from the chapter to complete the sentences.

1. A scientist who studies weather is called a/an _____ .
2. A/An _____ is used to measure wind speed.
3. A/An _____ is used to determine wind direction.
4. Air pressure is measured with a/an _____ .
5. Relative humidity is measured with a/an _____ .
6. Weather conditions over a large area are recorded on a/an _____ .
7. Rising currents of air containing much water vapor can result in the formation of a/an _____ .
8. A violent windstorm that can form within a thunderhead is called a/an _____ .
9. A large storm that forms over the ocean in tropical areas is called a/an _____ .
10. A scientist who studies worldwide weather conditions over a long period of time is called a/an _____ .

B. Identify each of the following.

1. I float on the water and record weather data. What am I?
2. I am a rapidly rising current of air. What am I?
3. I am a statement about what the weather will be like over the next few days. What am I?
4. I can show both wind speed and wind direction. What am I?

UNDERSTANDING IDEAS

A. Answer the questions that follow by studying the map.

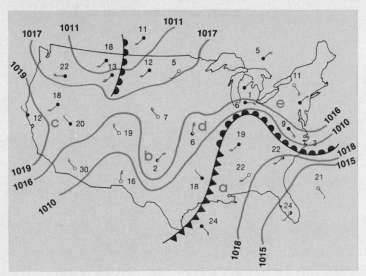

1. What are the temperature and cloud cover near point **b?**
2. What type of front is approaching point **a?**
3. What is the air pressure near point **c?**
4. What are the wind speed and wind direction near point **d?**
5. What is the air pressure near point **e?**

B. Explain the difference between the terms.

1. meteorologist, climatologist   2. isobar, isotherm
3. hurricane, tornado   4. updraft, downdraft

USING IDEAS

1. How can people prepare for a weather emergency?
2. Find out what the precipitation or temperature forecast is for the next 30-day period. Keep a record of the actual weather conditions, and compare it with the 30-day forecast.

Chapter 12

Exploring Space

The exploration of space took a huge step forward on February 7, 1984. It was on that day that Captain Bruce McCandless stepped away from the Space Shuttle Challenger. Captain McCandless became the first human to walk in space completely free of a spacecraft. He did this while wearing a Manned Maneuvering Unit, or MMU. In the near future, astronauts wearing MMUs will be able to build space stations. We will be able to learn a great deal about the stars and planets while observing them from these space stations.

In this chapter you will find out what has already been learned about the stars and planets. You will follow the exploration of space from early times to the present. You will also learn about future plans for using and exploring space.

Captain Bruce McCandless on his historic space walk

EXPLORING FROM EARTH

How do people on Earth gather information about space?

Astronomy (ə stron'ə mē) is the study of space and the many things it contains. Astronomy began when people first looked at the sky. Early people discovered many things about the sky. For example, they found that a star's location with respect to other stars does not change. They also found that certain stars were seen during certain seasons.

People noticed that a few objects seemed to move among the stars. They called these objects planets.

Some people developed models to explain what they saw. Ptolemy (tol'ə mē), an early astronomer, developed one of the first models. He taught that the sun, stars, and planets moved around Earth. His model was accepted for many centuries. This model was replaced in the 1500s by a sun-centered model.

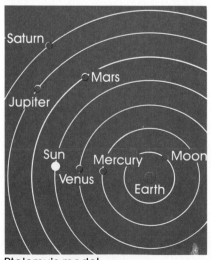

Ptolemy's model

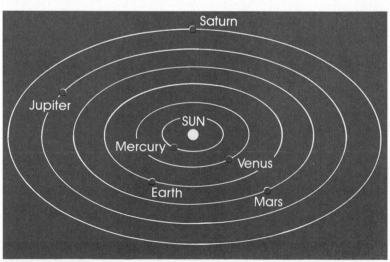

Sun-centered model

The first astronomers did not have special tools to help them study the sky. They had only their eyes to use in gathering information. Over the years, however, many tools have been developed to study the sky. One of the most useful of these tools is the telescope. Astronomers use telescopes to observe planets, stars, and other objects in the universe.

The most common telescope is the optical telescope. This telescope collects light from distant objects. The light forms an image, which is then magnified. There are two kinds of optical telescope. One kind uses a glass lens to gather light. It is called a **refracting telescope.** The other kind uses a curved mirror to gather light. It is called a **reflecting telescope.** Each kind uses a lens to magnify the image.

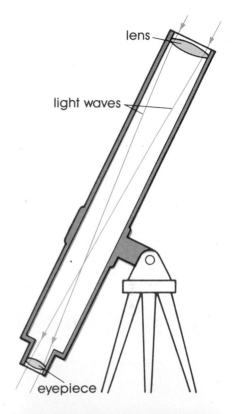

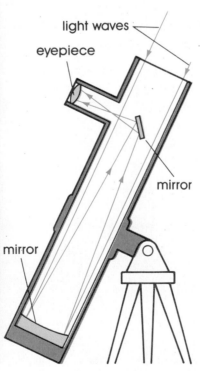

Reflecting telescope

Refracting telescope

Astronomers today use another item with their telescopes. They attach a camera so that images can be photographed. This allows observations to be saved for future examination.

Modern telescopes are housed in observatories (əb zër'və tôr ēz). An **observatory** is a building that is set up to study outer space. Pictures of stars, planets, and other objects in space are taken at observatories all around the world. Some of the pictures taken at observatories are shown on this page. Many scientists are able to study such pictures. The knowledge they gain helps all of us to understand the nature of the universe in which we live.

Spiral galaxy

Star cluster

Horsehead nebula

Mount Palomar Observatory

Radio waves that are given off by objects in space are also studied. These waves are collected by **radio telescopes**. Astronomers listen to and study these waves. The waves provide data about objects that cannot be seen as well as about objects that are visible. Such waves may give clues to how the universe began.

Do you know?

Are there other forms of intelligent life in the universe? No one knows. However, some attempts have been made to find out. In the early 1960s a radio telescope was used to pick up radio waves from outer space. The project, called Oz, was designed to detect any pattern in the waves. A pattern would be evidence of a message being sent by other beings. No pattern was ever detected. However, scientists have not given up. Other radio telescopes are now being used to listen in on the universe. Perhaps real creatures from outer space will send us a signal someday.

How does a radio telescope work?

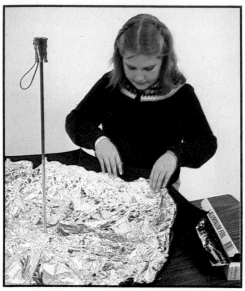

Materials umbrella / transistor radio / heavy-duty aluminum foil

Procedure
A. Open an umbrella, and line the inside with aluminum foil.

B. Place a transistor radio on your desk. Find a station that comes in weakly on the radio. Turn the radio until you get the best possible reception from this station.

C. Hold the umbrella behind the radio. The foil should face the incoming radio waves.

D. Move the umbrella to find the best reception.
   1. Why, do you think, did the radio reception improve?

E. Now find a strong station on the radio.

F. Hold the umbrella between the radio and the incoming waves. The foil should face the waves.
   2. What happened to the reception?

Conclusion
1. Why does a radio telescope have a large dish shape?
2. What is the function of the aluminum foil in this activity?

Using science ideas
Why are radio telescopes usually located away from large cities?

EXPLORING FROM SPACE

How is space explored using rockets and satellites?

Scientists continue to study space from Earth's surface. However, they also send objects out into space to gather data. This allows them to explore space in new ways.

Rockets are used to send objects into space. To launch something into space, a rocket must have enough power to overcome Earth's gravity. A rocket overcomes this force by burning a large amount of fuel. The fuel is burned in a **combustion chamber.** This is an enclosed chamber with an opening at the bottom. As the fuel burns, hot gas is produced. The gas pushes on the sides of the chamber, as shown in the drawing.

As you can see, gas pushes on the top of the chamber but not on the bottom. This is because the bottom end is open. Therefore, the gas escapes out the bottom. The force against the top of the chamber is not opposed by a force against the bottom. So the rocket moves up.

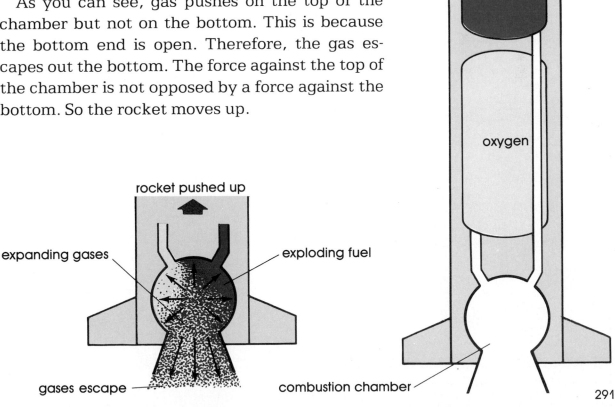

rocket pushed up

expanding gases

exploding fuel

gases escape

control systems

fuel

oxygen

combustion chamber

291

Satellites were among the first objects to be launched into space by rockets. A **satellite** is an object that orbits a larger object. The drawing shows a satellite being carried into space by a rocket and being released. The rocket usually falls back to Earth.

Sputnik 1, launched in 1957 by the Soviet Union, was the first satellite to be placed into Earth orbit. It sent data on the temperature of space back to scientists on Earth. Sputnik 1 worked in space for 22 days before its batteries died.

Explorer 1 was the first United States satellite. It was sent into space in 1958. Explorer 1 discovered that Earth is surrounded by radiation belts. Later satellites studied Earth's magnetic field, took pictures of the sun, and gathered data on meteorites.

Sputnik 1 (model)

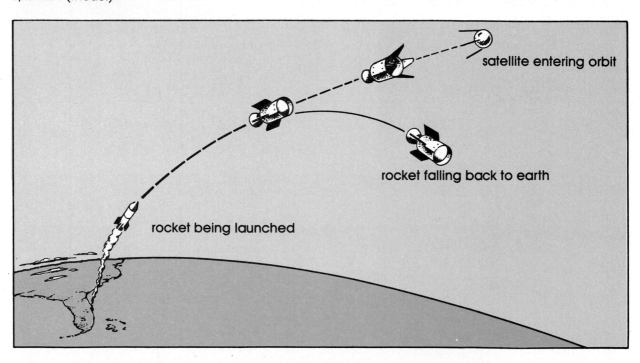
satellite entering orbit

rocket falling back to earth

rocket being launched

How does a rocket move?

Materials   fishing line / meterstick or metric tape / scissors / drinking straw / masking tape / balloon / twist tie

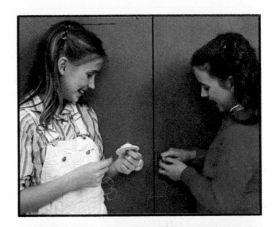

Procedure

A. Do this activity with a partner. Cut a 5-m length of fishing line. Attach one end of the fishing line to a door handle or an object of similar height.

B. Blow up a balloon. Attach a twist tie to the end so that air will not escape.

C. Tape a drinking straw to the balloon. The balloon and straw make up your rocket.

  1. Which part represents the combustion chamber?

D. Slide the loose end of the fishing line through the drinking straw.

E. Hold the string tight and in a straight line. Remove the twist tie. Observe how your rocket moves.

  2. How far did your rocket travel?

F. Repeat the activity. Try to make your rocket move farther this time.

  3. How far did it travel?

Conclusion

1. What makes your rocket move?
2. How could you make your rocket move farther?

Using science ideas

Make a rocket-powered car or boat. Test your rocket-powered vehicle.

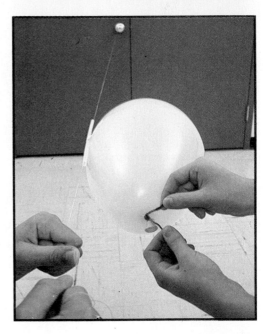

Satellites are also used for purposes other than exploring space. For example, Landsat satellites are used to give scientists information about Earth. Each Landsat contains special cameras. The cameras can detect areas of pollution on Earth. They can also show where minerals may be found. The Landsat pictures can even help farmers estimate how large their harvests will be. The Landsat picture on the left shows the area around Phoenix, Arizona. The picture on the right shows cornfields (reddish) in Nebraska and Iowa.

Landsat picture of Arizona

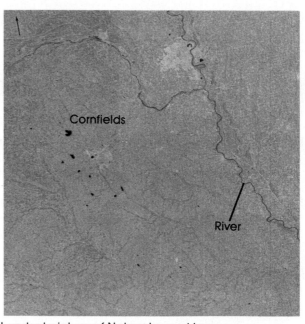

Landsat picture of Nebraska and Iowa

Some satellites are used to study weather. Weather satellites take pictures of Earth. Such pictures show where storms are located and how they are moving. This data helps scientists to forecast the weather for several days. Weather satellites keep watch on the weather all around the world.

Satellites are also used to send signals. One kind of satellite just reflects radio signals from one place on Earth to another. For example, such a satellite might reflect telephone signals.

Another kind of satellite receives radio waves and strengthens them. The waves can then be beamed to Earth or recorded for later use. One of the most famous satellites of this kind is Telstar. Telstar made possible the first TV broadcast across the Atlantic Ocean. Today, satellites can transmit live TV broadcasts almost anywhere in the world.

Rockets are also used to launch spacecraft that do not go into Earth orbit. Instead, these craft are sent out to gather data on the moon and the planets. Such spacecraft are called **space probes.**

Communications satellite

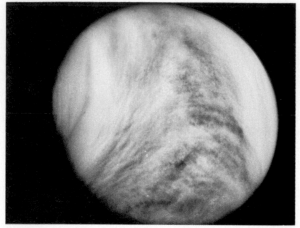
Venus

The surface of Mars

American probes have been sent to Venus. They sent back data about that planet's atmosphere. Two American Viking probes have landed on Mars. These probes tested the air and soil of Mars and sent the data to Earth. In addition, the Viking probes conducted experiments to search for life in the soil of Mars.

Two Voyager probes have been launched by the United States. The path of Voyager 2 is shown on the next page. Both Voyagers took close-up pictures of Jupiter and Saturn. The pictures showed moons that had never been seen before around these planets. The Voyagers also sent back close-up pictures of Saturn's rings.

Voyager 2 is scheduled to reach Uranus in 1986 and Neptune in 1989. Toward the end of this century, both probes will leave the solar system. Each Voyager spacecraft contains recordings of sounds on earth, messages in different languages, and pictures of earth scenes. These cargoes could serve as messages to whatever living beings find the probes about the place from which the probes were launched.

Saturn

Jupiter

Neptune
September 1, 1989

Uranus January 27, 1986

Saturn August 26, 1981

launched from Earth
August 20, 1977

Jupiter
July 9, 1979

Sun

The path of Voyager 2

Finding out

What path did Pioneer 10 follow? The first space probe to travel beyond our solar system was Pioneer 10. Pioneer 10 was launched in March 1972. Use a reference book to find out what path this space probe took from the earth. Use clay, yarn, and a piece of cardboard to make a model of this path. Also find out about the plaque Pioneer 10 took into space. Design a plaque that you would want to send on a spacecraft. Your plaque should tell other beings about our planet.

PEOPLE IN SPACE

What kinds of activities are performed by people in space?

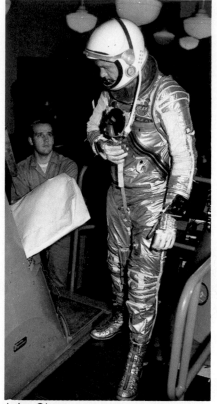

John Glenn

People have been journeying into space since 1961. As you may know, a person who travels into space is called an astronaut. Astronauts make observations, perform experiments, gather data, and test materials while in space.

The first person in space was Yuri Gagarin, a Soviet astronaut. The first American in space was Alan Shepard in 1961. He flew in the space capsule *Freedom 7* as part of the Mercury space program. Shepard did not orbit Earth. The first American to orbit Earth was John Glenn in 1962. Glenn orbited Earth three times during his flight in space.

One of the aims of the American space program was to find out if people could live in space. Astronauts in space are weightless. Scientists wondered how this would affect their muscles and bones. So far, it seems that calcium is lost from the bones during time spent in space. In addition, astronauts who remain in space for long periods may lose some strength in their muscles. Special programs have been designed to help correct these problems.

An early goal of the American space program was to send astronauts to the moon. This program was called Project Apollo. A new rocket, the Saturn V, was developed for the Apollo project. The Saturn V was the largest rocket ever built. With the Apollo spacecraft on top, the rocket stood almost 120 m high. It weighed about 3 million kg.

Astronaut in weightless state

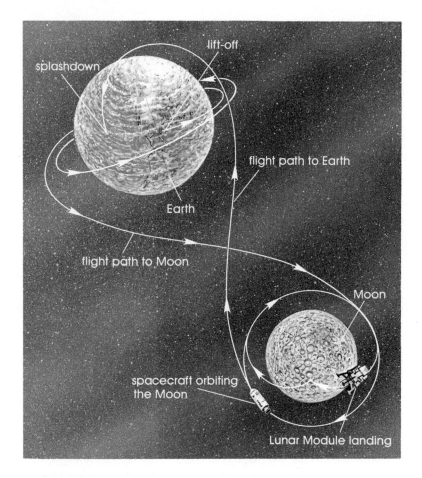

splashdown

lift-off

flight path to Earth

Earth

flight path to Moon

Moon

spacecraft orbiting the Moon

Lunar Module landing

The first landing on the moon was made in 1969. A Saturn rocket launched an Apollo spacecraft carrying three astronauts into Earth orbit. The spacecraft then carried the astronauts to the moon, a three-day journey. Two of the astronauts landed on the moon in a vehicle called the Lunar Module. The third remained in the Apollo spacecraft orbiting the moon. The astronauts on the surface gathered samples and took measurements. They then returned to the Apollo spacecraft for the journey home. In all, the United States has sent 12 astronauts to the moon's surface.

Skylab

In the early 1970s the United States launched Skylab. Skylab was an orbiting space laboratory. Astronauts traveled to and from Skylab in an Apollo spacecraft. Three astronauts could occupy Skylab for as long as three months. The astronauts performed experiments of many kinds aboard Skylab. In addition, they observed and took measurements of Earth and the sun. Three teams of astronauts worked aboard Skylab during its lifetime. Skylab eventually fell out of orbit. Most of it burned up on reentering Earth's atmosphere. Some pieces fell in Australia and in the Pacific Ocean.

America's Space Shuttle flights began in 1981. The Space Shuttle is the first reusable space vehicle. Twin rockets help to boost the Shuttle into space. The rockets then parachute to Earth and are recovered to be used again. The Shuttle can remain in orbit as long as two weeks. It can carry a crew of seven. After completing its mission, the Shuttle returns to Earth. Since it has wings, it lands much like an airplane. The Shuttle can then be flown again. Why is a reusable space vehicle helpful in the exploration of space?

The Shuttle can carry satellites into space. The crew members then launch the satellites into separate orbits. The Shuttle can also retrieve satellites from orbit. These can then be repaired and placed back into orbit. With the Shuttle, the cost of launching satellites has been reduced.

Scientists are planning to send a telescope into orbit aboard the Shuttle. Better observations of the solar system and of deep space will be possible with this telescope. Why will this be so?

Space Shuttle flight deck

THE FUTURE OF SPACE

How will space be explored and used in the future?

It seems probable that people will increase their activities in space in the future. For example, space shuttles could be used to carry building materials into orbit. Space stations could then be built there. Such space stations would allow people to work in space for many months. Some scientists aboard the stations would gather data about space. Others might experiment with new alloys or find ways to make new products.

Space colonies may also be developed in orbit. A colony might be made up of several large space stations. Rooms would be provided for the people living at the colony. Some of the people might run factories to produce goods in space. Others might be involved in mining on the moon or on asteroids. The minerals could be sent to Earth or used in the space factories to produce goods.

Mining in space

Space station

Space shuttles could also be used to build power plants in space. Such power plants would collect solar energy. The energy would then be beamed to Earth in the form of waves. These waves would be changed to electricity.

It is possible that hospitals may be built in space in the future. Some doctors feel that such hospitals could provide special care for patients with certain illnesses. In space there is no feeling of weight. Heart patients could benefit from this because their hearts would not have to work as hard. Patients with burns could also benefit from space hospitals. They would not have to lie in bed on their injuries. They could float freely in their weightless condition. Some doctors feel that this would help burns heal faster.

At some time people may move beyond the orbit of Earth to live and work. Colonies might be set up on the moon or Mars. These colonies would be like cities beyond Earth. Such a city might grow up around an observatory or a laboratory on another planet. In the future, then, people may live not only on the planet Earth.

Power plant in space

Lunar city

— HOW SPACE EXPLORATION —
AFFECTS YOU

How has the exploration of space changed people's lives on Earth?

It is possible that you will be a space traveler. However, whether you travel in space or not, the space age is affecting your life in many ways. For instance, materials that were developed for the space program are now used in many products here on Earth.

Much of the early work on tiny circuits was done for the space program. Computers and other electronic devices aboard a spacecraft must be small and light in weight. So miniature circuits were developed for these devices. Today, such tiny circuits are used in microcomputers, calculators, electronic games, and many other products.

Some clothlike fabrics that were developed for the space program have proved useful on Earth. For example, a lightweight fabric that reflects light and heat was used in the construction of a satellite. This material is now used to make emergency blankets.

Fabric roof

Fabrics used in spacesuits are also being used for other purposes. Fabric roofs have been built over sports stadiums and department stores. A fabric roof is light in weight and can help to keep the enclosed area cool. In addition, fabric roofs are low in cost.

Spacesuit fabric has also been used in new types of firefighting outfits. The new outfits will not burn or melt. They are waterproof yet allow

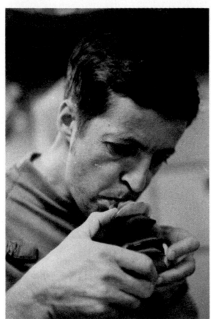

Collapsible drinking container

body heat and body moisture to pass out. The new clothing is being tested.

The food industry now uses some of the methods developed to keep food fresh during space flights. These methods produce good-tasting food that does not spoil at room temperature.

Special materials for cooking food have also come from the space program. These materials do not crack when heated or frozen. Therefore, they make very sturdy dishes for cooking and freezing food. Food can be stored in these dishes in the freezer. The dishes can be put into a hot oven right from the freezer.

A unit that purifies water on the Space Shuttle has been adapted for use on Earth. The new water filter can be attached to a faucet. It can kill bacteria in the water. It can also remove chemicals that cause water to taste bad.

The space program has led to new medical products. One of these is a medical unit in a briefcase. The unit is designed for use by a paramedic. It can be used to check a person's health signs, such as pulse and blood pressure. It can also be used to restore normal heartbeat in a person whose heart is not beating properly. The unit contains a two-way radio. So a paramedic treating a patient can contact a doctor for instructions. This new medical unit was developed from one that is used to check the health of astronauts.

Many other products have resulted from research in the space program. These include a new welding tool, new lighting systems, a new forestry vehicle, and a new camera. New products will continue to be developed in the future.

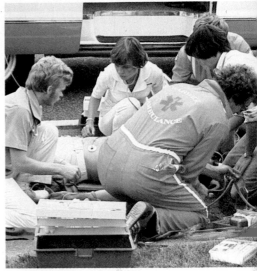

Paramedics

IDEAS TO REMEMBER

▶ Telescopes on Earth are used to gather data about space.

▶ Satellites are used to study both space and our own planet.

▶ Space probes have been sent to gather data about the moon and the planets.

▶ People travel in space. Some have explored the moon. Others perform experiments, test products, and gather data while in space.

▶ People may live and work in space in the future.

▶ Many products now in use on Earth were developed as a result of the space program.

Reviewing the Chapter

SCIENCE WORDS
A. Copy the sentences below. Use science words from the chapter to complete the sentences.

1. The study of space and the things it contains is called ____.

2. A/An ____ is a telescope that uses a glass lens.
3. A/An ____ is a telescope that uses a curved mirror.
4. A building that contains a telescope and that is set up to study space is called a/an ____.
5. Objects called ____ are placed into orbit to study the earth.
6. Rockets are used to launch ____ from the earth to gather data about the moon and the planets.
7. A rocket overcomes gravity by burning fuel in a/an ____.

8. In the future, people might live and work in space for months at a time while staying in ____.

B. Identify each of the following.

1. I am used to send an object into space. What am I?
2. I am a reusable spacecraft. What am I?
3. I am an object that orbits another object. What am I?
4. I am a space probe that landed on Mars. What am I?
5. I am a spacecraft that carried people to the moon. What am I?

UNDERSTANDING IDEAS

A. Describe ways in which the exploration of space has changed people's lives on Earth.

B. Drawings of three kinds of telescopes are shown. Identify the refracting telescope, the reflecting telescope, and the radio telescope.

C. Explain the difference between the terms.

    1. space probe, satellite   **2.** space station, space colony
    3. rocket,   **4.** optical telescope,
       combustion chamber   radio telescope

D. Describe ways in which people may use space in the future.

USING IDEAS

1. Collect newspaper articles about space exploration. Place them in a scrapbook. Include a short summary about each article.

2. Using scientific information and your imagination, create a detailed drawing or write a short story about a space colony.

Science in Careers

There are many careers in the fields of earth science and space science. Most of the jobs are highly technical and require advanced training. But some jobs require only on-the-job training.

Geologists study the structure of the earth itself. Some geologists study patterns of earthquake or volcanic activity. Others are involved in locating deposits of fossil fuels.

Meteorologist

Petroleum geologist

Many *meteorologists* work for the government. The National Oceanic and Atmospheric Administration (NOAA) employs meteorologists at weather stations all across the nation. The meteorologists take weather measurements and prepare weather forecasts. Commercial airlines also employ meteorologists.

Astronomers often combine research at observatories with teaching astronomy at the college level. Some astronomers work for the National Aeronautics and Space Administration (NASA). They may be involved in the study of the solar system. Their work sometimes includes analyzing data sent back by space probes. Other astronomers are interested in the study of objects deep in space, such as distant galaxies. Such astronomers do much of their work at observatories located around the country. As you can see, earth science and space science offer a variety of opportunities.

People in Science

Jakob Bjerknes (1897–1975)

Jakob was born in Stockholm, Sweden. His father, Vilhelm, was a famous meteorologist. Vilhelm identified air masses and fronts as causes of changes in weather. Jakob became a meteorologist too. He went on to study the conditions and movements of air masses and fronts. Jakob and Vilhelm worked out the idea of polar fronts. Jakob was the first person to suggest the existence of jet streams.

The movement of a hurricane can be predicted.

Developing Skills

WORD SKILLS

Many English words come from Latin, Greek, and other languages. If you know the meanings of words in other languages, you can often understand the meanings of English words. The tables list word parts that come from other languages and gives their meanings.

Use the tables for help in writing a definition for each of the following words. You can do this by breaking each word into parts. For example, the word *lithosphere* is made of these parts: *litho-* + *sphere.* Check your definitions by finding the meanings of the words in a dictionary.

1. lithosphere
2. asteroid
3. cosmology
4. agronomy
5. paleontology
6. luminous

Word part	Meaning
agro-	of fields, soil
aster-	star
cosmo-	universe
litho-	stone
lumin-	light
pale-	old, ancient
-onto-	organism

Word part	Meaning
sphere	ball, globe
-logy	science of
-nomy	knowledge of
-oid	like
-ous	full of
-scope	for seeing

READING A PICTOGRAPH

A pictograph is a graph that uses pictures to represent data. Look at the pictograph on the opposite page. It shows how much crude oil was produced in the United States between 1945 and 1980. Use this pictograph to answer the questions.

1. How many barrels of crude oil were produced in the United States during 1945?
2. In which year was the most oil produced in the United States?
3. How many more barrels of oil were produced in 1960 than in 1955?
4. During which five-year period did oil production decrease?
5. During which five-year period did oil production increase most?

APPROXIMATE AMOUNT OF CRUDE OIL PRODUCED IN THE UNITED STATES (1945-1980)

Year	Amount
1945	1.7 billion barrels
1950	2.0 billion barrels
1955	2.5 billion barrels
1960	2.6 billion barrels
1965	2.8 billion barrels
1970	3.5 billion barrels
1975	3.0 billion barrels
1980	3.1 billion barrels

Note: 🗼 is equal to 500 million barrels of oil

MAKING A PICTOGRAPH

Following is data for the average number of tornadoes occurring annually in five states. Make a pictograph to represent this data. You can use a small sketch of a tornado to represent 10 tornadoes. Include the symbol and what it equals at the bottom of the graph.

State	Number
Kansas	47
Missouri	30
Nebraska	34
Oklahoma	55
Texas	125

UNIT FOUR

Investigating the Human Body

Have you ever wanted a robot to do your work? Robots are run by computers. Today, robots are used for many jobs. They are used to mine coal, explore planets, and even to build cars.

Suppose a robot was built that looked and acted much like a person. It might have hands and fingers much like those of a person. It might even talk. But no matter how perfect it was, the robot still would not be human. It would not be able to think. It would not be able to reproduce. It would not be able to do many of the things that people can do. In this unit you will learn more about how special people are.

Chapter 13

Control Systems of the Body

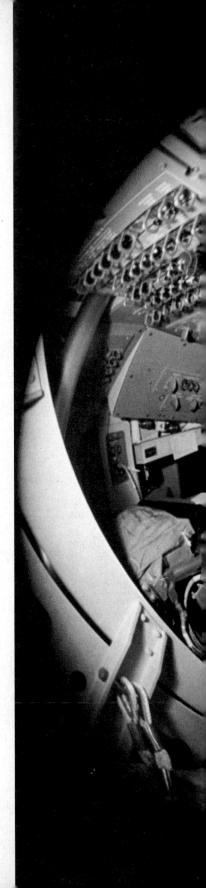

You have probably seen the launch or landing of the Space Shuttle. You know that such flights are controlled partly from the ground. There, Mission Control watches every second of the flight. However, much of the flight is controlled from aboard the Shuttle itself.

This is a picture of the flight deck of a Shuttle. The dials and knobs that you see are connected to many instruments. The instruments help to guide the Shuttle. They are also used to communicate with Mission Control. The Shuttle is controlled by complicated systems.

Your body, too, is controlled and guided by complicated systems. In this chapter you will learn about the way your body is controlled by your nervous system. You will also learn about another system that helps to regulate body activities.

—— THE NERVOUS SYSTEM ——
What are the parts of the nervous system?

Look at the picture below. The boy on the right is reading a book. He is also passing a pencil to the other boy. He must have heard him ask for the pencil. Both boys are breathing. Their hearts are beating. Some of these activities happen automatically. Others, such as passing the pencil, are voluntary actions.

What controls all of the body's activities? It is the nervous system. The **nervous system** is made up of the brain, spinal cord, and all the nerves of the body.

The nervous system can be divided into two main parts. The parts are named according to where they are located in the body. The **central nervous system,** as you may guess, is in the middle of the body, as shown in the drawing. It is made up of the brain and the spinal cord.

The other part is the **peripheral** (pə rif′ər əl) **nervous system.** The word *peripheral* means "outside" or "edge." This system includes all the nerves that extend from the central nervous system to the edges of the body. The drawing shows how these nerves extend from the central nervous system.

Some of your nerves control the actions you have to think about to do. Walking, talking, and eating are examples of such actions. Suppose you are sitting down and you want to get up and walk. You have to send a message from your brain to certain muscles in your body. Special nerves carry the messages. These nerves send messages to voluntary muscles.

Other nerves control the body activities you do not have to think about. Breathing and heartbeat are examples of such activities. Special nerves carry messages to the heart and to muscles near the lungs. The messages are sent without your having to think about them. The nerves carry the messages to involuntary muscles.

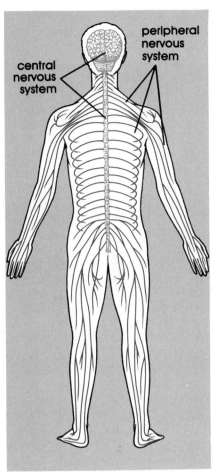

The nervous system

Voluntary muscles in action

── NERVE CELLS AND NERVES ──
What are the jobs of the three kinds of nerve cells?

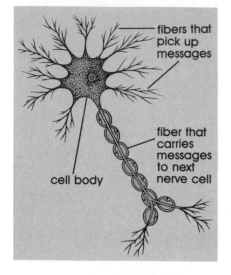

fibers that pick up messages

fiber that carries messages to next nerve cell

cell body

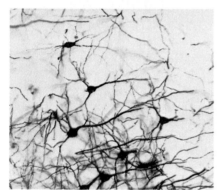

Nerve cells

Have you ever thought about how messages travel through the nervous system? Messages move through the system along a series of **nerve cells.** Each nerve cell has three main parts. These are shown in the drawing. There is a cell body at the center of each nerve cell. Many short fibers can be seen extending from the sides of the cell body. These fibers pick up messages and carry them to the cell body. A single long fiber extends from one side of the cell body. The long fiber carries messages from the cell body to another nerve cell. Compare the drawing of a nerve cell with the picture. What parts can you find?

Nerve cells are grouped in ''bundles'' that form nerves. This is something like the bundles of wires in a telephone cable. Nerves carry messages from parts of the body to the brain. They also carry messages from the brain to parts of the body. Some nerves in the fingers and toes are almost invisible. Others, like those that enter the spinal cord, are almost as thick as a pencil.

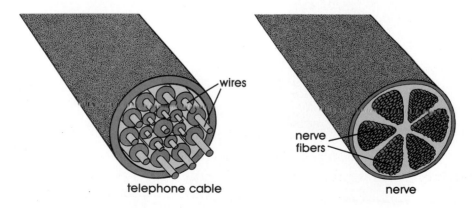

wires

telephone cable

nerve fibers

nerve

There are three kinds of nerve cells. Each kind does a different job. The first kind of nerve cell can respond to a stimulus from outside the body or from parts of the body. For example, nerve cells in the skin respond to pressure, pain, heat, and cold. These nerve cells send messages to the brain. Nerve cells that carry such messages are called **sensory nerve cells.** In the drawing, the brain is receiving a message that the hand has gripped the telephone receiver.

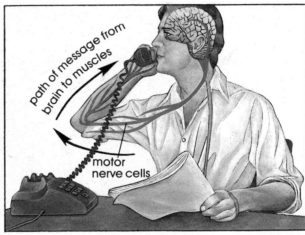

The second kind of nerve cell carries messages away from the brain and spinal cord. These nerve cells carry messages to parts of the body such as muscles. The messages can cause movement of the muscles. Nerve cells that carry such messages are called **motor nerve cells.** In the drawing, muscles in the arm have received a message to pick up the receiver.

The third kind of nerve cell connects sensory nerve cells to motor nerve cells. These cells are called **connecting nerve cells.** They are part of the central nervous system.

Messages sometimes take shortcuts. They can bypass the brain. For instance, you will quickly pull your hand away if you touch a hot pan. Such a reaction is called a **reflex.** In a reflex you respond without thinking. The message travels over sensory nerve cells to your spinal cord. In the spinal cord, it passes over connecting nerve cells to motor nerve cells. You instantly remove your hand when the muscles receive messages from the motor nerve cells. Follow the path of the message in the drawing of the reflex. Can you name other reflexes?

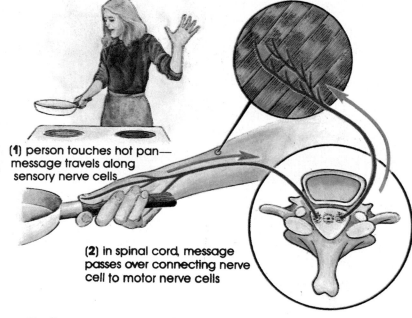

(3) motor nerve cells send message to muscles—person pulls hand away

(1) person touches hot pan—message travels along sensory nerve cells

(2) in spinal cord, message passes over connecting nerve cell to motor nerve cells

Reflex messages allow you to respond quickly. Messages that must travel to and from the brain result in delayed reaction. The time it takes for you to react is called **reaction time.** These basketball players must react quickly to actions around them. They need to have short reaction time.

How fast is your reaction time?

Materials meterstick

Procedure

A. Do this activity with a partner. Stand facing each other. Have your partner hold the meterstick from the top end (the 100-cm mark). The meterstick should be held high.

B. Place your thumb and forefinger around the meterstick, but do not touch it. Have your fingers at the 50-cm mark.

C. Your partner will drop the meterstick without warning. Try to catch it with your thumb and forefinger.
   1. At what mark did you catch it?

D. Find the distance the meterstick fell by subtracting 50 cm from the mark at which you caught it. This is a measurement of your reaction time.
   2. Record this measurement.

E. Repeat the activity four more times.
   3. Record each measurement.

Conclusion

1. Graph your reaction time (the distance the meterstick fell) versus the number of times you tried the activity.
2. How did your reaction time change with practice?

Using science ideas

1. How does a fast reaction time help a person when playing games or riding a bicycle?
2. Name some animals that depend on fast reaction times for survival.

— THE BRAIN AND SPINAL CORD —

What are the functions of the three main parts of the brain?

The central nervous system receives messages from all parts of the body. It also sends messages to all parts of the body. The brain and spinal cord are the two parts of the central nervous system.

The brain is the most important part of the nervous system. It is made up of delicate nerve tissue. The brain of an adult weighs about 1.5 kg. The brain is enclosed in the skull to protect it from damage.

The brain has three main parts. As you can see in the drawing, these are the brain stem, the cerebellum, and the cerebrum. The **brain stem** is the part of the brain that connects with the spinal cord. It controls many involuntary actions, such as breathing and heartbeat. It is also the control center for some actions that protect the body, such as sneezing, coughing, and blinking.

The brain stem at work

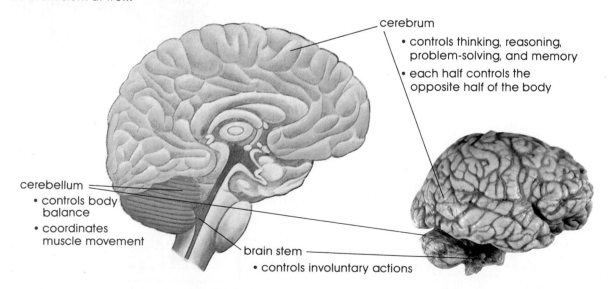

cerebrum
• controls thinking, reasoning, problem-solving, and memory
• each half controls the opposite half of the body

cerebellum
• controls body balance
• coordinates muscle movement

brain stem
• controls involuntary actions

The cerebellum at work

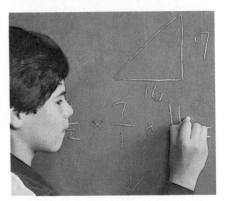

The **cerebellum** (ser ə bel'əm) is found above and behind the brain stem. The main job of the cerebellum is to control body balance and the movements of muscles. It helps the muscles work together.

The cerebellum sends messages to the right muscles so that they work together. When you catch a ball, the muscles of your eyes, arms, and hands must work together. Your cerebellum coordinates the movements of these muscles.

The largest and most important part of the brain is the **cerebrum** (ser'ə brəm). In fact, it makes up about 80 percent of the brain. It is divided into a right half and a left half. The right half controls the left side of the body. The left half controls the right side.

Look at the pictures on these pages. What parts of the brain are being used in each picture?

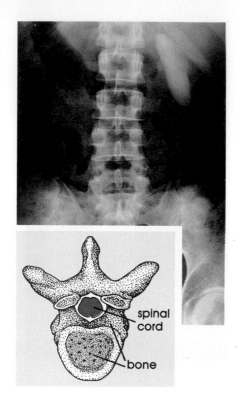

spinal cord

bone

The outer layer of the cerebrum has many deep folds and ridges. It looks something like a large walnut. This arrangement allows a great amount of nerve tissue to fit in the skull. In fact, half of the nerves in the body are located in the cerebrum. Thinking, reasoning, problem-solving, and memory are controlled by the cerebrum.

Messages travel to and from the brain along the spinal cord. The spinal cord is connected to the base of the brain. It is made up of bundles of nerve cells. The tissue of the spinal cord is soft and delicate. It is surrounded and protected by the backbone. The drawing shows how bone completely surrounds the spinal cord. Nerves from all parts of the body are connected to the spinal cord.

Finding out

How do folds and ridges increase the brain's surface area? Get a sheet of aluminum foil that is 50 cm square. If you do not have an extra-wide roll of foil, you can tape two pieces together. Be sure to cut them to the right size. This sheet is about the size of the outer layer of your brain if it were smoothed out. It is 2,500 square centimeters (cm²).

Now find a medium-size plastic bowl. It should be a little smaller than your head. A whipped-topping container—the 340-g size—is just right. It will be about the size of your brain.

"Fit" the sheet of foil around the bowl. Fold and pinch the foil so that it covers the outside surface of the bowl. How does this show how a large amount of brain tissue can fit inside your skull?

How good is your memory?

Materials   watch or clock with a second hand

Procedure

A. Do this activity with a partner. Have your partner hold up your book so that you can see Chart 1. Try to memorize the list of nonsense words. Your partner will give you 30 seconds to do this.

B. Try to write down the nonsense words in the correct order from memory.

   1. How many nonsense words did you remember?

C. Repeat the procedure, using Chart 2.

   2. How many words did you remember?

D. Repeat the procedure, using Chart 3.

   3. How many words did you remember?

Conclusion

1. Which chart was the easiest to memorize? Why do you think it was easiest?

2. Which chart was the hardest to memorize? Why do you think it was hardest?

Using science ideas

Make a chart containing 10 three-digit numbers. Repeat the activity with this chart. Is it easier to remember numbers or words?

Chart 1
wot
lom
eam
zel
kac
nik
bem
gur
fam
pon

Chart 2
milk
kitten
house
jump
school
many
star
work
sail
pen

Chart 3
only
a
scientific
people
can
survive
in
a
scientific
future

— DISORDERS OF THE NERVOUS — SYSTEM

What are three problems of the nervous system?

You know by now how important your nervous system is. Without it, you could not live. Problems with parts of the nervous system can be very serious. A cut finger will heal, but an injury to the spinal cord may never heal. Since the nervous system is the body's control center, damage to it can affect other parts of the body.

The brain and spinal cord can be damaged by an accident or an infection. Either trouble may cause paralysis. *Paralysis* means that one or more parts of the body cannot move.

Cerebral palsy (ser'ə brəl   pôl'zē) is a disorder of the brain. It may result from infection or injury to the part of the brain that controls the movement of muscles. A person with cerebral palsy has trouble moving. He or she may also have trouble speaking. This is because the muscles do

not work together. There is no cure for this disorder. But training can help a person with cerebral palsy to lead a nearly normal life.

Drugs that are misused affect the nervous system too. They may completely destroy the natural way the brain handles the messages it receives. A person who misuses drugs may not be able to think or reason normally. He or she may see things that are not there. He or she may hear sounds when there are no sounds. The parts of the body may not work together as they should. Drugs should be used only according to directions on the label.

Therapy for cerebral palsy

Do you know?

Computers may be able to help people walk. An Ohio woman, paralyzed from the ribs down, recently took several steps with the aid of a computer. Wires were used to connect the computer to muscles in her legs. The computer then triggered bursts of electricity that caused the muscles to work properly. The system is expensive and bulky. It is also limited, because it only allows the woman to put one foot in front of the other. However, it may be the first step in enabling those with paralysis of the legs to walk.

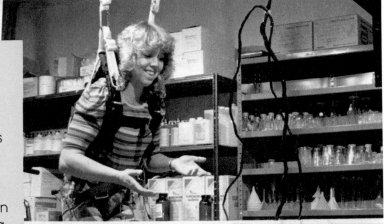
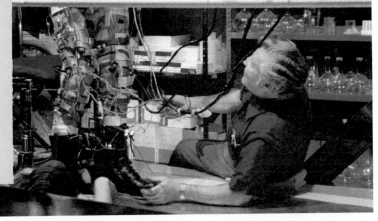

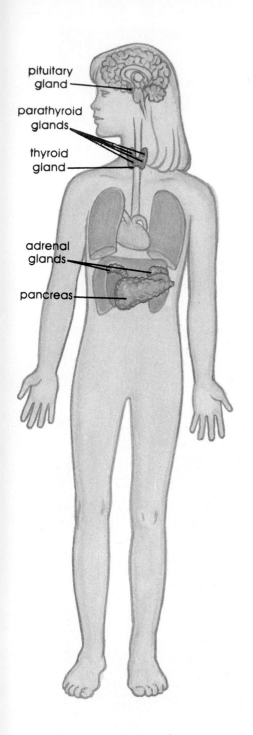

pituitary gland

parathyroid glands

thyroid gland

adrenal glands

pancreas

THE ENDOCRINE SYSTEM

What is the function of the endocrine system?

You have learned that much of what you do is controlled by your nervous system. But there is a second control system in your body. This system is the **endocrine** (en′dō krin) **system.** It controls the rate of many of your body's activities. For example, your endocrine system controls the rate at which you grow. It also controls how quickly energy is released from food in your body's cells. This system can both speed up and slow down activities in your body.

The endocrine system is made up of several glands. **Glands** are special organs or tissues in the body that make chemical substances. The chemical substances that the endocrine glands make are called **hormones** (hôr′mōnz). *Hormone* comes from a Greek word meaning "to excite." This is a good name, since the hormones do "excite" your body to do certain activities. Hormones are released into the blood by endocrine glands and then carried to the cells of the body.

The drawing shows some of the glands of the endocrine system. As you can see, the glands of the endocrine system are not directly connected to one another. How many kinds of these glands can you count? Let's look more closely at some of the endocrine glands and learn what they do.

The **pituitary** (pi tü′ə ter ē) **gland** may be the most important gland of the endocrine system. This gland is only about the size of a pea and is on the underside of the brain. Find the pituitary gland in the drawing. It produces several hormones. Some of these hormones control other endocrine glands in the body. For this reason the pituitary is often called the master gland.

One of the hormones from the pituitary gland regulates the growth of bones. Too much or too little of this growth hormone can affect a person's body size. Too much of the hormone can cause the bones to grow longer than their normal lengths. People with this condition grow to be very large. Some people grow as tall as 3 m. This condition is called giantism.

In some cases the pituitary does not make enough of the growth hormone. Then the bones do not grow to their normal lengths. This condition is known as dwarfism.

Giantism

Dwarfism

The **thyroid** (thī'roid) **gland** is in the neck. Can you feel your Adam's apple, or voice box? The thyroid is just below and in front of the voice box. Find the thyroid gland in the drawing on page 328. It makes an important hormone called thyroxine (thī rok'sēn). This hormone controls how fast the cells in your body obtain energy from food.

Too little thyroxine keeps the body from releasing energy from food fast enough. Some of the food is stored as fat. In this case a person would become overweight. He or she would also feel tired, since the body would not be getting enough energy from the food. People who have this problem can take medicine that contains thyroxine.

Too much thyroxine causes the body to use up food too quickly. In this case a person would lose weight and might have a lot of nervous energy.

The thyroid gland uses the chemical called iodine to make thyroxine. You usually get as much iodine as you need from the food you eat. But iodine is sometimes added to table salt. What does the label on this salt box tell you?

The **parathyroid** (par ə thī'roid) **glands** are on the back of the thyroid. There are four of these glands. Find them in the drawing on page 328. They are the smallest endocrine glands. They make hormones that control the amount of calcium and other minerals contained in the blood. These minerals are needed to make strong bones and tooth. Calcium is also needed for the blood to clot properly.

The **pancreas** (pan'krē əs) is a double-purpose organ. It is located behind the stomach. It makes substances that help to digest food.

The pancreas is also an endocrine gland. The pancreas makes a hormone that helps to control how the cells use sugar. This hormone is called insulin (in'sə lin). If the body does not have enough insulin, the cells cannot use the sugar in the blood. Then too much sugar builds up in the blood. This condition is called diabetes (dī ə-bē'tis). People with diabetes have to take medicine that contains insulin. A person with diabetes may wear a Medic Alert bracelet like the one shown. If a person with diabetes passes out, the bracelet can make others aware of the person's special medical problem.

Do you know?

By combining their knowledge of biology and electronics, scientists may be able to help people with diabetes someday soon. This drawing shows a biosensor surrounded by blood cells in the bloodstream. This biosensor will be connected to a device holding insulin. The tip of the sensor will contain a chemical that will react with sugar in the blood. The reaction will produce an electric signal. As the amount of sugar in the blood varies, so will the signal the sensor sends. As the signal varies, so will the amount of insulin that is released. By using a biosensor such as this, a person with diabetes might not have to worry about taking the correct amount of insulin again.

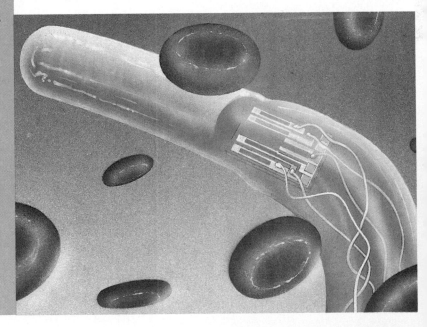

There are two **adrenal** (ə drē'nəl) **glands,** one on top of each kidney. Can you find these glands in the drawing of the endocrine system? The adrenal glands have an inner part and an outer part. The outer part makes hormones that help to control how the body uses food. These hormones also help the body to deal with stress. The inner part makes a special hormone in emergencies. This hormone is called adrenalin.

Adrenalin (ə dren'ə lin) is released when you are frightened, hurt, or in danger. The hormone triggers many body actions. Your eyes open wider. Your heart beats faster. You breathe faster. If you are cut, your blood clots faster. Also, your muscles can work harder and longer than they normally do.

Perhaps you have heard stories of unusual strength or endurance. For example, people have been known to lift very heavy objects to free trapped victims. Normally, they would not have been able to do so. But in an emergency, adrenalin causes many parts of the body to work harder.

Doctors sometimes inject adrenalin into someone whose heart has stopped working. The adrenalin can stimulate the heart and may start it beating again.

The table on page 333 is a summary of what you have learned about the endocrine system. Look at the table. What are the names of five endocrine glands? Which endocrine gland produces thyroxine? What is the function of the parathyroid glands? Where is the pituitary gland located? Which gland produces a hormone that is used by the body in emergencies?

THE ENDOCRINE SYSTEM

	Gland	Function
	Pituitary gland	• Produces hormones that control other glands • Produces growth hormone
	Parathyroid glands	• Produce a hormone that controls amounts of calcium and other minerals contained in the blood
	Thyroid gland	• Produces thyroxine, which controls how fast cells obtain energy from food
	Adrenal glands	• Produce hormones that help control how the body uses food, help the body deal with stress, and help in emergencies
	Pancreas	• Produces a hormone that helps to control how cells use sugar

IDEAS TO REMEMBER

▶ Body activities are controlled by the nervous system and the endocrine system.

▶ The nervous system consists of two main parts—the central nervous system and the peripheral nervous system.

▶ The thinking and reasoning actions of the body are handled by the cerebrum.

▶ Injury, disease, and the use of drugs can damage the nervous system.

▶ The endocrine system releases hormones that control some body functions.

▶ Some of the endocrine glands are the pituitary, thyroid, parathyroid, pancreas, and adrenal glands.

Reviewing the Chapter

SCIENCE WORDS

A. Use all the terms below to complete the sentences.

hormones

central nervous system

motor nerve cells

glands

peripheral nervous system

sensory nerve cells

reflex

connecting nerve cells

The __1__ is made up of the brain and spinal cord. The __2__ includes the nerves that extend to the edges of the body. Nerve cells that carry messages to the brain and spinal cord are called __3__. Nerve cells that carry messages from the brain and spinal cord to other body parts are called __4__. Messages passing between these two types of nerve cells travel over __5__. In a reaction called a/an __6__, messages bypass the brain. The rate of many body activities is controlled by chemical substances called __7__. These substances are produced by tissues and organs of the endocrine system called __8__.

B. Write the letter of the kind of endocrine gland that matches the function.

1. Controls the amount of calcium contained in the blood

2. Helps the body deal with stress

3. Controls how fast the cells obtain energy from food

4. Regulates the growth of bones

5. Regulates the use of sugar

a. thyroid gland

b. adrenal gland

c. pancreas

d. parathyroid gland

e. pituitary gland

UNDERSTANDING IDEAS

A. Write the correct term for each number in the diagram.

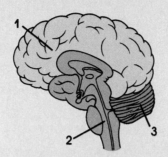

B. Suppose you watch a traffic light turn green. You then begin to cross the street. Describe the paths the messages take over your nerve cells so that you can begin to cross.

C. Explain the difference between the terms.

    1. reaction time, reflex   **2.** cerebrum, cerebellum
    3. hormone, gland   **4.** nerve cell, nerve

D. Both the nervous system and the endocrine system help to control body activities. How do they differ in the way they control body activities?

USING IDEAS

1. Use your library to find out how biofeedback is used to help control activities that are normally involuntary, such as blood pressure.
2. The pituitary gland is sometimes called the master gland. Find out which endocrine glands are controlled by the pituitary gland.

Chapter 14

Growth and Development

How are living things different from nonliving things? Perhaps one of the most important differences is that living things can reproduce. Living things produce other living things of the same kind. Nonliving things cannot do this.

The picture shows a family. Each person is a special individual. And you can see that the family members are alike in some ways. But why do living things resemble their parents? In this chapter you will learn how living things reproduce. You will also learn why parents and their young are alike in certain ways.

REPRODUCTION
Why is reproduction important?

Suppose plants could not form seeds. Suppose birds could not lay eggs. Suppose people could not have children. Suppose no living things could reproduce. What would happen? Soon there would be no living things left on Earth. It would be a barren planet of rock, water, and air.

Reproduction is the process by which living things produce other living things of the same kind. It is important for living things to reproduce. If a certain kind of living thing stopped reproducing, it would die out, or disappear. For example, if pandas stopped reproducing, they would die out, or become extinct.

Different living things may reproduce in different ways. In some kinds of living things, reproduction requires only one parent. In some cases a new living thing can grow from a part of the parent organism. For example, a new plant can often be grown from a leaf taken from the parent. If certain kinds of worms are cut in pieces, the pieces will grow into new worms. How many new worms have formed in the drawing?

Planting a cutting

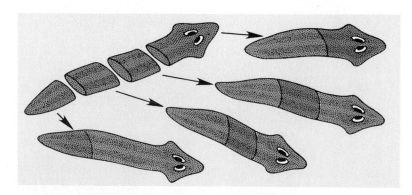

Some single-celled organisms reproduce by dividing. The parent cell simply divides into two new cells. The amoeba in the pictures is reproducing by dividing. If the two new amoebas that have formed divide again, how many amoebas will there be?

Some living things reproduce by growing buds. The buds grow out from the parent organism. The buds grow larger and then break off from the parent. Yeasts, shown in the picture, reproduce by budding. The hydra shown in the picture has a bud growing from it. The bud will break off and a new hydra will have formed.

Photographs by Carolina Biological Supply Company.

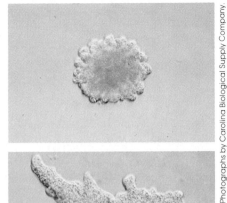
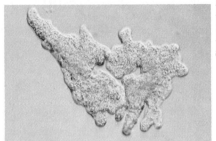
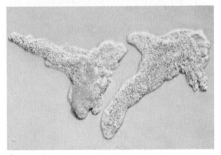

Amoeba reproducing

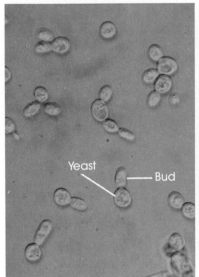
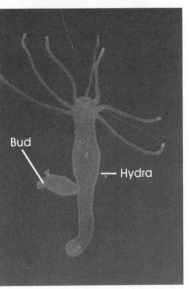

Yeast — Bud

Bud Hydra

In many other kinds of living things, reproduction requires two parents. In this kind of reproduction, cells from a male and a female must join. When they join, a new living thing—an offspring—begins. To understand how an offspring forms, you must know something about male and female reproductive cells.

— REPRODUCTION AND CELLS —

How are reproductive cells different from other kinds of cells?

You know that all living things are made up of cells. Some living things are made up of only one cell. Others, like people, are made up of trillions of cells. A person may have as many as 50 trillion cells. Most are so small that 100,000 would fit on the head of a pin!

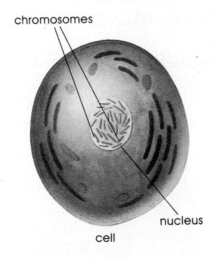

chromosomes

nucleus

cell

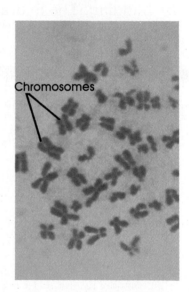

Chromosomes

The control center for a cell is the nucleus. It is also the information center for a cell. It stores all the information the cell needs to grow, reproduce, and do its job. This information is found inside the nucleus, on the threadlike structures called chromosomes.

Each cell in a living thing has a certain number of chromosomes. The chromosomes are usually arranged in pairs. Different organisms have different numbers of chromosome pairs. In a person, there are 23 pairs of chromosomes in the nucleus

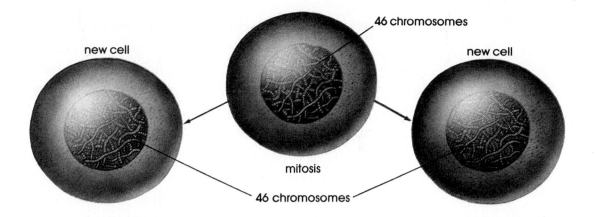

new cell

46 chromosomes

new cell

mitosis

46 chromosomes

of every body cell. This means that each of your body cells contains 46 chromosomes. As you grow, your body forms more and more cells. These cells are produced by mitosis. Mitosis is a process in which one cell divides to form two cells. Mitosis is shown in the drawing above.

Before a cell undergoes mitosis, it makes a duplicate set of chromosomes. So the cell at that time contains two complete sets of chromosomes. The cell then divides into two new cells. Each new cell receives a complete set of chromosomes. In this way all the body cells have the same information. When a cell with 16 chromosomes undergoes mitosis, how many chromosomes will each new cell have?

Mitosis is a very important body process. You add new cells as you grow. New cells also replace worn-out cells. Mitosis supplies these new cells.

In many living things reproduction requires two parents. Each parent produces a special kind of cell called a reproductive cell. The male parent produces a **sperm cell.** The female parent produces an **egg cell.** The sperm cell is a tiny cell. The egg cell is the largest cell in the body.

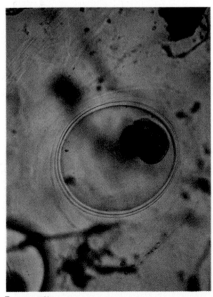

Egg cell

Reproductive cells differ from other cells in the body. They are not formed by mitosis. Instead, they are formed by a special kind of cell division that reduces the number of chromosomes by one half. So sperm cells and egg cells have only half the number of chromosomes that other cells have. In a person, the body cells have 46 chromosomes. How many chromosomes would each egg cell or sperm cell have in a person?

When an egg cell and a sperm cell join, or unite, they make a cell called a **zygote** (zī′gōt). The zygote has as many chromosomes as were in both the sperm cell and the egg cell. Half of the chromosomes come from the egg cell, and half come from the sperm cell. Look at the drawing below. The egg cell and the sperm cell each have 20 chromosomes. How many chromosomes would the zygote have?

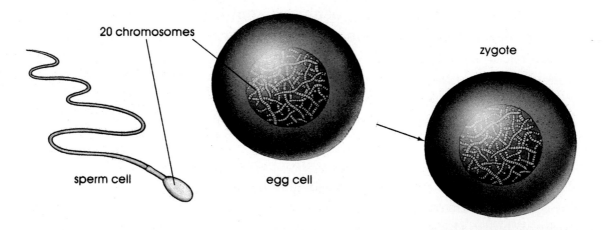

20 chromosomes

zygote

sperm cell   egg cell

A new organism begins when a sperm cell joins with an egg cell and forms a zygote. This process is called **fertilization** (fėr tə lə zā′shən). The zygote that is formed has a complete set of chromosomes. And it is able to divide by mitosis.

— A NEW ORGANISM DEVELOPS —

How does a new organism develop from a single cell?

After fertilization, the zygote develops into a new organism. It begins as a single cell, with chromosomes from both parents. This cell then undergoes mitosis. In other words, it begins to divide and to form new cells. Each new cell then divides. In this way many new cells are formed. The organism grows and develops as new cells are added.

As new cells form, they begin to carry out different jobs. Many different kinds of cells form. For example, in humans some of the new cells become skin cells. Others become muscle cells and bone cells. What other kinds of cells can you name?

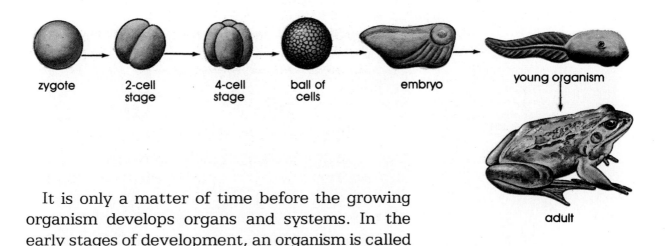

zygote   2-cell stage   4-cell stage   ball of cells   embryo   young organism

adult

It is only a matter of time before the growing organism develops organs and systems. In the early stages of development, an organism is called an **embryo** (em′brē ō). By the time of birth or hatching, the embryo has developed into a young

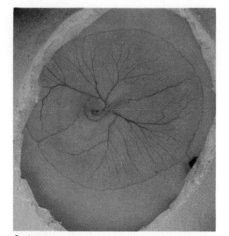
3 days

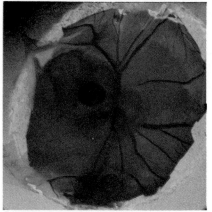
7 days

organism that resembles its parent. The pictures show several stages in the development of a chicken.

The amount of time the embryo needs before birth or hatching varies from one kind of organism to another. In humans the embryo usually needs 280 days. Look at this table. How much time does a cat embryo need to develop?

DEVELOPMENT TIME BEFORE BIRTH	
Animal	Approximate time (days)
Mouse	21
Rabbit	30–43
Kangaroo	40–45*
Dog	58–65
Cat	60
Lion	106
Armadillo	150
Horse	330–380
Whale	334–365
African elephant	641

* Young are born undeveloped; growth continues in a pouch.

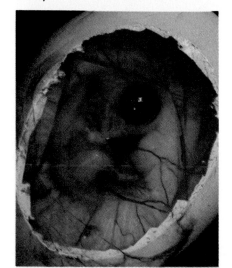
14 days

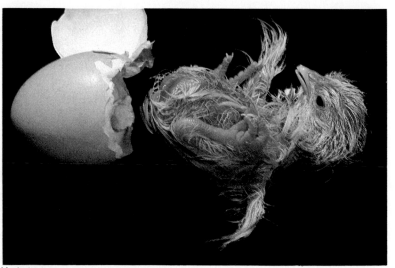
Hatching

— PASSING ON INFORMATION —

How are features of parents passed on to their offspring?

Perhaps someone has said to you, "You look just like your mother." Or, "You look like your uncle when he was a boy." Almost all of us have heard statements like these. We all have features of our parents and other relatives. You may be tall like your father, or you may have blue eyes like your mother. Such features are called traits.

As you have learned, half of your chromosomes came from your mother. Half came from your father. So your chromosomes carry information from both parents. This information determines many of your traits. The information helps to determine your height. It determines traits such as your hair color and eye color. What other traits are passed along on chromosomes? What traits do the mother and child in the picture below have in common?

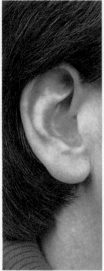

Free earlobes   Attached earlobes

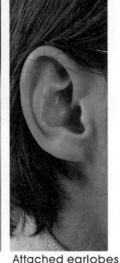

Scientists estimate that each cell carries between 10,000 and 100,000 different instructions. Besides body features, traits such as ability in art, music, or sports may be partially determined by information on chromosomes. Traits or features that are passed on from parents to offspring are often called **inherited traits.**

There are some traits you inherit that may not seem important. For example, look at the ears of the other people in your class. In some people, the earlobes may be attached to their heads. In others the earlobes may hang free. The pictures show free and attached earlobes.

Finding out

Can you roll your tongue? The picture shows a person who can roll up the sides of her tongue. Most people can do it. But if you cannot, it is because of chromosomes in your cells. Check your classmates. Also check members of your family. Check friends in your neighborhood. Keep a record of the number of tongue rollers and nonrollers you find. No amount of practice can make a roller out of a nonroller. How important do you think this inherited trait is?

What traits do your classmates have?

Procedure

A. Copy the chart on a sheet of paper.

B. Look at your classmates to find out what color eyes each one has. Record the numbers in the chart. Don't forget to include yourself.

    1. What is the most common eye color among your classmates?

C. Fill in the rest of the chart after observing the remaining traits in each of your classmates.

    2. What is the most common hair color among your classmates?

    3. Do more of the students have straight hair or curly hair?

    4. Do more of the students have earlobes that are attached or not attached?

Conclusion

1. For each trait that you studied, identify the variation that is the most common.

2. Based on your data, identify the trait expressions that you think are dominant.

Using science ideas

Make bar graphs showing your data for eye color and hair color.

Trait	Number

Eye color:
  Brown
  Blue
  Green
  Gray
  Other	

Hair color:
  Black
  Brown
  Blond
  Red	

Hair:
  Straight
  Curly	

Earlobes:
  Attached
  Not attached	

You know that you received chromosomes from both parents. Often, the chromosomes from both parents contain the same information for a trait. For instance, both parents may have brown hair. In such a case there is a strong likelihood that their offspring will have brown hair. But in some cases the information coming from the parents is not the same for a trait. One parent may have black hair and the other may have red hair. What happens in such a case?

To understand how the traits of an offspring are determined, let's look more closely at chromosomes. On the chromosomes are special units called genes. The genes are the units on the chromosomes that carry information about an organism's traits.

When a sperm cell and an egg cell join, genes from both parents are brought together. The genes for hair color that are received from both parents may be the same or different.

When two genes carrying different information for a trait join, one gene may determine that trait in the offspring. Such a gene is said to be dominant. A **dominant gene** is one that, when present, always determines a trait of an offspring. A gene that does not determine a trait when paired with a dominant gene is called a **recessive gene.** A recessive gene can only determine a trait when paired with the same kind of recessive gene.

Eye color is a good example of a trait for which there are dominant and recessive genes. The gene for brown eyes can cover up the gene for blue eyes. So we say brown eye color is dominant. Blue eye color is recessive.

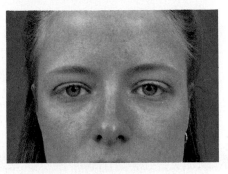

Do you know?

Certain kinds of diseases can be inherited. For example, sickle-cell anemia, a blood disease, can be inherited. In this disease some of the red blood cells are shaped like sickles, or crescents, so they cannot carry oxygen. The disease is caused by a recessive gene that controls the formation of the sickle-shaped cells. Sickle-cell anemia occurs mostly among black people. Scientists are searching for ways to prevent this and other inherited diseases.

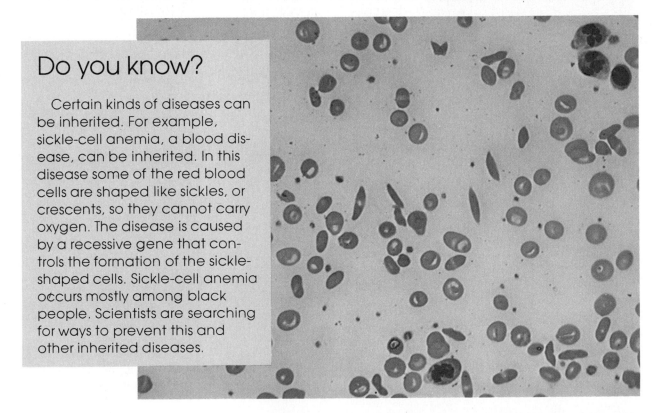

You can trace how eye color is inherited by looking at the drawings. Because the gene for brown eyes is dominant, we use the symbol **B** for it. Because the gene for blue eye color is recessive, we use the symbol **b** for it. Remember that you get a gene for eye color from each parent.

If you get a **B** from each parent, you will have brown eyes (**BB**). If you get a **B** from one parent and a **b** from the other, you will also have brown eyes (**Bb**). As you know, the gene for brown eyes (**B**) covers up the gene for blue eyes (**b**). The only way you can have blue eyes is if you get a **b** gene from each parent. Then the message for eye color that your cells carry will be **bb**.

The study of inherited traits is an interesting part of science. Scientists use what they have learned to develop special kinds of plants and animals. For example, someone who breeds show dogs can determine the traits of the offspring by selecting parents with certain traits.

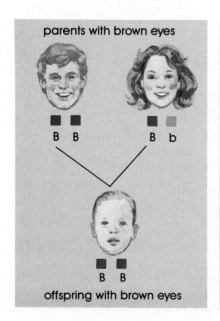

parents with brown eyes

B B   B b

B B

offspring with brown eyes

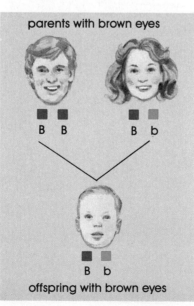

parents with brown eyes

B B   B b

B b

offspring with brown eyes

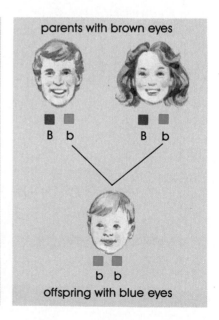

parents with brown eyes

B b   B b

b b

offspring with blue eyes

How is color inherited in bean seeds?

Materials 2 brown paper bags / 10 brown bean
seeds / 10 white bean seeds

Procedure

A. The brown beans and white beans will be used
to represent genes for seed color. Each brown
seed represents a gene for the dominant color
brown (B). Each white bean represents a gene for
the recessive color white (b).

B. Label one paper bag *Parent A.* Label the other
one *Parent B.*

C. Put 10 brown beans in bag *A.* Put 10 white
beans in bag *B.*

D. Take one bean from each bag. Record the
combination you drew and the seed color that
would result from this combination. Replace the
beans in their proper bags. Repeat the procedure
nine times.

E. Empty the bags. Place five brown beans and
five white beans in bag *A.* Do the same with bag *B.*

F. Repeat step **D.** Record your results.
  1. Compare your two trials. How do they differ?

Conclusion

1. What would the seed color be if both parents
are brown?
2. What would the seed color be if both parents
are white?
3. What would the seed color be if one parent is
brown and the other parent is white?

THE LIFE CYCLE

What are the stages of the human life cycle?

You have learned that all living things reproduce. Living things also grow and change. The stages that a living thing goes through make up the **life cycle** of the organism.

A person goes through a life cycle too. A person begins as a single cell. The cell divides again and again as an embryo. After about 9 months, a new baby is born. For several months after birth, a baby is in the stage called **infancy.** An infant depends on its parents for food and protection.

An infant grows as more and more cells are produced. In about a year an infant enters the stage called **childhood.** A child depends less on its parents than does an infant. A child continues to grow and develop. During this stage a child learns many skills. For example, a child learns to walk and talk. A child also learns many of the social skills needed to get along with others.

Infancy

Childhood

Adolescence

After childhood a person enters a stage of rapid growth and change. This stage is called **adolescence** (ad ə les'əns). Adolescence occurs when a person is in his or her teens. During this stage he or she begins to take on new responsibilities. A person also begins to learn to make his or her own decisions.

Adulthood

The stage that follows adolescence is **adulthood.** This is the longest stage in the life cycle. As an adult a person is fully grown. While in this stage, some adults have offspring. The cycle then begins for the offspring. Like all other organisms, people grow old. They also die. When this happens, the life cycle for an individual ends.

IDEAS TO REMEMBER

▶ The nucleus of a cell stores the information for the growth and development of the cell. This information is carried on the chromosomes.

▶ Sperm cells and egg cells have half the number of chromosomes that regular body cells have.

▶ A new living thing begins when a sperm cell joins with an egg cell.

▶ Many traits are passed on from parents to offspring. These are called inherited traits.

▶ Traits are carried on units on the chromosomes called genes.

▶ Each living thing goes through a life cycle.

▶ The human life cycle includes infancy, childhood, adolescence, and adulthood.

Reviewing the Chapter

SCIENCE WORDS

A. Use all the terms below to complete the sentences.

adulthood   reproduction   childhood
life cycle   adolescence   fertilization
infancy   zygote

The process by which living things produce other living things of the same kind is called __1__. In humans, a new organism begins when a sperm cell joins with an egg cell, a process called __2__. The cell that is formed is called a/an __3__. All living things go through changes that make up the __4__ of the organism. In humans, the stage that occurs immediately after birth is called __5__. During __6__, an individual learns many skills, such as the ability to walk and talk. During __7__, rapid growth and change occur. During the stage called __8__, physical growth stops.

B. Copy the sentences below. Use science words from the chapter to complete the sentences.

1. The female reproductive cell is the _____.
2. During the early stages of its development, an organism is called a/an _____.
3. Features or traits that are passed on from parents to offspring are called _____.
4. The male reproductive cell is the _____.
5. A gene that, when present, always determines a trait of an offspring is called a/an _____.

UNDERSTANDING IDEAS

A. Study the drawing. The gene for brown hair (**B**) is dominant. The gene for red hair (**b**) is recessive. Determine the hair color of the offspring in each case.

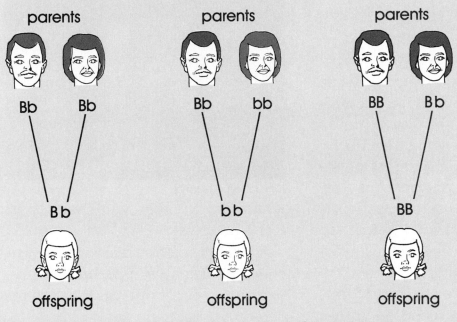

B. Explain why offspring have traits of both parents.

C. In what ways do egg cells and sperm cells differ from the other cells of the body?

D. What changes occur in an organism during the time it is an embryo?

USING IDEAS

1. How can keeping records on milk production help a farmer to develop the best possible herd of cows?

2. Find out about some genetic diseases, such as Tay-Sachs and phenylketonuria. For each disease, state whether the gene that causes it is dominant or recessive.

Science in Careers

Did you visit a doctor the last time you were sick? A *doctor* is well trained in how the organs and systems of the human body work. A doctor can usually recognize problems in the body and frequently can help to heal the body. But a doctor is just one member of the team of workers who provide health care.

A *nurse* is another member of the health-care team. A nurse may assist a doctor in treating patients. Some nurses take special training to care for special cases, such as heart patients or burn victims.

A *medical technologist* performs laboratory tests on blood and other body tissues. These tests help to determine which disease a person may have. A *laboratory assistant* is a

Inhalation therapist

laboratory worker who helps perform the tests.

A *pharmacist* is trained in the science of drugs. A pharmacist prepares drug prescriptions that are ordered by a doctor.

A *physical therapist* works with people who must rebuild their muscles or relearn to walk. A physical therapist teaches exercises and may use special equipment to help strengthen a person's muscles.

People who have become addicted to drugs often need counseling to help them with problems. A *drug counselor* can help a person understand why he or she was using drugs.

If the functioning of the human body interests you, perhaps a career in health care is for you.

Doctors and nurses

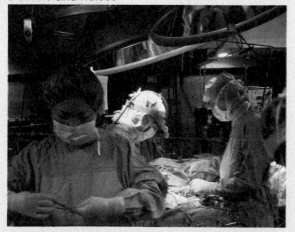

People in Science

Ko Kuei Chen (1898–   )

Dr. Chen has been involved in research in pharmacy, the science of drugs. His studies have led to the development of a medicine that helps to relieve the symptoms of asthma and bronchitis. He has also developed drugs for treating cyanide poisoning. In addition to doing research, Dr. Chen has also taught at several universities.

Drugs being manufactured at a pharmaceutical company

Developing Skills

WORD SKILLS

Use the tables for help in writing a definition for each of the following words.

1.	histology	2.	spermatocyte
3.	neural	4.	ambidextrous
5.	epidermis	6.	psychology
7.	somatic	8.	osteocyte

Word part	Meaning
ambi-	both
epi-	on the outside
histo-	tissue
neur-	nerve
osteo-	bone
psycho-	mind
somat-	body
spermato-	sperm, seed

Word part	Meaning
dextr-	toward the right
-al	of, like
-cyte	cell
-dermis	skin
-ic	having to do with
-logy	science of
-ous	full of

READING A TABLE

A table is used to organize data so that needed information can be easily picked out. The table on the opposite page identifies five physical skills that can be improved by participation in certain activities. Use the table to answer the questions.

1. Which activity—bicycling or handball—would help you develop better balance?

2. Identify the best activities to participate in if you want to improve (shorten) your reaction time.

3. Suppose you wish to develop better coordination. However, you want to choose an activity that can be done at home. Identify those activities that are either good or excellent at improving coordination at home.

4. Suppose a person with excellent coordination develops a medical problem that weakens the muscles. What activities will help the person improve power as well as retain top form in coordination?

EFFECT OF ACTIVITIES ON IMPROVING PHYSICAL SKILLS

	Improves balance	Improves coordination	Improves reaction time	Improves power	Improves speed
Backpacking	Fair	Fair	Poor	Fair	Poor
Baseball	Good	Excellent	Excellent	Excellent	Good
Basketball	Good	Excellent	Excellent	Excellent	Good
Bicycling	Excellent	Fair	Fair	Poor	Fair
Dancing, Aerobic	Fair	Good	Fair	Poor	Poor
Dancing, Social	Fair	Good	Fair	Poor	Fair
Fencing	Good	Excellent	Excellent	Good	Excellent
Football	Good	Good	Excellent	Excellent	Excellent
Golf	Fair	Excellent	Poor	Good	Poor
Gymnastics	Excellent	Excellent	Good	Excellent	Fair
Handball	Fair	Excellent	Good	Good	Good
Horseback Riding	Good	Good	Fair	Poor	Poor
Racquetball	Fair	Excellent	Good	Fair	Good
Skating, Ice	Excellent	Good	Fair	Fair	Good
Skating, Roller	Excellent	Good	Poor	Fair	Good
Skiing, Cross-country	Fair	Excellent	Poor	Excellent	Fair
Skiing, Downhill	Excellent	Excellent	Good	Good	Poor
Soccer	Fair	Excellent	Good	Good	Good
Softball	Fair	Excellent	Good	Good	Good
Surfing	Excellent	Excellent	Good	Good	Poor
Swimming	Fair	Good	Poor	Fair	Poor
Tennis	Fair	Excellent	Good	Good	Good
Volleyball	Fair	Excellent	Good	Fair	Fair
Walking	Fair	Fair	Poor	Poor	Poor

MAKING A TABLE

The length of an organism's life cycle is called the life span. Average life span varies from one kind of organism to another. Collect data about the average life span of different kinds of animals. Organize the data into a table. Group the animals in the table as mammals, birds, reptiles, and so on.

Units of Measurement

Two systems of measurement are used in the United States, the metric system and the English system. Feet, yards, pounds, ounces, and quarts are English units. Meters, kilometers, kilograms, grams, and liters are metric units. Only metric measurements are used in science. The following tables list some metric and English units. The tables show what each unit is approximately equal to in the other system. The metric mass/English weight relationships hold true for objects on the earth.

MEASUREMENT	METRIC UNITS (symbol)	EQUAL TO IN ENGLISH UNITS (symbol)
Length	1 millimeter (mm)	0.04 inch (in.)
	1 centimeter (cm)	0.4 inch (in.)
	1 meter (m)	39.4 inches (in.) or
		1.1 yards (yd)
	1 kilometer (km)	0.6 mile (mi)
Mass (weight)	1 gram (g)	0.035 ounce (oz)
	1 kilogram (kg)	2.2 pounds (lb)
Volume	1 liter (L)	1.06 quarts (qt)

MEASUREMENT	ENGLISH UNITS (symbol)	EQUAL TO IN METRIC UNITS (symbol)
Length	1 inch (in.)	2.5 centimeters (cm) or
		25 millimeters (mm)
	1 foot (ft)	30.5 centimeters (cm)
	1 yard (yd)	0.91 meter (m)
	1 mile (mi)	1.6 kilometers (km)
Weight (mass)	1 ounce (oz)	28.4 grams (g)
	1 pound (lb)	0.45 kilogram (kg)
Volume	1 quart (qt)	0.95 liter (L)

Lesson Questions

To the student

Reading your book will help you learn more about the world around you. Your book will provide answers to many questions you may have about living things, the earth, space, matter, and energy.

On the following pages you will find questions from each lesson in your book. These questions will help test your understanding of the terms and ideas you read about.

There are two kinds of questions. You can answer the first kind by using the information you read in each lesson. Careful reading will help answer these questions.

The second type of question is called "Thinking like a Scientist." These questions are more challenging. The answer may not be found just by reading the lesson. You may have to think harder.

1 *Living Things*

LIVING AND NONLIVING
(pp. 4–6)

1. All living things carry out certain activities called life processes. List these life processes.
2. Describe each life process.

Thinking like a Scientist

Scientists identify unknown organisms by comparing them with known organisms. Suppose a scientist looking at the blood of an astronaut saw a strange new particle. How could the scientist determine whether the particle was living or nonliving?

ANIMAL CELLS
(pp. 7–9)

1. Identify the parts of the animal cell in the drawing.

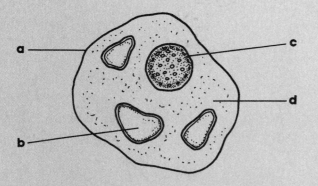

2. Describe each part of the animal cell you labeled.

Thinking like a Scientist

Scientists classify objects according to their common characteristics. Suppose you were looking at five cells. What characteristics would you look for to classify some of them as animal cells?

PLANT CELLS
(pp. 10–13)

1. Plant cells contain some structures not found in animal cells. Identify these structures in the drawing below and explain their jobs.

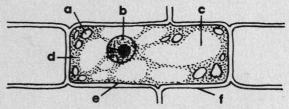

2. Name those structures that are found in both plant cells and animal cells.

Thinking like a Scientist

Not all plants are able to make their own food. If you were given 12 plants, how could you determine which plants could make their own food?

HOW CELLS REPRODUCE

(pp. 14–16)

1. What is mitosis?
2. Describe each of the steps in mitosis.

Thinking like a Scientist

What is the fewest number of cells that are needed to make 256 cells through mitosis? Explain your answer.

SINGLE CELLS

(pp. 17–20)

1. What is a single-celled organism called?
2. What are animallike protists called?
3. What can plantlike protists make?
4. How do scientists classify bacteria?
5. Give an example of how bacteria can be helpful.

Thinking like a Scientist

Why is it an advantage for a large animal to be made of billions of cells rather than just one cell?

TISSUES, ORGANS, AND SYSTEMS

(pp. 21–23)

1. What is a tissue? Give three examples.
2. What is an organ? Give three examples.
3. What is a system? Give three examples.

Thinking like a Scientist

What do you think is the most important organ in the human body? Write a paragraph explaining your choice.

2 Plant Growth and Responses

HOW PLANTS GROW
(pp. 28–31)

1. Where are growth regions found in plants?

2. Study the tree stems shown here. How old is each tree? How did the amount of rainfall vary during the lifetime of each tree?

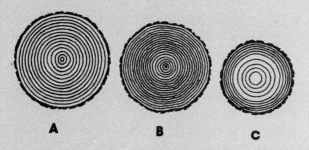

A   B   C

3. Why don't plants grow during the winter?

Thinking like a Scientist

Suppose a beaver gnawing on the trunk of a tree was suddenly frightened away and didn't return. If the tree grew 30 cm taller in the next two years, where would the scar from the beaver's teeth be? Why?

GROWTH AND SURVIVAL
(pp. 32–35)

1. Plants respond to things in their environment. List three stimuli to which most plants respond.

2. Why does light stimulate plants to respond the way they do?

3. Describe what is happening here. Is it an adaptation? Explain your answer.

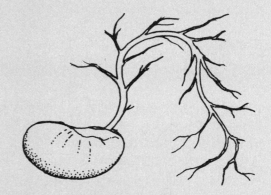

Thinking like a Scientist

The trunks of young trees bend easier than the trunks of older trees. Why might this be an advantage? Explain your answer.

OTHER ADAPTATIONS OF PLANTS

(pp. 36–41)

1. Why do seeds that land on the soil near the parent plant have little chance to survive?
2. Explain how each adaptation shown below helps the plant survive.

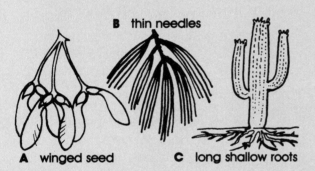

B   thin needles

A   winged seed   C   long shallow roots

Thinking like a Scientist

What adaptations would a maple tree need to grow in a desert? Make a drawing of a maple tree that has these adaptations.

BIOLOGICAL CLOCKS

(pp. 42–45)

1. What is a biological clock?
2. Crocuses bloom in the early spring. Would crocuses bloom in the tropics? Give a reason for your answer.

Thinking like a Scientist

Design an experiment that could be done to prove that plants have biological clocks.

3 Animal Adaptations

STRUCTURAL ADAPTATIONS
(pp. 50–58)

1. How are the porcupine and armadillo protected from enemies?
2. Describe the adaptations for movement of the kangaroo, cheetah, and vulture.
3. Study these drawings. Identify three types of teeth in each drawing. Identify each animal as either a meat eater or a plant eater.

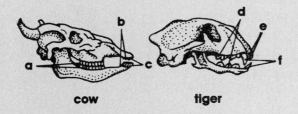

cow   tiger

Thinking like a Scientist

An animal's eyes, ears, and nose are adaptations that help the animal find and identify its predators and prey. Look at the pictures in Chapter 3. Choose three animals. Describe how each animal's eyes, ears, or nose help the animal survive.

LOOKS THAT PROTECT
(pp. 59–61)

1. Describe what is meant by protective coloration. Give two examples.
2. Give an example of protective resemblance.
3. Define *mimicry*. Give an example.

Thinking like a Scientist

About 100 years ago there was a certain species of moth that lived in England. Although most of the moths were whitish-gray in color, some of them were dark gray as you can see below. The lighter colored moths were nearly invisible to birds against the bark of white birch trees. But as England became industrialized, the trees became covered with dark soot. What do you think happened to this species of moth?

BEHAVIOR AND INSTINCT
(pp. 62–63)

1. What does the word *instinct* mean?
2. Give one example of a simple instinctive behavior and one example of a complex instinctive behavior.

Thinking like a Scientist
How could you determine whether the nest-building behavior of a certain type of bird was instinctive?

ANIMAL MIGRATION
(pp. 64–65)

1. What is migration?
2. Give two reasons why an animal migrates.

Thinking like a Scientist
People called nomads live in the desert. They travel from place to place to follow animals, to look for sources of water, and to avoid harsh weather. Would you classify this behavior as migration? Explain your answer.

HIBERNATION
(pp. 66–69)

1. What changes take place in an animal's body during the time it is hibernating?
2. How does a woodchuck hibernate differently from a chipmunk?

Thinking like a Scientist
What are some dangers a hibernating animal might face?

LEARNED BEHAVIOR
(pp. 70–73)

1. List the steps needed for learning to take place.
2. What are the two types of reinforcement?

Thinking like a Scientist
Why is it important that animals have the ability to learn? What would happen if all animal behavior was instinctive behavior?

4 Climate and Life

BIOMES
(pp. 78–80)

1. Look at this graph. What is the average temperature and amount of precipitation in this biome in June?
2. What type of biome is represented by this graph?

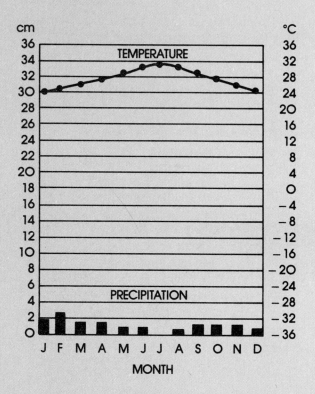

THE TUNDRA
(pp. 81–82)

1. Why aren't there any tall trees in the tundra?
2. How are musk oxen adapted to life in the tundra?

Thinking like a Scientist

The Alaskan pipeline was built to bring oil from Alaska to the other states. What problems do you think the engineers who worked on the pipeline faced?

THE TAIGA
(pp. 83–84)

1. What is an important resource of the taiga? Why?
2. How do insects, squirrels, bears, lynx, and wolves adapt to winter in the taiga?

Thinking like a Scientist

How was the taiga useful in the production of this book?

Thinking like a Scientist

The map on page 78 shows the locations of six major biomes. Do you think it is possible to find a biome outside the area described in this map? Explain your answer.

THE DECIDUOUS FOREST
(pp. 85–87)

1. Describe the climate in a deciduous forest.
2. How is the deciduous forest biome different from the taiga?

Thinking like a Scientist

The gypsy moth is an insect pest that eats the leaves from many trees in a deciduous forest. How might this pest affect the other plants and animals in the forest?

THE TROPICAL RAIN FOREST
(pp. 88–90)

1. Why do the trees of the tropical rain forest stay green all year?
2. Why are there so many animals found in a tropical rain forest?

Thinking like a Scientist

If you have ever seen a movie filmed in a jungle, you know how noisy a jungle can be. Why are jungle animals so noisy? Why aren't animals in a grassland or desert so noisy?

THE GRASSLAND
(pp. 91–93)

1. What is the major difference between the climates of the grassland and the deciduous forest?
2. Name two ways the grasslands are used.

Thinking like a Scientist

Prairie fires are common in the grasslands. Why are they important? What features of the grasslands help the fires to spread easily and help make them hard to fight?

THE DESERT
(pp. 94–96)

1. How are animals adapted to live in a desert?
2. How are plants adapted to live in a desert?

Thinking like a Scientist

Even though there are no trees in a desert, birds are common. Where might birds build their nests in a desert?

AQUATIC HABITATS
(pp. 97–101)

1. Put the following members of an ocean food chain in the correct order. Begin with the sun.

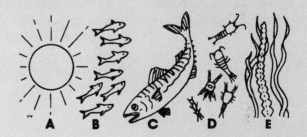

2. Name three types of aquatic habitats. Describe each habitat.

Thinking like a Scientist

Some scientists predict that the average temperature on the earth will increase at least several degrees in the near future. How would such an increase affect aquatic habitats? How would it affect each of the six major biomes?

5 Matter and Atoms

MATTER AND MASS
(pp. 112–114)

1. Which object on the balance has more mass, A or B?

2. What is weight?
3. How would an object's mass and weight be affected if it were taken from the earth to the moon?

Thinking like a Scientist

Suppose that you have two 1-L containers filled with water. You freeze one container. Which weighs more—the container of ice or the container of water? Explain your answer. Which has more mass? Explain your answer.

ATOMS
(pp. 115–116)

1. Identify the parts of the atom in the following drawing.

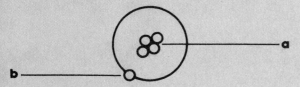

2. What kinds of particles can be found in the central part of an atom?
3. What are the paths in which particles travel around the central part of an atom called?

Thinking like a Scientist

The diameter of a golf ball is about half the diameter of an orange. If the nucleus of a hydrogen atom were the size of a golf ball, about how far away would the orbiting electron be?

GROUPING THE ELEMENTS
(pp. 117–121)

1. What is an element?
2. What would the atomic number of an atom be if it had 10 protons and 11 neutrons in the nucleus?
3. What is the atomic number of this atom?

4. What is the periodic table?

Thinking like a Scientist

Nearly 2,000 electrons equal the mass of 1 proton. About how many electrons would it take to equal the mass of the protons in one atom of the element neon?

COMPOUNDS AND MOLECULES

(pp. 122–123)

1. What is a compound?
2. What is a particle with two or more atoms that are chemically joined called?
3. Copy the following table. Use the formula for glucose, which is $C_6H_{12}O_6$, to fill in the table.

ELEMENT	SYMBOL	NUMBER OF ATOMS IN GLUCOSE
Carbon		
Hydrogen		
Oxygen		

Thinking like a Scientist

A mystery compound contains 100 atoms of carbon and 200 atoms of oxygen. What is the compound? Explain your answer.

KINDS OF COMPOUNDS

(pp. 124–129)

1. Identify each of the following as an acid or a base.
   a. Substance X has a bitter taste.
   b. Substance M turns blue litmus paper red.
   c. Substance G feels slippery.
   d. Substance Z turns red litmus paper blue.
2. What is an indicator?
3. What kind of compound is formed from an acid and a base?
4. Which of these are acids? Which are bases?
   a. lemon juice
   b. vinegar
   c. ammonia
   d. tea
   e. bleach
   f. baking soda

Thinking like a Scientist

About 100 years ago, coin collectors shined copper coins by using a mixture that included lemon juice. Why do you suppose lemon juice was used?

6 Chemical Changes in Matter

PROPERTIES AND CHANGES
(pp. 134–137)

1. Name two types of changes that matter can undergo. Give three examples of each.
2. Give three examples of physical properties.
3. Is this a physical change or is it a chemical change? Explain your answer.

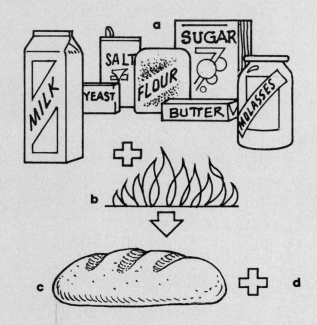

Thinking like a Scientist

Every chemical change is accompanied by a physical change. Describe three chemical changes that involve a change in one physical property, color.

CHEMICAL REACTIONS
(pp. 138–142)

1. Identify each part of the chemical reaction shown here.

2. Describe two kinds of chemical reactions.
3. What is meant by the law of conservation of matter?
4. What is meant by the law of conservation of energy?

Thinking like a Scientist

Explain how people in the following professions are involved with chemical reactions: auto-body mechanic, grocer, photographer, steelworker.

CHEMICAL BONDS
(pp. 143–144)

1. What are chemical bonds?
2. How is making a chemical compound like building a model with plastic blocks?
3. Explain what is happening here.

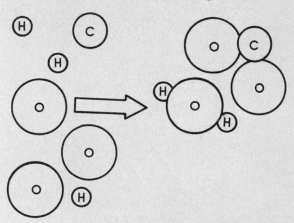

Thinking like a Scientist
Why is it easier to separate a mixture into its various elements than it is to separate a compound into its various elements?

OTHER CHANGES IN MATTER
(pp. 145–149)

1. What is nuclear energy?

2. Identify the following nuclear reactions.

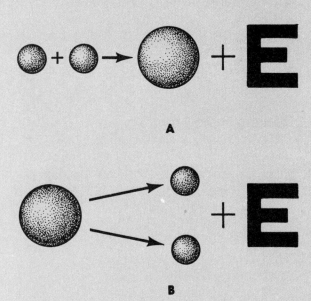

A

B

3. What is a radioactive element?

Thinking like a Scientist
Suppose the underground water supply in your area was found to be slightly radioactive. What could have caused this?

7 Light Energy

THE NATURE OF LIGHT
(pp. 154–159)

1. Which form of radiant energy is visible?
2. How does light travel?
3. Draw and label a diagram of a light wave.
4. What protects us from the ultraviolet rays of the sun?
5. What is the important difference between light and sound waves?

Thinking like a Scientist

What would happen if the sun suddenly disappeared? How long would it take for people on the earth to know that it disappeared? How would life on Earth be different?

THE BEHAVIOR OF LIGHT
(pp. 160–163)

1. Study the drawings below. Tell what happened to the light when it struck each object.

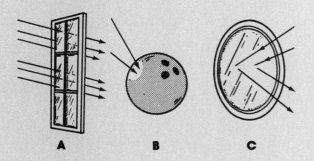

A   B   C

2. Give an example of transparent matter, an example of translucent matter, and an example of opaque matter.

Thinking like a Scientist

Suppose you were going to build the solar heater shown here. Tell whether you would make each of the labeled parts from a transparent material, a translucent material, or an opaque material.

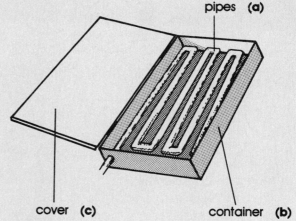

pipes (a)

cover (c)   container (b)

SEEING COLORS
(pp. 164–167)

1. How do colors of light differ?
2. If an object reflects green light and absorbs all other colors, what color will it be?
3. How can a prism affect white light?

Thinking like a Scientist

In 1819 Dr. Jan Purkinje observed that at twilight, red objects appear to fade faster than blue objects of the same brightness. Describe a simple experiment you could do to test this observation.

REFLECTION AND MIRRORS
(pp. 168–169)

1. What type of mirror produces a wide field of vision?
2. What type of mirror produces enlarged images?
3. Explain what is happening here.

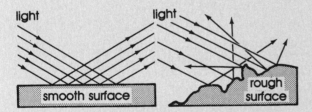

Thinking like a Scientist

Why does a trick mirror, such as the type found at fairs and circuses, make people look taller or shorter, and skinnier or fatter?

BENDING LIGHT WAVES
(pp. 170–172)

1. Why does a pencil appear to be bent when placed in a glass of water?

2. Identify the following lenses as being either concave or convex. Copy the lenses on another sheet of paper. Draw lines to show how light passes through each lens.

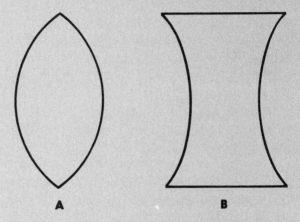

Thinking like a Scientist

A hawk hunts for food by soaring high above the ground. What kind of lens do you think a hawk's eyes have? Explain your answer.

MODERN USES OF LIGHT
(pp. 173–175)

1. List five uses of lasers.
2. How can the sun be used to produce electricity?

Thinking like a Scientist

In which areas of the world would solar heating be most difficult? Explain your answer.

8 Using Electricity

ELECTRONS AND ELECTRICITY
(pp. 180–181)

1. Describe a direct current.
2. Describe an alternating current.

Thinking like a Scientist
A galvanometer like the one shown here is an instrument that detects electric current. How do you think this instrument works?

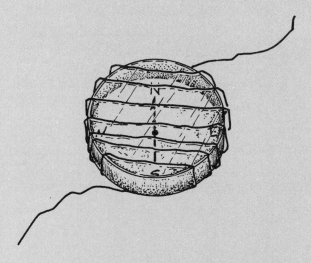

CIRCUITS
(pp. 182–184)

1. Name two types of circuits.
2. Make a drawing of a series circuit and a drawing of a parallel circuit.

Thinking like a Scientist
Which do you think produces more electricity—two batteries connected in a series circuit or two batteries connected in a parallel circuit? Explain your answer.

ELECTRICITY AND THE TELEPHONE
(pp. 185–188)

1. Explain how a telephone sends messages.
2. Explain how a telephone receives messages.

Thinking like a Scientist
Why do you suppose it is difficult to distinguish sounds such as "b" and "v" through a telephone receiver?

COPYING SOUND WAVES
(pp. 190–191)

1. Name two ways sound waves may be recorded.
2. How does a phonograph reproduce sound?

Thinking like a Scientist
Why do phonograph records that are warped produce distorted sounds?

RADIO AND TELEVISION
(pp. 193–195)

1. Identify the parts of the following drawing.

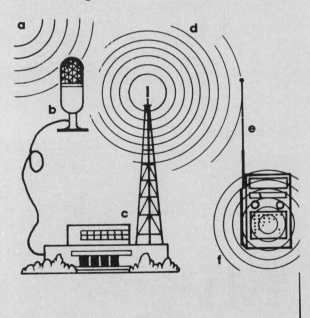

2. How are radio signals sent and received?

Thinking like a Scientist
How do you suppose wireless telephones work?

STORING AND USING INFORMATION
(pp. 196–201)

1. Name the parts of a computer that do each of the following jobs: input, control memory, display information, process information, store information.
2. List two things that microprocessors do for us.

Thinking like a Scientist
In what way is a computer like a human brain? How is it different?

9 The Earth's Resources

LIVING RENEWABLE RESOURCES
(pp. 212–213)

1. What is a renewable resource?
2. Why are plants and animals renewable resources?

Thinking like a Scientist

New inventions can have both good and bad effects on renewable resources. Name an invention that has had a good effect on a renewable resource. Name an invention that has had a bad effect on a renewable resource.

NONLIVING RENEWABLE RESOURCES
(pp. 214–215)

1. Give an example of a nonliving renewable resource and explain how it is renewed.
2. What would happen if there were no green plants on the earth?

Thinking like a Scientist

Farmers often vary the crop they plant in a field from year to year. Sometimes they plant crops and plow them under the ground without harvesting them. They might also plow their fields in curved rather than straight lines and plant rows of trees between fields. How does each of these practices protect or renew resources?

NONRENEWABLE RESOURCES
(pp. 216–219)

1. Copy the following chart. Classify the following items as renewable or nonrenewable: natural gas, granite, water, aluminum, gold, soil, limestone, trees, coal, people, air, diamond.

RENEWABLE	NONRENEWABLE

2. Define the term *minerals*. Give two examples of minerals.

Thinking like a Scientist

By using instruments on satellites, scientists have located places on the earth where many nonrenewable resources can be found. How will people benefit from this information? What problems might arise from obtaining this information?

RECYCLING
(pp. 220–221)

1. What is recycling?
2. Name three types of materials that can be recycled. Describe how each recycled material can be used.

Thinking like a Scientist
Some states have a law that requires all soft-drink containers be returnable. What is good about such a law? What problems might result from such a law?

FOSSIL FUEL RESOURCES
(pp. 223–226)

1. What are fossil fuels?
2. Identify the things shown here that are made from fossil fuel feedstocks.

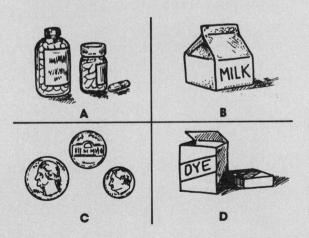

Thinking like a Scientist
Oil companies employ many scientists. What skills would scientists be able to offer the oil companies?

RESOURCES FROM THE OCEANS
(pp. 227–233)

1. Why is desalination useful?
2. What are nodules from the ocean floor? How are they used?
3. What is mariculture? Give two examples.
4. Copy the following chart. List examples of ocean resources in the first column. Describe a use for each resource in the second column.

RESOURCE	USE

Thinking like a Scientist
Choose one type of ocean food. Describe a way to farm the food. Describe several uses for your farm product. Describe problems that might come from farming the food.

10   Changes in the Earth's Crust

THE FLOATING CRUST

(pp. 238–243)

1. Describe the theory of continental drift.
2. Use the drawing below to describe the process of sea-floor spreading.

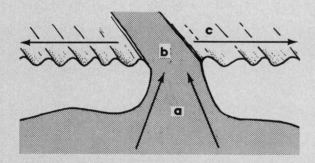

3. What is the plate tectonic theory?

Thinking like a Scientist

Many scientists before Alfred Wegener, had noticed how the continents seemed to fit together like pieces in a jigsaw puzzle. However, not many scientists supported Wegener's theory of continental drift. What do you think most scientists look for in a theory before they support it? Why has the plate tectonic theory gained support from most scientists?

EARTHQUAKES

(pp. 244–247)

1. Where do most earthquakes occur?
2. What causes earthquakes?
3. What is a seismograph and how is it used?
4. What signs may occur that can help predict earthquakes?

Thinking like a Scientist

Why is fire often a problem after an earthquake? Do earthquakes start fires?

VOLCANOES

(pp. 248–253)

1. Identify the three types of volcanoes in the drawing and explain how each is formed.

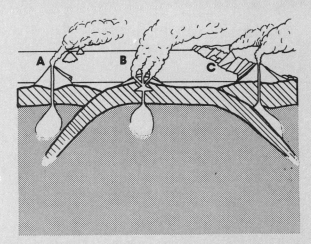

2. What is the Ring of Fire?

Thinking like a Scientist

Explain a way in which volcanoes might benefit people.

MOUNTAIN BUILDING

(pp. 254–257)

1. Describe the difference between folded mountains and fault-block mountains.
2. What is a dome mountain?
3. How can you tell an old mountain from a young mountain?

Thinking like a Scientist

What would the earth be like if all volcanoes, earthquakes, and mountain building stopped?

11 Forecasting the Weather

WEATHER INSTRUMENTS

(pp. 262–266)

1. What is meteorology?
2. Name and describe three instruments used to measure wind conditions.
3. What is relative humidity?
   Use these drawings of barometers to answer questions 4 through 7.

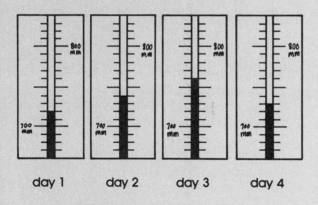

day 1   day 2   day 3   day 4

4. How did the air pressure change from day 1 to day 3?
5. What caused the changes from day 1 to day 3?
6. What probably caused the change from day 3 to day 4?
7. What was the weather probably like on day 4?

Thinking like a Scientist

Two people in different cities hang their clothes to dry on a clothesline. The temperature in city A is 25°C. The relative humidity is 50 percent. The temperature in city B is 25°C. The relative humidity is 90 percent. Which person's clothes will probably dry faster? Why?

COLLECTING WEATHER DATA

(pp. 267–269)

1. What kind of information is gathered by weather stations? How is this information used?
2. What instruments do weather stations use to collect data?
3. How are satellites used to collect weather data?

Thinking like a Scientist

Scientists make and save detailed records of their observations. Meteorologists, for example, keep detailed notes about weather conditions. Meteorologists in many cities have weather records for every day of the past 100 years. Why are these old records important to meteorologists?

WEATHER MAPS
(pp. 270–271)

1. Identify these symbols used on a weather map.

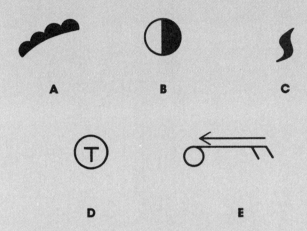

A   B   C

D   E

2. How are the movements of high- and low-pressure areas helpful in predicting weather changes?

Thinking like a Scientist

Look at the weather map on page 271. In general, weather systems move from west to east in North America. Predict the weather in your area during the 24 hours after this weather map was made.

WEATHER FORECASTS
(pp. 272–275)

1. What is the National Weather Service?
2. What is meant by visibility?
3. How is climate different from weather?

Thinking like a Scientist

On September 1 a computer is directed to make two forecasts. The first forecast is for the average temperature in the state of Texas for the entire month of September. The second forecast is for the exact high temperature in Dallas on September 22. Which forecast is likely to be more accurate? Why?

STORMS
(pp. 276–281)

1. What two conditions are necessary for a thunderstorm to form?
2. How are a tornado and a hurricane similar? How are they different?

Thinking like a Scientist

Why do pilots avoid flying through thunderheads?

12 Exploring Space

EXPLORING FROM EARTH
(pp. 286–290)

1. Name three things early people discovered about the sky.
2. Identify each kind of telescope shown here.

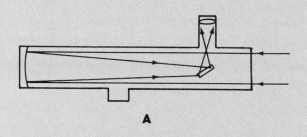

A

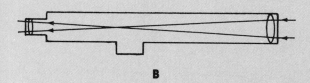

B

Thinking like a Scientist

Many scientists are looking forward to the day when observatories will be located on orbiting space stations. What advantages would there be to having these observatories? What problems might come from having them?

EXPLORING FROM SPACE
(pp. 291–297)

1. Use this drawing to explain how a rocket moves.

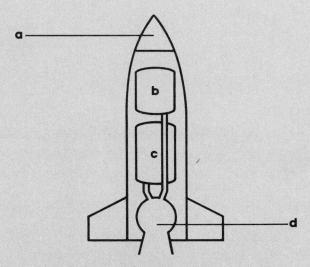

2. What is the difference between a satellite and a space probe?
3. What kind of information was gathered by early satellites?
4. How are satellites used today?

Thinking like a Scientist

Of all the satellites that have been launched, which do you think is the most important? Why? Many uses for satellites were discussed in this lesson. Describe another way you would like satellites to be used in the future.

PEOPLE IN SPACE
(pp. 298–300)

1. How does being in space affect a person's bones and muscles?
2. Identify the steps in this journey to the moon and back. Use the labels *liftoff, flight to moon, spacecraft orbiting moon, lunar module landing, flight to Earth, splashdown.*

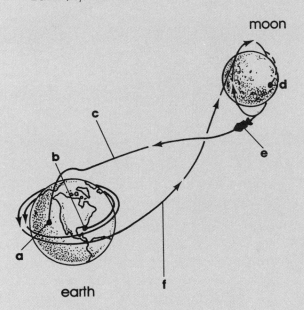

moon

earth

Thinking like a Scientist
Scientists consider as much information as possible before making a decision. Why do you think scientists chose Florida as a site for launching spacecraft?

THE FUTURE OF SPACE
(pp. 301–302)

1. What kind of activities might people be doing in space in the future?
2. Why may orbiting space stations be important in the future?

Thinking like a Scientist
In the future, many of the materials we use every day may come from space. Name three items that might have a ''Made in Space'' label in the future.

HOW SPACE EXPLORATION AFFECTS YOU
(pp. 303–305)

1. Describe some clothlike fabrics that were developed for use in space but are now being used on Earth.
2. Describe two developments from the space program that have been used in kitchens on Earth.

Thinking like a Scientist
Scientists who are involved with the space program are pleased to see the ways that space research has changed people's lives on Earth. But suppose that the space program did not benefit people on Earth immediately. Would the work done by scientists still be important? Why?

13 Control Systems of the Body

THE NERVOUS SYSTEM

(pp. 316–317)

1. What parts make up the nervous system?
2. What is the difference between the central nervous system and the peripheral nervous system? Name the parts that make up each type of nervous system.
3. Describe the difference between voluntary actions and involuntary actions. Give an example of each kind of action.

Thinking like a Scientist

What voluntary and involuntary actions take place to help your body produce and conserve heat when you are cold?

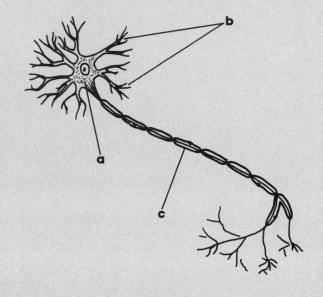

NERVE CELLS AND NERVES

(pp. 318–321)

1. Identify the parts of this drawing. Use the labels *cell body, fiber that carries messages to the next nerve cell,* and *fibers that pick up messages.*

2. Name three kinds of nerve cells. Tell what each kind of cell does.
3. What is a reflex?

Thinking like a Scientist

Suppose a mosquito was biting your left hand and you slapped it with your right hand. Is this a voluntary response, an involuntary response, or a reflex? Draw a diagram to show what pathways the nerve messages involved followed.

THE BRAIN AND SPINAL CORD

(pp. 322–325)

1. Identify the parts of the brain shown.

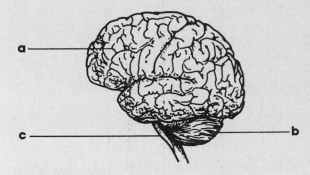

2. Describe the function of each brain part.

Thinking like a Scientist

Scientists do not do experiments on the brains of human beings. How do you think they learned what each part of the brain controls?

DISORDERS OF THE NERVOUS SYSTEM

(pp. 326–327)

1. Why is injury to the spinal cord very serious?

2. What causes cerebral palsy? What does cerebral palsy affect?

Thinking like a Scientist

When people suffer head injuries, a doctor will usually flash a bright light into the person's eyes. What do you think the doctor is observing?

THE ENDOCRINE SYSTEM

(pp. 328–333)

1. Describe the function of the pituitary gland.
2. Describe the function of the pancreas.
3. Describe the function of the adrenal gland.

Thinking like a Scientist

A doctor has recommended the following to two patients. Identify what might be wrong with each patient.

Patient 1: Take thyroxin tablets as prescribed. Use iodized salt.

Patient 2: Take insulin as required. Do not eat foods containing sugar.

14 Growth and Development

REPRODUCTION

(pp. 338–339)

1. Why is it important for living things to reproduce?
2. How is reproduction in a hydra similar to reproduction in a yeast?
3. How do many kinds of single-celled organisms reproduce?

Thinking like a Scientist

Sometimes pollution prevents living things from reproducing. For example, the eggshells of some pelicans were so thin that they often broke before the baby birds could hatch. A chemical called DDT is known to cause this problem. DDT is used to fight insects. But pelicans eat fish, not insects. How might the pelicans have taken in the DDT? Why is it important to protect living things from this type of pollution?

REPRODUCTION AND CELLS

(pp. 340–342)

1. What is the function of the nucleus in a cell?
2. This drawing shows a cell undergoing mitosis. The cell has 46 chromosomes. How many chromosomes would be found in each of the new cells?

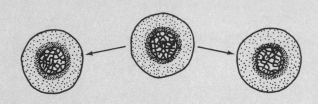

3. How are reproductive cells different from other cells in the body?
4. What is a zygote?

Thinking like a Scientist

Suppose a scientist observes three cells through a microscope. One cell contains 46 chromosomes, another contains 23 chromosomes, and the third contains 92 chromosomes. Explain what the scientist is observing.

A NEW ORGANISM DEVELOPS

(pp. 343–344)

1. How does a zygote develop into an organism with millions of cells?
2. What is an embryo? How is an embryo different from a zygote?

Thinking like a Scientist

Tables and graphs help scientists come to conclusions about what they observe. Study the table on page 344. What can you conclude about the relationship between an organism's development time and its size?

PASSING ON INFORMATION

(pp. 345–351)

1. What are inherited traits? Give three examples.
2. What are genes? Where are they found?
3. Study these drawings. The gene for brown eyes (B) is dominant over the gene for blue eyes (b). Determine the eye color of each offspring.

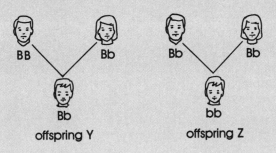

offspring Y   offspring Z

Thinking like a Scientist

Some horse-stable owners pay large amounts of money for a colt or mare before it is born. Why are the offspring of famous racehorses so valuable?

THE LIFE CYCLE

(pp. 352–353)

1. Describe childhood.
2. Describe adulthood.
3. Describe infancy.
4. Describe adolescence.

Thinking like a Scientist

Children who are 13 years old usually seem much older than children who are 8 years old. Yet when these people are adults, a 5-year difference in age is hardly noticed. Why is this so?

GLOSSARY

absorbed   Action in which light waves are trapped by matter. *p. 161*

acid   A compound that contains hydrogen and that has a sour taste. *p. 124*

adaptation (ad ap tā′shən)   Any structure or response that helps an organism to survive. *p. 35*

adolescence (ad ə les′əns)   Stage of human life that follows childhood and that involves rapid growth and change. *p. 353*

adrenal (ə drē′nəl) **glands**   Two glands, one at the top of each kidney, that release hormones that help a person deal with stress and emergencies. *p. 332*

adulthood   The final stage of human life. *p. 353*

air pressure   The push of air on all surfaces. *p. 266*

alternating (ôl′tər nā ting) **current**   Current electricity in which the electrons flow first in one direction and then in the opposite direction. *p. 180*

anemometer (an ə mom′ə tər)   An instrument that is used to measure wind speed. *p. 263*

annual rings   Rings of wood that are produced yearly by growth tissue in the stems of trees. *p. 31*

aquatic (ə kwat′ik) **habitat**   A body of water where organisms live. *p. 97*

astronomy (ə stron′ə mē)   The study of space and the many things it contains. *p. 286*

atom   The smallest particle of an element. *p. 117*

atomic number   The number of protons in the nucleus of an atom. *p. 118*

bacteria (bak tir′ē ə)   The simplest protists. *p. 19*

barometer (bə rom′ə tər)   An instrument that is used to measure air pressure. *p. 266*

base   A compound that contains oxygen and hydrogen and that has a bitter taste and feels slippery. *p. 125*

behavior   The activities and actions of an animal. *p. 62*

biological clock   A chemical clock by which an organism controls the timing of certain activities. *p. 43*

biome (bī′ōm)   All the plants and animals that live in a region that has a particular climate. *p. 78*

brain stem   The part of the brain that controls such involuntary actions as breathing and heartbeat. *p. 322*

breeding grounds   Regions to which certain animals migrate to reproduce and to raise their young. *p. 64*

buoys (boiz)   Objects that float on the ocean and that record and transmit weather data. *p. 269*

canines (kā′nīnz)   Sharp pointed teeth found near the front of the mouth. Such teeth are large in meat-eating animals. *p. 52*

cell   The smallest living part of an organism *p. 6*   A device in which chemical energy is changed to electrical energy. *p. 307*

cell wall   The thick wall that is found outside the plasma membrane of a plant cell. *p. 10*

central nervous system   The brain and spinal cord. *p. 316*

cerebellum (ser ə bel′əm)   The part of the brain that controls body balance. *p. 323*

cerebrum (ser′ə brəm)   The part of the brain that controls thinking and reasoning. *p. 323*

chemical bonds   The forces that hold together the atoms in a compound. *p. 143*

chemical change   A change in which one or more different kinds of matter are formed. *p. 135*

chemical energy   Energy stored in chemical bonds. *p. 144*

chemical property   A property that determines how an element or compound reacts with other elements or compounds. *p. 136*

chemical reaction (rē ak′shən)   A chemical change. *p. 138*

childhood   Stage of human life following infancy. *p. 352*

chlorophyll (klôr′ə fil)   The chemical in plant cells that traps energy from sunlight. *p. 11*

chloroplast (klôr′ə plast)   The structure in a plant cell that contains the green chemical called chlorophyll. Food is made in chloroplasts. *p. 11*

chromosomes (krō′mə sōmz)   Threadlike structures found in the nucleus that contain a cell's genes. *p. 7*

climate   The average weather for a large region over a long period of time. *p. 78*

climatologist (klī mə tol′ə jist)   A scientist who studies climate. *p. 275*

cold-blooded animal   An animal whose body temperature changes as the temperature of the environment changes. *p. 66*

combustion chamber   The chamber in a rocket in which fuel is burned. *p. 291*

compound (kom′pound)   A substance made up of two or more elements that are chemically joined. *p. 122*

computer   A device that can store and use information. *p. 196*

concave lens   A lens that is thinner in the middle than at the edge. *p. 171*

concave (kon kāv′) **mirror**   A mirror in which the reflecting surface curves inward. *p. 169*

conifers (kō′nə fərz)   Trees that produce seeds in cones. *p. 83*

connecting nerve cells   Nerve cells that connect sensory nerve cells with motor nerve cells. *p. 319*

continental (kon tə nen′təl) **drift theory**   The theory that the continents were once part of a single land mass that broke up, with the continents then drifting apart. *p. 239*

convex lens   A lens that is thicker in the middle than it is at the edge. *p. 171*

convex (kon veks′) **mirror**   A mirror in which the reflecting surface curves outward. *p. 169*

crest   The top of a wave. *p. 155*

cytoplasm (sī′tə plaz əm)   The jellylike material outside the nucleus of a cell. *p. 7*

deciduous (di sij′ü əs) **forest**   A biome in which broad-leaved trees are prominent. *p. 85*

desalination (dē sal ə nā′shən)   The process by which salt is separated from seawater. *p. 227*

desert   A biome that receives little or no rain. *p. 94*

direct current   Current electricity in which the electrons flow in only one direction. *p. 180*

dome mountain   A mountain that forms when magma pushes the crust up and then hardens under the crust. *p. 256*

dominant gene   A gene that, when present, determines a trait of an offspring. *p. 349*

downdraft (doun′draft)   A falling air current. *p. 277*

earthquake   A movement of the earth's crust. *p. 244*

egg cell   The female reproductive cell. *p. 341*

electrons (i lek′tronz)   Particles that move around the nucleus of an atom. *p. 116*

element (el′ə mənt)   A substance made up of only one kind of atom. *p. 117*

embryo (em′brē ō)   An organism during the early stages of its development. *p. 343*

endocrine (en′dō krin) **system**   A system that helps control the rate of many body activities by releasing chemicals called hormones. *p. 328*

environment (en vī′rən mənt)   The conditions that are found where an organism lives. The environment includes all the living and nonliving things in an area. *p. 32*

estuary (es′chü er ē)   An aquatic habitat where a freshwater river flows into the ocean. *p. 100*

fault-block mountains   Mountains that form when blocks of crust on one side of a fault move up while blocks of crust on the other side move down. *p. 255*

faults   Cracks in the earth's crust where blocks of rock have moved. *p. 245*

feedstock   A raw material from which other materials are made. *p. 223*

fertile (fẻr'təl)   Condition in which soil is rich in the minerals that plants need to grow. *p. 215*

fertilization (fẻr tə lə zā'shən)   The process by which a sperm cell and an egg cell join. *p. 342*

focus   The place where blocks of rock slip during an earthquake. *p. 245*

folded mountains   Mountains that form as a result of collisions between plates. *p. 255*

forecast   A statement of what the weather will probably be like in the next few days. *p. 262*

fossil fuels   Fuels that have formed from the bodies of dead plants and animals. *p. 223*

frequency (frē'kwən sē)   The number of waves that pass a point in a certain period of time. *p. 156*

freshwater habitat   An aquatic habitat such as a pond, lake, or stream. *p. 97*

genes   The units that control a cell's activities. Genes control the growth and development of an organism. *p. 7*

glands   Special organs or tissues in the body that make chemical substances. *p. 328*

grassland biome   A biome in which grasses are prominent and trees are scarce. *p. 91*

growth regions   The areas within a plant where growth takes place. Such areas contain growth tissue. *p. 28*

hibernation (hī bər nā'shən)   The very deep sleep in which some animals spend the winter. *p. 66*

hormones (hôr'mōnz)   Chemicals produced by the endocrine glands. *p. 328*

hurricane (hẻr'ə kān)   A large storm involving strong winds and heavy rain that develops over the ocean in a tropical area. *p. 280*

incisors (in sī'zərz)   Sharp front teeth used by meat-eating animals to tear off chunks of flesh. *p. 52*

indicator (in'də kā tər)   A substance that changes color when it is added to an acid or a base. *p. 126*

infancy   Stage of human life occurring after birth and lasting for several months. *p. 352*

infrared (in frə red') **waves**   Waves of radiant energy with lower frequencies than light waves. *p. 157*

inherited traits   Traits or features that are passed on from parents to offspring. *p. 346*

instinct (in'stingkt)   Any behavior pattern that an animal is born with. *p. 62*

integrated circuit   A circuit in which all parts and connections are contained on a chip. *p. 184*

isobar (ī′sə bär)   A line on a weather map connecting places that have the same air pressure. *p. 270*

isotherm (ī′sə therm)   A line on a weather map connecting areas that have the same temperature. *p. 270*

laser (lā′zər)   A device that strengthens light. *p. 173*

lava   Magma that reaches the earth's surface. *p. 249*

law of conservation of energy   The law that states that energy is neither created nor destroyed during a chemical reaction. *p. 142*

law of conservation of matter   The law that states that matter is neither created nor destroyed during a chemical reaction. *p. 142*

lens (lenz)   A transparent material having at least one curved surface. *p. 170*

life cycle   The stages that a living thing goes through during its life. *p. 352*

magma (mag′mə)   Melted rock that forms below the earth's crust. *p. 249*

mariculture   Farming of the oceans for food. *p. 231*

marine habitat   An aquatic habitat in which the water is salt water. *p. 98*

mass   A measure of the amount of matter in an object. *p. 112*

matter   Anything that has mass and takes up space. *p. 112*

memory circuits   Circuits in a computer that store information. *p. 197*

meteorologist (mē tē ə rol′ə jist)   A scientist who studies weather. *p. 262*

meteorology (mē tē ə rol′ə jē)   The study of weather. *p. 262*

microprocessor (mī krō pros′es ər)   A chip, found in many kinds of computers and other devices, that contains problem-solving circuits. *p. 197*

migration (mī grā′shən)   The movement of an animal or a group of animals over a long distance. *p. 64*

mimicry (mim′ik rē)   An adaptation in which an animal looks like a dangerous or poisonous animal. *p. 61*

mineral (min′ər əl)   Any useful material that is found in the earth's crust. *p. 217*

mitosis (mī tō′sis)   The process by which a cell divides to form two cells. *p. 14*

molars (mō′lərz)   The flat teeth found along the sides of the mouth. Such teeth are large in grazing animals. *p. 52*

molecule (mol′ə kyül)   A chemical unit made up of two or more atoms. *p. 122*

motor nerve cells   Nerve cells that carry messages from the central nervous system to parts of the body such as muscles. *p. 319*

native metals   Metals that are not chemically combined with other materials. *p. 218*

natural resource (ri sôrs′)   A valuable material that is found in nature and used by people to meet their needs. *p. 212*

nerve cells   Cells that carry messages in the nervous system. *p. 318*

nervous system   A system that helps control body activities. It includes the brain, spinal cord, and a network of nerve cells. *p. 316*

neutral (nü′trəl)   The condition of a substance that is neither an acid nor a base. *p. 126*

neutron (nü′tron)   A particle found in the nucleus of an atom. *p. 116*

nodules (noj′ülz)   Round lumps found on the ocean floor that contain certain metals. *p. 230*

nonrenewable (non ri nü′ə bəl) **resource** A resource that exists in a limited amount. *p. 216*

nuclear energy   Energy that is stored in the nucleus of an atom. *p. 145*

nuclear fission (fish′ən)   The splitting of a nucleus into smaller parts. *p. 145*

nuclear fusion (fyü′zhən)   The joining, or combining, of nuclei. *p. 147*

nuclear (nü′klē ər) **reaction**   A reaction involving the nuclei of atoms. *p. 145*

nucleus (nü′klē əs)   A round body inside the cell. It contains the genes. *p. 7*   The central part of an atom. *p. 116*

observatory (əb zėr′və tôr ē)   A building that is set up for the study of outer space. *p. 288*

opaque (ō pāk′)   Condition of matter through which light cannot pass. *p. 162*

orbits   The paths that electrons move in. *p. 116*

ore   Rock or mineral from which useful metal can be obtained. *p. 217*

organ (ôr′gən)   A group of tissues working together to carry out a body activity. *p. 22*

organism (ôr′gə niz əm)   A living thing. *p. 6*

pancreas (pan′krē əs)   An organ that produces substances that help digest food and that also produces a hormone which controls how the cells use sugar. *p. 330*

parathyroid (par ə thī′roid) **glands**   Four small endocrine glands that produce hormones which control the amount of calcium and other minerals found in the blood. *p. 330*

periodic table   A chart containing many facts about elements and their atoms. *p. 120*

peripheral (pə rif′ər əl) **nervous system** The nerves that extend from the central nervous system to the edges of the body. *p. 317*

phototropism (fō tō trō′piz əm)   The response of a plant to light. *p. 33*

physical change   A change in the size, shape, or state of matter. *p. 134*

physical property   A property that can be identified without causing a chemical change in the matter. *p. 135*

pituitary (pi tü′ə ter ē) **gland**   An endocrine gland that is important to normal growth. *p. 328*

plankton (plangk′tən)   Microscopic plants that float on the surface of the ocean. *p. 98*

plasma membrane (plaz′mə   mem′brān) The structure that surrounds the cell and helps to control the movement of materials into and out of the cell. *p. 8*

plate tectonic (tek ton´ik) **theory**   The theory that the crust of the earth is made up of sections, called plates, that are in motion. *p. 241*

plates   The sections of crust that move over the earth, according to the plate tectonic theory. *p. 241*

printed circuit   Circuit in which the transistors and all other parts are connected with flat wires. *p. 183*

prism (priz´əm)   A specially shaped transparent object that is used to separate light. *p. 164*

program   A set of instructions that tells a computer what to do. *p. 198*

protective coloration (prə tek´tiv   kul-ə rā´shən)   The structural adaptation in which an animal has a color similar to the color of its environment. *p. 59*

protective resemblance (ri zem´bləns)   The adaptation in which an animal looks similar to something in its environment. *p. 60*

protist (prō´tist)   A single-celled organism. *p. 17*

proton (prō´ton)   A particle found in the nucleus of an atom. *p. 116*

protozoans (prō tə zō´ənz)   Animallike protists. *p. 17*

radiant (rā´dē ənt) **energy**   Energy that travels through space in the form of waves. Light is one kind of radiant energy. *p. 154*

radio telescope   A telescope that collects radio waves given off by objects in space. *p. 289*

radio transmitter   A device for producing radio waves. *p. 194*

radioactive (rā dē ō ak´tiv) **elements**   Elements that break down into other elements. *p. 148*

reaction time   The time it takes for a person to react when messages travel to and from the brain. *p. 320*

receiver   The part of a telephone that changes electric current to sound waves. *p. 186*

recessive gene   A gene that does not determine a trait when paired with a dominant gene. *p. 349*

recycling (rē sī´kling)   The collecting and re-treating of materials so that they can be reused. *p. 220*

reflected   Action in which light waves are bounced off matter. *p. 161*

reflecting telescope   A telescope that uses a curved mirror to gather light. *p. 287*

reflex   A response in which messages travel over sensory nerve cells to the spinal cord and directly back to motor nerve cells. *p. 320*

refracting telescope   A telescope that uses a lens to gather light. *p. 287*

refraction (ri frak´shən)   A change in the direction of a light wave as it travels from one transparent material to another. *p. 170*

relative humidity   The amount of water vapor in the air compared with the most the air can hold at that temperature. *p. 264*

renewable (ri nü´ə bəl) **resource**   A resource that is replaced naturally. *p. 212*

reproduction   The process by which living things produce other living things of the same kind. *p. 338*

response (ri spons′)   A reaction of an organism to something in its environment. *p. 32*

rocket   A vehicle that is used to send objects into space. *p. 291*

salt   A compound made from an acid and a base. *p. 126*

satellite (sat′ə līt)   An object that orbits a larger object. Satellites are used to study space and also to study conditions on earth, such as weather. *p. 292*

sea-floor spreading   Process by which hot liquid rock flows up through cracks in the ocean floor, hardens to new ocean floor, and pushes older floor material outward. *p. 240*

seismograph (sīz′mə graf)   An instrument that can measure and record earthquake waves. *p. 246*

sensory nerve cells   Nerve cells that carry information to the brain and spinal cord. *p. 319*

solar still   A device that uses energy from the sun to separate salt from sea water. *p. 228*

space probe   A spacecraft sent out to gather data about the moon or the planets. *p. 295*

spectrum (spek′trəm)   The bands of color that when mixed produce white light. *p. 164*

sperm cell   The male reproductive cell. *p. 341*

stimulus (stim′yə ləs)   A condition in the environment that can cause a response. *p. 33*

structural adaptation   An adaptation that involves some part of an organism's body. *p. 50*

system   A group of organs that work together to do a major job that keeps an organism alive. *p. 22*

taiga (tī′gə)   A large biome south of the tundra. Conifers are abundant in the taiga. *p. 83*

theory (thē′ər ē)   An idea that is used to explain observed facts. *p. 239*

thunderstorm (thun′dər stôrm)   A storm in which violent air currents, rain or hail, and lightning are produced. *p. 276*

thyroid (thī′roid) **gland**   An endocrine gland located in the neck. It produces a hormone that controls how fast cells obtain energy from food. *p. 330*

tissue (tish′ü)   A team of cells in a plant or animal that does a special job. *p. 21*

tornado   A very violent, short-lived windstorm. *p. 278*

translucent (trans lü′sənt)   Condition of matter in which light is scattered as it passes through. *p. 162*

transmitted   Action in which light waves are passed through matter. *p. 161*

transmitter (trans mit′ər)   The part of a telephone that changes sound waves to electric current. *p. 186*

transparent   Condition of matter in which light can pass through without being scattered. *p. 162*

tropical rain forest　A biome that has a warm, rainy climate and that contains a rich variety of plant and animal life. *p. 88*

tropisms (trō′piz əmz)　Plant responses that involve growth. *p. 33*

trough (trôf)　The bottom of a wave. *p. 155*

tundra (tun′drə)　A large biome of the Far North. It is the coldest biome. *p. 81*

ultraviolet (ul trə vī′ə lit) **waves**　Waves of radiant energy with higher frequencies than light waves have. *p. 157*

updraft (up′draft)　A rising air current. *p. 276*

upwelling　Action in which ocean water from the bottom rises to the surface. *p. 99*

vacuoles (vak′yü ōlz)　Clear structures in a cell that contain stored food. *p. 8*

vacuum (vak′yüm)　Any space that contains little or no matter. *p. 159*

visibility (viz ə bil′ə tē)　The distance an average person can see under existing weather conditions. *p. 273*

volcano　An opening in the earth's crust through which magma, ash, and steam erupt. *p. 248*

warm-blooded animal　An animal that has a fairly constant body temperature. *p. 67*

wavelength　The distance between the crest of one wave and the crest of the next wave. *p. 156*

weather map　A map on which the weather conditions over a large area are recorded. *p. 270*

weight　A measure of the force of gravity on an object. *p. 113*

wet-and-dry-bulb thermometer　An instrument that is used to measure relative humidity. *p. 264*

wind sock　An instrument that can show both wind speed and wind direction. *p. 263*

wind vane　An instrument that is used to determine wind direction. *p. 263*

zygote (zī′gōt)　Cell formed when a sperm cell and an egg cell join. *p. 392*

INDEX

CREDITS

Cover: Taylor Oughton
Portrait art: Gregory Hergert
Other art: Ralph Brillhardt, Gail Eisnitz, Robert Jackson, Phillip Jones, Joseph LeMonnier, John Lind, Alan Neider, Taylor Oughton, Sally Schaedler, Ric Del Rossi, Rebecca Merrilees, Heidi Palmer
Map, b.242, adapted from DISCOVER Magazine, ©1982, Mark Kaplan

Unit One vi–1: E.R. Degginger; except 1 *l.* Robert Ross/E.R. Degginger

Chapter 1 2–3: ©Spike Haller/Photo Researchers, Inc. 4: *t.* Z. Leszczynski/ Breck P. Kent; *m.* © Gilbert Grant/Photo Researchers, Inc.; *b.* © Thomas W. Martin/Photo Researchers, Inc. 5: *t.l.* E.R. Degginger; *t.r.* © Jeff Apoian/Photo Researchers, Inc.; *b.* © Cosmos Blank, National Audubon Society Collection/ Photo Researchers, Inc. 6: *t.* Silver Burdett; *b.* E.R. Degginger. 9: Silver Burdett. 11: *l.* Roland Birke/Peter Arnold, Inc.; *r.* Alfred Owczarzak/Taurus Photos. 12: *l.* Alfred Owczarzak/Taurus Photos; *r.* Manfred Kage/Peter Arnold, Inc. 13: Silver Burdett. 16: *t.* E.R. Degginger; *b.* Silver Burdett. 17: Phil Degginger. 18: *l.* Manfred Kage/Peter Arnold, Inc. 19: E.R. Degginger; *inset* Alfred Pasieka, Science Photo Library/Taurus Photos. 20: James Somers, Science Photo Library/ Taurus Photos. 21: Manfred Kage/Peter Arnold, Inc. 22: Rita Meyers/Tom Stack & Associates. 23: Ginger Chih/Peter Arnold, Inc.

Chapter 2 26–27: Dr. G.J. Chafaris/E.R. Degginger. 28: Manfred Kage/Peter Arnold, Inc. 29: L.L.T. Rhodes/Taurus Photos. 30: Imagery. 31: J. Dermid/Bruce Coleman, Inc. 32: Imagery. 33: *t.* Grant Heilman Photography; *b.* Breck P. Kent. 34–35 *t.:* Silver Burdett; 35 *b.* Hickson-Bender Photography for Silver Burdett. 36: *l.* Stephen J. Krasemann/Peter Arnold, Inc.; *r.* Breck P. Kent. 37: *t.* E.R. Degginger; *b.* © Harald Sund. 38: Dan De Wilde for Silver Burdett. 39: E.R. Degginger; *r.* Stephen J. Krasemann/Peter Arnold, Inc. 42: *l.* Grant Heilman Photography; *r.* Breck P. Kent. 43: *t.* Imagery; *b.* Grant Heilman Photography. 44: Silver Burdett. 45: Grant Heilman Photography

Chapter 3 48–49: W. Perry Conway/Grant Heilman Photography. 51: *l.* Hans Pfletschinger/Peter Arnold, Inc.; *r.* Stephen J. Krasemann/Peter Arnold, Inc. 52: *t.* Norman O. Tomalin/Bruce Coleman; *b.* Steve Allen/Peter Arnold, Inc. 53: Jen and Des Bartlett/Bruce Coleman. 54: *t.* © Tom McHugh/Photo Researchers, Inc.; *b.* M. P. Kahl/Bruce Coleman. 55: *t.* Norman O. Tomalin/Bruce Coleman; *b.* John Mac-Gregor/Peter Arnold, Inc. 56: *t.* C. Allan Morgan/Peter Arnold, Inc.; *b.* Jerry L. Hout/Bruce Coleman. 57: *t.* Stephen J. Krasemann/Peter Arnold, Inc.; *m.* A. Blank/Bruce Coleman; *b.* Breck P. Kent. 58: Silver Burdett. 59: Breck P. Kent/ Bruce Coleman. 60: *t.* © Alan Carey/Photo Researchers, Inc.; *m.* © Charlie Ott/ Photo Researchers, Inc.; *b.* G. Ziesler/Peter Arnold, Inc. 61: *t.* Lynn M. Stone/ Bruce Coleman; *b.* Kevin Byron/Bruce Coleman. 62: R.R. Pawlowski/Bruce Coleman. 63: *t.* E.R. Degginger; *b.* Larry Riley/Bruce Coleman. 64: E.R. Degginger. 65: *t.* Gordon Langsbury/Bruce Coleman; *b.* Blum/Peter Arnold, Inc. 66: E.R. Degginger/Bruce Coleman. 67: *t.* E.R. Degginger; *b.* Norman O. Tomalin/Bruce Coleman. 68: *t.* Breck P. Kent; *b.* Tom Brakefield/Bruce Coleman. 70: Laura Riley/ Bruce Coleman. 71: *t.* Walter Chandoha; *b.* Stephen J. Krasemann/Peter Arnold, Inc. 72: Life Nature Library *Animal Behavior;* photographed by Nina Leen; © 1965 Time Inc., Time-Life Books, publisher. 73: Courtesy The Seeing Eye, Inc., Morristown, N.J.

Chapter 4 76–77: Lester Tinker/Taurus Photos. 81: Gary Meszaros/Bruce Coleman; *inset* © Charlie Ott/Photo Researchers, Inc. 82: *t.* Laura Riley/Bruce Coleman; *m.* Ralph Hunt Williams/Bruce Coleman; *b.* Clara Calhoun/Bruce Coleman. 83: K. Gunnar/Bruce Coleman; *inset* Breck P. Kent. 84: *t.l.* Wayne Lankinen/Bruce Coleman; *t.r.* Bob and Clara Calhoun/Bruce Coleman; *b.* © Tom McHugh/Photo Researchers, Inc. 85: George Rockwin/Bruce Coleman; *inset* © John Serrao/ Photo Researchers, Inc. 86: *t.* S.L. Craig/Bruce Coleman; *b.l.* E.R. Degginger/ Bruce Coleman; *b.r.* Harry Engels/Bruce Coleman. 87: *t.l.* © Leonard Lee Rue III, National Audubon Society Collection/Photo Researchers, Inc.; *t.r.* Tom Brakefield/Bruce Coleman; *b.* E.R. Degginger/Bruce Coleman. 88: J. Ehlera/Bruce Coleman; *inset* E.R. Degginger. 89: *t.l.* M. P. Kahl/Bruce Coleman; *t.r.* Joe McDonald/Bruce Coleman; *b.* E.R. Degginger/Bruce Coleman. 90: *t.* C.B. and D.W. Frith/Bruce Coleman; *b.l.* K.W. Fink/Bruce Coleman; *b.r.* Michael Fogden/ Bruce Coleman. 91: Joy Spurr/Bruce Coleman; *inset* Grant Heilman Photography. 92: *t.l.* George and Lois Cox/Bruce Coleman; *t.r.* Hans Reinhard/Bruce Coleman; *b.* Jeff Foott/Bruce Coleman. 93: *t.* Joseph Van Wormer/Bruce Coleman; *b.* E.R. Degginger. 94: *t.* John Shaw/Bruce Coleman; *b.* Martin Grosnick/Bruce Coleman. 95: *t.* M.P.L. Fogden; *b.l.* E.R. Degginger; *b.r.* Lynda M. Stone/Bruce Coleman. 97: *t.* © Rod Planck/Photo Researchers, Inc.; *m.* © Patricia Caulfield/Photo Researchers, Inc.; *b.* Larry Ditto/Bruce Coleman; *inset* © Tom Evans/Photo Researchers, Inc. 98: *t.* Jack Dermid/Bruce Coleman; *inset* Kim Taylor/Bruce Coleman; *m.* Chris Newbert/Bruce Coleman; *b.* Jeff Foott/Bruce Coleman. 99: Jeff Rotman/Peter Arnold, Inc. 100: *t.* D.J. Lyons/Bruce Coleman; *t.r.* F. Simon/Bruce Coleman; *b.l.* Jeff Foott/Bruce Coleman; *b.r.* Michael Gallagher/Bruce Coleman. 101: Werner Muller/Peter Arnold, Inc. 104: *l.* Phil Degginger; *r.* E.R. Degginger. 105: Ron and Valerie Taylor/Tom Stack & Associates.

Unit Two 108: Michael Marlow/Bruce Coleman. 108–109: David Madison/Bruce Coleman. 109: *t.l.* Vito Palmisano/Taurus Photos; *t.r.* Runk/Schoenberger/Grant Heilman Photography; *b.* E.R. Degginger.

Chapter 5 110–111: D. Brewster/Bruce Coleman. 112: Silver Burdett. 113: NASA. 114: Silver Burdett. 115: Courtesy Brookhaven National Laboratory. 117: Hickson-Bender Photography for Silver Burdett. 124–128: Silver Burdett.

Chapter 6 132–133: Ron Singer/Shostal Associates. 134: *t.* W.E. Ruth/Bruce Coleman; *b.l.* Jonathan Wright/Bruce Coleman; *b.m.* Leo DeWys, Inc.; *b.r.* D. Brewster/Bruce Coleman. 135: *t.* Jay Hoops/Leo DeWys, Inc.; *b.* E.R. Degginger. 137: Silver Burdett. 138: *t.* J. Gerard Smith; *b.* Charles E. Rotkin/Photography for Industry. 139–140: Silver Burdett. 141: Silver Burdett; except *l.* D. Brewster/ Bruce Coleman. 142: Hickson-Bender Photography for Silver Burdett. 144: Silver Burdett. 146: *t.* E.R. Degginger; *b.* George D. Lepp/Bruce Coleman. 148: *t.* Jay Lurie/Bruce Coleman; *b.* © Paolo Koch/Photo Researchers, Inc. 149: NASA.

Chapter 7 152–153: Andy Levin/Black Star. 154: Silver Burdett. 155: J. Gerard Smith. 157: Phil Degginger. 158: *t.* Jeffrey Reed/The Stock Shop; *b.* E. Johnson/ Leo DeWys, Inc. 159: NASA. 160: *t.l., t.r.* Silver Burdett; *b.* Hickson-Bender Photography for Silver Burdett. 161: Tom Stack & Associates. 162–163: Silver Burdett. 164: Runk/Schoenberger/Grant Heilman Photography. 165: H. Oizinger/ Leo DeWys, Inc. 166–172: Silver Burdett. 173: *t.* Gary Millburn/Tom Stack & Associates; *b.* David York-Larry Mulvehill/The Stock Shop. 174: *t.* Dick Luria/The Stock Shop; *b.* courtesy Bell Laboratories. 175: Alec Duncan/Taurus Photos.

Chapter 8 180–181: Jim Nachtwey/Black Star. 182: Dan De Wilde for Silver Burdett. 183: *t.* Vince Streano/Bruce Coleman; *b.r.* John Crosley/Shostal Associates. 185: Peter Bryon for Silver Burdett. 186: *t.* John V.A.F. Neal/Photo Researchers, Inc. 188: Princeton University Plasma Physics Laboratory. 191: *t.* Silver Burdett; *b.* Richard Choy/Peter Arnold, Inc. 192: *t.* T. Zimberoff/Sygma; *b.* NASA. 193: Sygma. 194: Dan De Wilde for Silver Burdett. 195: Breck P. Kent. 196: Photo Trends. 198: *l.* Jen and Des Bartlett/Bruce Coleman; *r.* Kurt Scholtz/Shostal Associates. 199: *l.* Heinz Herfort/Bruce Coleman; *r.* Dick Garvey/West Stock. 200–201: Silver Burdett. 202: *t.* © Paolo Koch/Photo Researchers, Inc.; *b.* Breta Westlund/ Tom Stack & Associates. 204: *t.* Tom Tracy/The Stock Shop; *b.* Warren D. Coleman/Tom Stack & Associates. 206: *l.* A. D'Arazien/Shostal Associates; *r.* Don Arms/Tom Stack & Associates. 207: Schomburg Center for Research in Black Culture, New York Public Library.

Unit Three 208–209: *t.* S.J. Flannery/Bruce Coleman; *b.* Tersch Enterprises. 209: *t.m.* © 1985 Ira Block/Woodfin Camp & Associates; *t.r.* © Dan Guravich/ Photo Researchers, Inc.; *b.r.* G.D. Plage/Bruce Coleman.

Chapter 9 210–211: Philip Wallick/Alpha. 213: *t.* Jeff Foott/Bruce Coleman; *b.* Robert P. Carr/Bruce Coleman. 215: George Riley/Stock, Boston. 216: *l.* D.P. Hershkowitz/Bruce Coleman; *r.* E.R. Degginger/Bruce Coleman. 217: Hickson-Bender Photography for Silver Burdett. 218: Owen Franken/Stock, Boston; *inset* Rick Smolen/Leo DeWys, Inc. 220: Silver Burdett; except *b.r.* Bohdan Hrynewych/Stock, Boston. 221–222: Silver Burdett. 224: Nicholas DeVore III/Bruce Coleman. 225: Bob Evans/Peter Arnold, Inc. 227: Andy Rakoczy/Shostal Associates. 229: Silver Burdett. 230: Courtesy Dr. N.L. Zenkevitch; *inset* Christopher Springman. 231: W.H. Hodge/Peter Arnold, Inc.; *inset* M. Timothy O'Keefe/Bruce Coleman. 232: W.H. Hodge/Peter Arnold, Inc.

Chapter 10 236–237: © 1985 Kal Muller/Woodfin Camp & Associates. 238: Silver Burdett. 239: Courtesy Dr. Takeo Susuki, UCLA. 244: Dan De Wilde for Silver Burdett. 245: © 1985 George Hall/Woodfin Camp & Associates. 246: *t.,* *inset* Hickson-Bender Photography for Silver Burdett; *b.* Norman O. Tomalin/ Bruce Coleman. 248: *l.* James Balog/Bruce Coleman; *r.* © 1985 Roger Werths/ Woodfin Camp & Associates. 249: Silver Burdett. 250: Courtesy Water Resources Center Archives, University of California, Berkeley, CA. 252: *l.* Leo DeWys, Inc.; *r.* Ken Sakamoto/Black Star. 253: Keith Gunnar/Bruce Coleman. 254: C.B. Frith/ Bruce Coleman. 255: Helen Byram/Leo DeWys, Inc. 256: *t.* Hickson-Bender Photography for Silver Burdett; *b.* R.E. Pelham/Bruce Coleman. 257: *l.* Nicholas DeVore III/Bruce Coleman; *r.* Ronald F. Thomas/Bruce Coleman.

Chapter 11 260–261: © Russ Kinne/Photo Researchers, Inc. 262: *t.l.* © Ronny Jaques/Photo Researchers, Inc.; *b.l.* © 1985 Ed Zirkle/Woodfin Camp & Associates; *r.* © Sepp Seitz/Woodfin Camp & Associates. 263: E.R. Degginger/Bruce Coleman. 264: *l.* Owen Franken/Stock, Boston; *r.* Runk/Schoenberger/Grant Heilman Photography. 265: Silver Burdett. 267: NASA. 268: *t.* © 1985 Jim Brandenberg/Woodfin Camp & Associates; *b.* Gerald Davis/Contact Press Images. 269: *t.l.* NASA; *t.r.* © Carleton Ray/Photo Researchers, Inc.; *b.* Gerald Davis/Contact Press Images. 272: Jim McNee/Tom Stack & Associates. 273: *t.* © Will McIntyre/Photo Researchers, Inc.; *r.* E.R. Degginger/Bruce Coleman. 275: W.H. Hodge/Peter Arnold, Inc. 276: © Cliff Dolfinger/Photo Researchers, Inc. 277: *t.* Runk/Schoenberger/Grant Heilman Photography; *b.* Joe DiMaggio-J. Kalish/Peter Arnold, Inc. 278: E.R. Degginger. 279: Robert Screnco/Shostal Associates. 280: *t.* Herman J. Kokojan/Black Star; *b.* NASA.

6 7 8 9 10—VH—90 89 88 87 86